THE STRESSED SEX

the
stressed

Uncovering the Truth About Men,
Women, & Mental Health

sex

DANIEL FREEMAN &
JASON FREEMAN

OXFORD
UNIVERSITY PRESS

OXFORD
UNIVERSITY PRESS

Great Clarendon Street, Oxford, OX2 6DP,
United Kingdom

Oxford University Press is a department of the University of Oxford.
It furthers the University's objective of excellence in research, scholarship,
and education by publishing worldwide. Oxford is a registered trade mark of
Oxford University Press in the UK and in certain other countries

First Edition published in 2013

Impression: 1

British Library Cataloguing in Publication Data

Data available

Library of Congress Cataloging in Publication Data

Data available

ISBN 978–0–19–965135–1

Printed in Great Britain by
Clays Ltd, St Ives plc

CONTENTS

PREFACE

The real voyage of discovery consists not in seeking new landscapes, but in having new eyes.

Marcel Proust

This book sets out to answer a simple question: are rates of psychological disorder different for men and women?

Although the question is straightforward enough, the implications—for individuals and society alike—are far-reaching. Yet, much to our initial surprise, the topic has been largely ignored by mental health specialists. And the picture that emerges from the relatively few texts that do allude to the issue is frustratingly contradictory. Moreover, though the appetite for books on gender differences seems as keen as ever, the issue of mental health is conspicuous by its absence.

The Stressed Sex, therefore, represents our attempt to clarify the links between gender and mental health. Is one sex more likely to develop problems than the other? And if so, why? To help us try to answer these questions, we draw on the best scholarship from a range of disciplines, including epidemiology, genetics, neuroscience, psychiatry, and cognitive, social, and clinical psychology. This makes *The Stressed Sex* the first evidence-based book on the topic—that is, grounded in high-quality scientific research.

Because it's the first book of its type, *The Stressed Sex* has inevitably been a voyage of discovery. We've journeyed through the available evidence, gradually—and sometimes necessarily tentatively—fitting together the pieces of the puzzle. And in seeking to answer the question at the beginning of this Preface, we've found ourselves tackling others too. What is mental illness? How prevalent is it in society? How are such conditions best defined and diagnosed? What causes psychological disorders? How do we integrate the various contributions of social, biological, and psychological factors? How should we go about researching such issues?

Every day millions of people struggle with psychological and emotional problems. Given the scale of the distress, understanding what causes these conditions is an urgent priority. We think gender can play a critical role in such problems. Over the course of this book, you'll discover why.

ACKNOWLEDGEMENTS

The Stressed Sex ranges over considerable scientific ground. It was therefore invaluable to receive expert comment and opinion on the text. We would very much like to thank the following researchers for reading the book and sharing their views with us: Claire Hughes, Angelica Ronald, Sally McManus, Helen Startup, Paul Bebbington, Sarah Reeve, Emma Cernis, Katherine Pugh, and Rachel Lister. We are also grateful to Sarah Reeve for her assistance with the literature searches for Part 2 of the book, and to Gail Freeman for her perceptive comments on an earlier draft of the text.

We thank the excellent team at Oxford University Press: our editor Latha Menon, Emma Marchant, Kate Farquhar-Thomson, Phil Henderson, and Rosanne Dawkins. And we are, as ever, indebted to Zoe King, our agent at the Blair Partnership.

The central focus of Daniel's work is developing the understanding and treatment of severe mental health problems, and he would like to thank the funders of this research: the UK Medical Research Council (MRC), the Wellcome Trust, and the NHS National Institute for Health Research. Jason thanks Eleanor for her love, encouragement, and support, and awards well-deserved gold stars to Ethan, Evelyn, and Jude. His work on this book, just like the others, is for them.

ABOUT THE AUTHORS

Daniel Freeman is a Professor of Clinical Psychology, and a Medical Research Council (MRC) Senior Clinical Fellow, in the Department of Psychiatry at Oxford University, and a Fellow of University College, Oxford. He is also an honorary consultant clinical psychologist in Oxford Health NHS Foundation Trust.

Jason Freeman is a writer and editor in the areas of popular psychology and self-help.

Daniel and Jason are the authors of:

- *How to Keep Calm and Carry on: Worry Less, Live Better*
- *Anxiety: A Very Short Introduction*
- *You Can Be Happy: The Scientifically Proven Way to Change How You Feel*
- *Use Your Head: A Guided Tour of the Human Mind*
- *Know Your Mind: The Complete Family Reference Guide to Emotional Health*
- *Paranoia: The 21st-Century Fear*
- *Overcoming Paranoid and Suspicious Thoughts*

PART 1

*Differences between Men & Women
in Mental Health*

What Does the Data Tell Us?

1

Introduction
The Stressed Sex?

The book you are now reading is the product and culmination of a journey that began five years ago.

Back in 2008 we were busy writing *Know Your Mind*, a self-help guide to the most common psychological and emotional problems. Each of the entries—and there were more than fifty—followed a set formula. We described the problem; offered a case study; presented a self-assessment questionnaire; and finished up by explaining the practical steps the reader could take to improve their personal situation.

Alongside these details, we included some basic data on prevalence. We noted how common a particular disorder was in the population, and highlighted any epidemiological patterns detected by scientists. So, for example, in the entry on depression we noted that 10–20 per cent of people will experience the illness at some point in their life—indeed depression is so widespread that, according to the World Health Organization, it is the number one cause of disability in the world. We mentioned that depression normally strikes for the first time in the mid-20s. And we reported that women are twice as likely as men to develop the condition.

That last statistic (and others very similar to it) is one that we found ourselves including in the entries with an almost monotonous regularity. It appears, for instance, that the risk of developing generalized anxiety disorder (a severe and persistent type of worry) is twice as high for women as it is for men. Ditto for panic disorder, phobias, and insomnia. Women are more prone than men to certain sexual disorders, specifically loss of desire, arousal problems, and pain during sex. They are more vulnerable to chronic fatigue syndrome. They are three times more likely than men to develop anorexia and *ten* times more likely than men to suffer from bulimia.

It's not always a one-way street: some problems appear to affect men and women equally (obsessions and compulsions, for example, or bipolar disorder). But the picture that inadvertently emerged from *Know Your Mind* is one in which the burden of psychological illness is principally borne by women. Indeed, looking back over the problems covered in the book, we were able to find just one that is more common in adult males than females (that problem being drug and alcohol abuse).

Sometimes it takes a little distance to see what's been staring you in the face all along. We had been dutifully researching the data on prevalence, problem by problem, entry by entry. Yet it was only when *Know Your Mind* was published that we were given cause to stop and think about the implications. In one promotional interview after another, journalists would remark on the imbalance in, say, depression or anxiety and ask why women were more likely to develop these psychological problems than men. And we would have to agree that yes, the difference was very striking but admit that no, we didn't really know why.

Then we saw the wider implications. Given that insomnia, anxiety, and depression are the most common problems, and that women clearly outnumber men for all three, then surely women suffer more mental health problems than men? Granted many women will experience insomnia, anxiety, and depression at the same time. And men are more susceptible to drug and alcohol problems. But would these factors be sufficient to make total rates of disorder for men and women equal? We thought it unlikely, but we wanted to find out for sure.

Over recent years a lively debate has been taking place regarding psychological differences between the sexes ('lively' being a euphemism for an argument that has sometimes been downright acrimonious). Do these differences exist? And, if they do, what explains them? Some experts, and many popular science writers, have argued that male and female brains are fundamentally dissimilar in certain key ways, and that this is why, for example, males are supposedly better at mathematics, and females more adept at sensing how other people are feeling. Others, however, argue that psychological differences—where they exist at all—are essentially the product of social and cultural factors. We were aware of this debate yet also conscious that, though fascinating, it had paid little if any attention to the issue we considered the most pressing: that of gender and mental health.

But you may be wondering how we arrived at the figures for prevalence given in *Know Your Mind*. Where do these statistics come from? Are they up to date? Can we trust them? We're going to sift the data, and carry out some new analyses, in Chapters 2 and 3. By the time we have finished you will, we believe, possess about as clear a picture of what the figures tell us about gender and psychological illness as it's currently possible to have. But, for now, bear in mind that our sources were the published results of epidemiological surveys carried out in various countries, together with expert summaries of the data in academic articles and books. Here, first, are some examples of those surveys.

The main US epidemiological survey is something called the National Comorbidity Survey Replication (NCS-R), which assessed the psychological health of a nationally representative sample of around 9,200 adults in 2001–2002. (It's called a 'replication' because it followed on from the National Comorbidity Survey conducted between 1990 and 1992.) It is important to note that the NCS-R and the other surveys we are going to discuss are based on interviews with members of the general population. They aren't studies of those receiving treatment for problems; instead they attempt to show the mental health of the country as a whole. According to the NCS-R, in the twelve months leading up to the survey, 8.6 per cent of women had suffered from depression, as compared to 4.9 per cent of men; for panic disorder, the figures were 3.8 per cent for women and 1.6 per cent for men; and for post-traumatic stress disorder, prevalence was 5.2 per cent (women) and 1.8 per cent (men).

The UK equivalent of the NCS-R (though in fact its most recent incarnation only covers England) is the Adult Psychiatric Morbidity Survey (APMS), which was last carried out in 2007 and covered 7,400 people. On the issue of gender, the APMS concluded that: 'Women were more likely than men to have a common mental disorder (19.7 per cent and 12.5 per cent respectively).'[1] For example, 11 per cent of women were found to have suffered from mixed anxiety and depression disorder in the previous week as compared to 6.7 per cent of men.

Our final example is the National Health and Social Life Survey, conducted in 1992, which assessed sexual behaviour in a demographically representative group of US adults aged 18 to 59. (Sexual problems comprise one of the fifteen main categories of psychological disorder in the key classificatory systems.) Just over 1,400 men and 1,749 women were interviewed about their experiences over the previous twelve months. A large proportion of both men and women reported sexual problems—for example, loss of desire, difficulties with arousal or orgasm, or ejaculating too quickly. But women were more likely to have experienced such problems than men (43 per cent compared to 31 per cent).

So much for the epidemiological surveys. Let's now take a look at a sample of typical expert opinion on the issue of gender and mental illness.

In the world of mental health, there are two principal reference books. One is the *International Classification of Diseases and Health Related Problems* (ICD), published by the World Health Organization, and the other is the American Psychiatric Association's *Diagnostic and Statistical Manual of Mental Disorders*, commonly known as the DSM. If you see a health professional about a psychological problem, it's the categories set out in the DSM and ICD (the two are broadly similar) that they'll be using to decide what exactly you're suffering from and how best to treat it. The most recent edition of the DSM was published in 1994 (a fifth edition is due in 2013). Each section deals with a specific psychological disorder and is written by a team of experts who survey current research and clinical practice.

We consulted the DSM while researching *Know Your Mind*. To give you a flavour of its findings, here's what it has to say about the prevalence of clinical depression (or 'major depressive disorder' to use the official term):

The lifetime risk for Major Depressive Disorder in community samples [that is, among the general population] has varied from 10% to 25% for women and from 5% to 12% for men. The point prevalence [i.e. the proportion of individuals suffering from the problem at any given time] of Major Depressive Disorders in adults in community samples has varied from 5% to 9% for women and from 2% to 3% for men.[2]

More support for the idea that depression affects many more women than men can be found in *The Mindful Way Through Depression*, one of the most successful self-help books to be published in recent years. Self-help books are regarded with suspicion in some quarters, and it's certainly possible to find rather flakey, unscientific, vacuously feel-good examples of the genre. *The Mindful Way Through Depression*, co-written by experts at the universities of Oxford, Cambridge, Toronto, and Massachusetts, is not one of those books. Based on decades of research and clinical practice, it's a thoughtful, wise, and sensible look at how meditation can tackle low mood. And it expresses the view that: 'Around 12 per cent of men and 20 per cent of women will experience major depression at some point in their lives.'[3]

Moving from depression to sleep disorders, Maurice Ohayon, director of the Stanford University Sleep Epidemiology Research Center, has written:

> Epidemiologists have published more than 50 studies of insomnia based on data collected in various representative community-dwelling samples or populations. These surveys provide estimates of the prevalence of insomnia according to four definitions: insomnia symptoms, insomnia symptoms with daytime consequences, sleep dissatisfaction and insomnia diagnoses. The first definition, based on insomnia criteria as defined by the DSM-IV [as we write, the most recent edition], recognizes that about one-third of a general population presents at least one of them. The second definition shows that, when daytime consequences of insomnia are taken into account, the prevalence is between 9% and 15%. The third definition represents 8–18% of the general population. The last definition, more precise and corresponding to a decision-making diagnosis, sets the

prevalence at 6% of insomnia diagnoses according to the DSM-IV classification. These four definitions of insomnia have higher prevalence rates in women than in men.[4]

Nowhere is the apparent disparity between the sexes' psychological health more starkly displayed than in the finding of the 2007 Adult Psychiatric Morbidity Survey (APMS) that women in England are more likely than men to have considered suicide. Almost one in five of the women interviewed (19.2 per cent) had, at some point in their life, experienced suicidal thoughts. The figure for men was 14 per cent. And the data suggests that the situation for women may be getting worse. The APMS found that the number of people who had contemplated suicide in the previous twelve months had risen since the previous survey in 2000. That change was entirely accounted for by an increase in the rate for women (4.2 per cent in 2000, 5.2 per cent in 2007). The figure for men remained unaltered at 3.5 per cent. (It is true, however, that men are more likely than women to actually kill themselves.)

Women certainly seek treatment more frequently than men. This might be further evidence that women suffer more psychological distress than men. Or it might, as some commentators have asserted, simply reflect the fact that wild horses couldn't drag many men into a doctor's surgery—and especially not for a psychological problem. We'll look at this debate in more detail in Chapter 3, but for now let's just note the fact that when a GP sees a patient with anxiety or depression or sleep problems, that patient is likely to be female.

So the established view, emerging from national surveys and accepted by leading mental health professionals, is that men and women differ in their susceptibility to specific psychological problems. It's the view we presented in *Know Your Mind*. Generally speaking, women are seen to be at greater risk of many of the most common disorders, including depression, certain anxiety problems, and sleep and sexual difficulties. Only for alcohol and drug problems do men outnumber women. And unless these substance disorders are enough to correct the gender imbalance, it seems that women may well be more vulnerable to psychological problems per se.

Yet, as we continued to dip our toes into this particular stretch of water, things became less, rather than more, clear. How puzzling, for example, to find on the World Health Organization's website, in a section headed 'Gender Disparities and Mental Health: The Facts', the following statement:

> Overall rates of psychiatric disorder are almost identical for men and women[5]

This authoritative view has filtered down. According to the Mental Health Foundation, a prominent UK charity:

> The same numbers of women and men experience mental health problems overall, but some problems are more common in women than men, and vice versa.[6]

And on the website of the Priory, which describes itself as 'one of Europe's leading independent providers of care for adults and children with a wide range of psychiatric, psychological and mental health related issues, including addictions, eating disorders and depression', and which most of us know as the favoured retreat of countless beleaguered celebrities, we found the following:

> Rates of severe mental illness do not vary significantly between men and women. However, a range of physical, socio-economic and psychological factors operate which increase women's vulnerability to various psychological difficulties and illnesses.[7]

Clearly something intriguing was afoot. We had begun by assuming that the answers to our questions about gender and psychological problems were there in the literature: all we had to do was look in the right place. Now it seemed that the consensus we had thought we would find might not actually exist. Were women more likely to develop psychological conditions, as the evidence seemed to imply? The most authoritative sources were either quiet on the issue or insisted that there were no differences in overall rates of disorder. It didn't add up. What *was* the evidence on mental health and gender? The literature we had consulted seemed contradictory, the picture curiously incomplete. So we decided to investigate for ourselves.

We had three principal questions:

- How do specific psychological disorders affect men and women?
- In which sex is the rate of overall psychological disorder higher: men, women, or neither?
- If there are differences—in susceptibility to specific problems and/ or to psychological disorders in general—what are the reasons?

Our focus was on adults rather than children. We wanted to look at the main stretch of life, rather than a temporary developmental stage. And research tends to deal with adults and children separately, with surveys of the former much more common.

Of course, you might want to ask some rather different questions. For instance, why does any of this matter? Are we merely dancing on the head of a statistical pin? Aren't there more pressing issues in mental health? We believe there are at least two compelling reasons for such an investigation. The first is clinical. According to a 2012 report by the UK Centre for Economic Performance, psychological disorders account for nearly half of all ill health in the under-65s: 'In other words, nearly as much ill health is mental illness as all physical illnesses put together.'[8] If our hunch is correct and women truly are more vulnerable to psychological problems at present, that's a major public health issue—one that should inform treatment, guide research, and perhaps necessitate social change.

The second reason relates to our theoretical understanding of psychological problems. If the statistics we came across when writing *Know Your Mind* are accurate, it seems that gender may play a significant role in mental health, influencing the kind of conditions we develop, and perhaps even whether we experience problems at all. We need to identify, therefore, precisely how this works. In what ways does gender affect mental health, and why? In tackling these questions, we may actually shine a light on the causes of psychological problems in general. There's much uncertainty about these causes; but following the thread of gender may both lead us to other factors, and help us understand how these factors interact to produce disorder. Given the distress these problems bring to so many people, men and women alike, understanding them is critical. Our theoretical knowledge, after all, allows us to develop more effective treatments and even to reduce the chances of individuals suffering from problems in the first place. Clearly, there's much more at stake here than merely trying to sort out apparent inconsistencies in the academic literature.

The topic of gender and mental health has been something of a battleground for many years. Back in the 1970s, for instance, a notable spat took place between, in the blue corner, the sociologists Walter Gove and Jeanette Tudor and, in the red corner, the epidemiologists Bruce Dohrenwend and Barbara Snell Dohrenwend. Gove and Tudor argued that:

> in modern Western industrial nations, women, because of stress associated with their sex roles, [have] higher rates of mental illness than men.[9]

Gove and Tudor speculated that this gender difference might be a relatively recent phenomenon, the result of 'drastic changes' in the social role of women in the years following World War II. The burden of these changes had been shouldered by *married* women (unmarried women were no worse off psychologically than men, and in fact healthier than unmarried men), who increasingly found themselves expected not only to run the house and raise a family, but to work outside the home too. Moreover Gove and Tudor noted that housework and homemaking can often be tedious, exhausting, solitary, and undervalued—exactly the sort of activity that's likely to lower one's mood.

The Dohrenwends, on the other hand, argued that since at least 1900 men and women have experienced broadly similar levels of psychological disorder. Where the sexes differ is in the *type* of problem they typically develop. Specifically, women tend to fall prey to 'neurosis and manic-depressive psychosis' while men are prone to personality disorders. (The DSM defines the latter as the product of a personality that is 'inflexible or maladaptive, and causes[s] significant functional impairment or subjective distress',[10] but it's an area fraught with controversy.) Although the years since World War II had seen an increase in recorded rates of psychological disorders, the Dohrenwends attributed this not to social changes, but to new methods of defining and recording mental illness.

With hindsight, this was an argument that neither party could win. For a start, each had a different view of what constituted mental illness, with the principal area of contention being whether to include the personality disorders (the Dohrenwends did so; Gove and Tudor did not). As a result, like was not being compared with like. Moreover, whatever one might decide counts as mental illness, the methods available to decide whether an individual was suffering from a problem were a lot less reliable in the 1960s and 70s than they are now.

Appropriate, standardized interview questions weren't generally used in mental health surveys of the general population until the 1980s.

Indeed the sort of nationally representative surveys we've quoted from in this chapter didn't exist in the 1970s. Gove and Tudor, for example, drew their conclusions from statistics on 'first admissions to mental hospitals, psychiatric treatment in general hospitals, and psychiatric treatment in outpatient clinics'.[11] They did also analyse a number of 'community surveys', but such surveys were generally pretty unreliable, not least because of the absence of diagnostic questionnaires. This means that anyone analysing historical patterns of mental health is forced to work with relatively short timescales. It's impossible, for example, to judge whether psychological problems are more widespread today than they were in, say, the 1960s or World War II or the Great Depression, let alone any further back. To put it in a nutshell, psychology and epidemiology in the 1970s weren't yet able to provide anything like a definitive answer to the question of whether women suffer from more psychological problems than men, or vice versa. This may have contributed to the sense of mutual miscomprehension one gets now from reading the Gove and Tudor/ Dohrenwends' papers. Or of heads being banged repeatedly, and futilely, against walls.

In the 1970s and 80s, feminists from a range of academic disciplines began to tackle the issue of women's mental health in earnest, often going back to the 18th and 19th centuries to trace the formation of attitudes towards gender and psychological disorder. These critics noted the disproportionately high numbers of women traditionally treated for mental illness; highlighted the fact that psychiatry was an overwhelmingly male-dominated profession; attempted to identify the distinctive social and cultural pressures that might cause women to seek treatment; and pointed to a long-standing cultural association between femininity and madness.

One of the key books to emerge from this wave of feminist scholarship was Elaine Showalter's *The Female Malady: Women, Madness, and English Culture, 1830–1980*, published in 1985. Showalter is a literary critic, but her analysis extended way beyond the usual parameters of her academic discipline to take in areas as diverse as social history, the development of psychiatry, and the visual arts. Here's how Showalter summarized her findings:

> Madness is a female malady because it is experienced by more women than men...But how should we interpret this statistical fact? There have always been those who argued that women's high rate of mental disorder is a product of their social situation, both their confining roles as daughters, wives and mothers and their mistreatment by a male-dominated and possibly misogynistic profession...By far the more prevalent view, however, sees an equation between femininity and insanity that goes beyond statistical evidence or the social condition of women...women, within our dualistic systems of language and representation, are typically situated on the side of irrationality, silence, nature and body, while men are situated on the side of reason, discourse, culture and mind....[Feminist philosophers, literary critics, and social theorists] have analyzed and illuminated a cultural tradition that represents "women" *as* madness, and that uses images of the female body...to stand for irrationality in general.[12]

Were one to discuss the issue with a typical 19th-century medical man, he would probably explain that it was hardly surprising women suffer more psychological problems than men: they are fundamentally unstable. It's not their fault, mind you: thanks largely to the peculiarities of the sexual and reproductive systems, women are prey to huge and unsettling emotional volatility. 'Madness', for women, is always close at hand. Showalter argued that this identification of madness as inherently female only truly took root at the end of the 18th century. It was then that 'the appealing madwoman gradually displaced the repulsive madman, both as the prototype of the confined lunatic and as a cultural icon'.[13] And the plentiful representations of female insanity in art, literature, and opera 'operated as ways of controlling and mastering feminine difference itself'.[14]

This cultural linking of femininity and psychological disorder had its corollary in real-life care of the mentally ill. Prior to the mid-19th century, men made up the majority of asylum inmates. There then began a sizeable shift in the opposite direction. Charles Dickens, visiting St Luke's Hospital in 1851, noted:

> The experience of this asylum did not differ, I found, from that of similar establishments, in proving that insanity is more prevalent among women than among men. Of the eighteen thousand seven hundred and fifty-nine inmates St Luke's Hospital has received in the century of its existence, eleven thousand one hundred and sixty-two have been women.[15]

And at the same time as the asylums were filling with women, the treatment and control of those psychiatric patients became increasingly dominated by men.

Ah, but that was the Victorian age, you might be thinking: those attitudes have long since disappeared, haven't they? In 1985 Showalter was far from convinced that the link between women and madness had weakened, nor indeed that women and men were being treated equally in the mental health system: 'In modern literature and art, the schizophrenic woman stands for the alienation and fragmentation of the age. In medical psychiatry...women appear to be the prime subjects of shock treatment, psychosurgery, and psychotropic drugs.'[16] More than twenty-five years later, many feminist critics argue that even now nothing much has changed. In her recent book *The Madness of Women*, the health psychologist Jane Ussher writes:

Women outnumber men in diagnoses of madness, from the 'hysteria' of the eighteenth and nineteenth centuries, to 'neurotic' and mood disorders in the twentieth and twenty-first. Women are also more likely to receive psychiatric 'treatment', ranging from hospitalisation in an asylum, accompanied by restraint, electro-convulsive therapy (ECT) and psychosurgery, to psychological therapy and psychotropic drug treatments today. Why is this so? Some would say that women *are* more mad than men, with psychiatric treatment a beneficent force that sets out to cure the disordered female mind. I proffer an alternative explanation – that women are subject to misdiagnosis and mistreatment by experts whose own pecuniary interests can be questioned, as can their use (or abuse) of power.[17]

Ussher doesn't dispute the fact that a great many women suffer psychological and emotional distress. But she argues that this unhappiness is more accurately interpreted as a 'reasonable response' to 'restricted and repressive'[18] lives than as a sign of illness.

Some critics have argued that you can detect psychiatry's problematic—perhaps even antagonistic—attitude towards femininity in its judgements as to what constitutes mental illness. Writing of the third edition of the American Psychiatric Association's *Diagnostic and Statistical Manual* (published in 1980), Marcie Kaplan argued that:

> masculine biased assumptions about what behaviors are healthy and what behaviors are crazy are codified in diagnostic criteria and thus influence diagnosis and treatment patterns.[19]

Kaplan's article produced an irate response from two of the leading figures in the creation of DSM-III, Janet Williams and Robert Spitzer, who insisted that the text had been reviewed with a fine-tooth comb to avoid any suggestion of 'sex bias'. They noted that the American Psychiatric Association's Committee on Women had scrutinized drafts, that 'many of the hypothetical clinical examples that she uses to illustrate her point have no relationship to the actual content of DSM-III',[20] and that for some conditions the gender imbalance worked in the opposite direction.

The DSM continues to grapple with the problems posed by gender. You can get a sense of the complexity of the issue—and the resultant perplexity of those trying to navigate their way through it—in an article co-written by the editor of the most recent version, Michael First:

> Most of the DSM-IV criteria sets are intended to be used with both males and females. However it is unclear whether these criteria sets are always equally valid for males and females…Given the likely impact of gender on the etiology and expression of most mental disorders, the development of gender-neutral diagnostic criteria sets can be quite problematic.[21]

Although one might aim for gender neutrality, it may not always be appropriate. First and his co-author Thomas Widiger use the example of somatization disorder (an uncommon problem characterized by physical ailments without any detectable medical cause): 'if irregular menses, excessive menstrual bleeding, and vomiting throughout pregnancy are clinically important and valid symptoms of somatization disorder in women, it could be problematic to remove them for the sake of "gender neutrality"'.[22] First and Widiger conclude, perhaps a little wearily, that more research is needed into just how psychological problems present in males and females.

If the DSM is striving for gender neutrality, not everyone is convinced. Here's Jane Ussher, writing in 2011:

> Representations of madness encapsulated within the DSM not only define the boundaries of what it means to have a 'disordered' mind, but also function to construct the subject position 'mad woman',

legitimising the right of particular experts to speak about and treat her condition, and defining which particular 'truths' are accepted as explanations for her disordered state.... [T]his means positioning the problem solely within the woman, and legitimising bio-psychiatry and Big Pharma—the drug companies which profit from the now ubiquitous biochemical 'cures'.[23]

Certainly it's not difficult to find examples of women who've experienced inaccurate diagnosis, ineffective therapies, and sometimes downright cruel and exploitative treatment at the hands of male mental health professionals. Several are highlighted in Lisa Appignanesi's award-winning *Mad, Bad, and Sad: A History of Women and the Mind Doctors from 1800 to the Present*. (On the other hand, whether men have fared better is an open question.)

Feminist critics have also drawn attention to the fact that, if women are more likely to be treated for psychological problems, that often puts them first in line for whichever type of treatment is currently in vogue. Diazepam, better known under the trade name Valium, was arguably *the* drug of the 1970s. One of the new type of 'minor tranquillizers' called benzodiazepines prescribed to treat minor anxiety problems and depression, Valium was frequently aimed at women. Often this was the harassed housewife but unmarried women were also targeted, as an advert placed by its manufacturer Roche in the *Archives of General Psychiatry* (and quoted by Jane Ussher) makes abundantly clear:

> *Jan, 35, single and psychoneurotic* You probably see many such Jans in your practice. The unmarrieds with low self esteem, Jan never found a man to measure up to her father. Now she realises she's in a losing position – and that she may never marry. Valium (Diazepam) can be a useful adjunct in the therapy of the tense, over anxious patient who has a neurotic sense of failure, guilt, or loss.[24]

It's perhaps not surprising that the public were so keen on Valium: benzodiazepines produce a sense of relaxation that resembles the feeling produced by alcohol. Pour yourself a glass of wine with your breakfast and you'll soon get the kind of reputation you'd rather do without. Popping a pill, on the other hand, is *so* much more discreet. But in the end Valium became a synonym for overmedication, apparently handed out like aspirin by doctors too busy or uninterested to enquire properly into the problems affecting their patients. Moreover, unpleasant side effects were common, and stopping the drug could result in nasty withdrawal symptoms. As the 1980s wore on, the tide of scientific and popular opinion turned so conclusively that the brand name Valium was dropped.

Feminist critics have devoted a great deal of time to analysing the connections between gender and mental health. (Understandably, however, their focus has been on women's experience.) For these writers, the idea that women are more likely than men to be diagnosed with a psychological problem isn't controversial, though they see it principally as the result of women's rational behaviour being mistakenly stigmatized as mental illness. And yet, among the mainstream of mental health professionals, psychologists, and psychiatrists the question of gender differences receives surprisingly little attention. Is it discussed in the population at large? We think probably not. And if it is generally accepted that women are more prone to certain problems, there's a marked reluctance to look at the bigger picture: to do, as the phrase has it, the maths. Perhaps this stems from an awareness of the sometimes shabby treatment of women in former days. If to portray women as generally less mentally healthy than men runs the risk of providing the justification to deny women access to positions of status and power, naturally one might think twice about raising the matter. And yet it's surely too important an issue to ignore or gloss over, not least because it bears so directly on the suffering of so many people.

We wanted to find out whether the picture that emerged while writing *Know Your Mind* really added up to a gender difference. And what that would then tell us about psychiatric problems. Of course, we aren't the first to address the question of gender differences in mental health. But what no one has yet done is to assess those differences by analysing the data generated by the wave of nationally representative epidemiological studies carried out over the last twenty years.

What we focus on is not hospital admissions, or visits to doctors, but the prevalence of psychological problems in the general adult population. It's this evidence that makes it possible to uncover the truth about men, women, and mental health, giving us an unprecedented view of exactly how—and how many—ordinary men and women are affected by these issues. This analysis comprises the first part of the book: an in-depth look at what the best and most comprehensive epidemiological surveys tell us about rates of specific psychological problems, and mental ill health in general, in men and women across a range of countries. In Part 2, we assess the possible explanations for what we've found.

Like all the most rewarding journeys, this one will take us via an assortment of fascinating places. Attempting to answer the big question about gender differences in mental health inevitably means tackling a host of other, equally significant issues. What, for instance, do we understand by the terms 'mental illness' or 'psychological disorder'? Which problems count? Indeed, is it helpful to think of psychological distress in terms of individual conditions? Rather than seeing a person's symptoms in the round, are we simply squeezing them into reductive and relatively arbitrary diagnostic categories ('Ms X has depression,' 'Mr Y is suffering from generalized anxiety disorder')? And what factors cause mental illness? Does gender play a part and, if so, in what ways?

Incidentally, we ought to add a word here about our use of the terms 'sex' and 'gender'. 'Sex' is often a biological concept, used to distinguish creatures as male or female. 'Gender', on the other hand, is cultural: it's a socially constructed idea of what it means to be male or female. The epidemiological surveys we analyse present data on gender. Rather than ascertaining the biological sex of the person being interviewed, the survey simply records whatever that individual reports. (And thank goodness, you might think, for that.) However, it often proves extremely tricky to determine whether a difference between the sexes is a product of biological or sociocultural influences. As Michael Rutter and colleagues have written:

> It is unlikely that gender-differentiated social influences will have arisen completely independently of biological features. Equally, it is implausible that all biological influences will operate in ways that are free of social-contextual pressures.... [I]t is important to seek to determine the relative importance of constitutional and socio-cultural influences...but the differentiation has to arise out of the empirical findings; it cannot be imposed by fiat through terminology.[25]

For this reason, we use the terms 'sex' and 'gender' interchangeably throughout this book.

Our first task in our exploration of gender and mental health is to find out what the data really tells us about rates of psychological disorder in men and women. Which problems are more common in men? Which disorders crop up predominately in women? And what about the overall prevalence of psychological problems in males and females? To find the answers to these questions, let's turn now to a detailed investigation of national surveys of mental health across the globe. No one has ever analysed this data to discover overall rates of disorder by gender. Some surprises may lie in store.

2

Number Crunching
The Pattern and Prevalence of Psychiatric Problems

Until recent decades, psychiatric diagnosis could be a highly personal, idiosyncratic affair. As David Barlow and V. Mark Durand have noted: 'As late as 1959 there were at least nine different systems of varying usefulness for classifying psychological disorders worldwide.'[1] The diagnosis one might receive would thus depend on which system a given psychiatrist used—assuming, that is, they adhered to a particular system at all.

The first tentative steps towards standardization were taken in 1948 when the World Health Organization included information on mental illness in their *International Classification of Diseases and Health Related Problems* (ICD). This was followed in 1952 by the American Psychiatric Association's *Diagnostic and Statistical Manual of Mental Disorders* (DSM). Neither, however, made much impact at first. Although a second edition of the DSM appeared in 1968, the real leap forward occurred with the third edition, published in 1980. In place of contentious and distracting speculations about the causes of psychological problems, the emphasis switched to a detailed enumeration of symptoms, designed to make the clinician's task of diagnosis much easier and more consistent. This was an effort that continued in what is as we write the current edition, DSM-IV, published in 1994. By 2000, DSM-IV had sold almost a million copies—which indicates just how influential it had become. And as the DSM evolved, increasing efforts were made to coordinate its approach and content with that of the ICD. As a result, though the two aren't identical, they are now very similar.

Both the DSM and ICD have changed radically over the years, and it's a fair bet that they'll continue to do so. Each edition, though now developed over several years and in consultation with hundreds of experts, triggers a wave of debate about both details and overall philosophy. One common criticism, for example, centres on the slicing up of psychological distress into what seems like an endlessly proliferating collection of discrete conditions (the first edition of the DSM, for example, listed around 100 disorders; the second 182; the third 265; and the 2000 revision of the fourth edition almost 300, though this includes subcategories of basic disorders and thus significantly overestimates the number of main diagnoses actually used in clinical settings). The result may resemble a kind of periodic table of psychological problems, but no one would argue that it's based on the same kind of hard science as the schema used in chemistry. This is why some experts argue that it would make more sense to think in terms of broad clusters of symptoms, rather than separate disorders.

These kinds of reservation about the approach of the DSM and ICD are important, and we'll discuss them in detail in Chapter 3. But if we want to know how widespread mental health problems are, we first have to decide what counts as a problem. And to do that it makes sense to begin with the rubric laid out in the DSM and ICD, not least because they're the definitive reference works on mental illness, used by health services worldwide (including the NHS). Visit your doctor with an emotional or psychological problem, and they'll make a diagnosis using the categories set out in the DSM or ICD. Need to claim on your sickness insurance? It's the DSM/ICD classification that your insurer will use. Want to find out more about your symptoms and how to tackle them? The vast majority of the reputable books on the topic will also use the DSM/ICD systems as their starting point.

Because the DSM and ICD are so well established, it's these categories that are used by national surveys of mental health. To get a sense of how they work, let's look at how the DSM defines depression—or 'major depressive episode' to use the official term. There are nine possible symptoms, and a person will need to report at least five of them to warrant a diagnosis:

- depressed mood most of the day, nearly every day
- markedly diminished interest or pleasure in all, or almost all, activities most of the day, nearly every day
- significant weight loss when not dieting or weight gain... or decrease or increase in appetite nearly every day
- insomnia or hypersomnia [i.e. excessive sleepiness] nearly every day
- psychomotor agitation or retardation nearly every day [i.e. appearing extremely on edge or, alternatively, very listless and withdrawn]
- fatigue or loss of energy nearly every day
- feelings of worthlessness or excessive or inappropriate guilt nearly every day
- diminished ability to think or concentrate, or indecisiveness, nearly every day
- recurrent thoughts of death (not just fear of dying), recurrent suicidal ideation without a specific plan, or a suicide attempt or a specific plan for committing suicide.

These symptoms need to 'cause clinically significant distress or impairment in social, occupational, or other important areas of functioning'.[2] And they must have persisted for at least two weeks.

So depression, like other disorders in the DSM, involves a set number of specified symptoms. These symptoms must be sufficiently intense to really interfere with a person's life. And they must have lasted for a while. The effect of this three-pronged approach is to emphasize the severe end of a spectrum that also includes relatively mild psychological problems. The DSM criteria won't capture everyday fluctuations in mental health. And they won't pick up people with, say, four symptoms rather than five. Or those who manage to keep going with work and other commitments in spite of their problems.

The DSM uses fifteen broad categories of mental illness, which you can see listed in Table 2.1. Our consideration of rates of mental health problems in men and women omits dementias and certain childhood conditions. In the case of dementias, it's questionable whether they're really best thought of as psychological disorders. They're caused, after all, by organic damage to the brain. There's some evidence to suggest that women are more at risk of Alzheimer's disease, but when you look at the dementias as a whole the rates for men and women are very similar. We've also chosen to exclude those childhood problems that don't last into adulthood, such as bed-wetting (known as enuresis) and separation anxiety, a fairly common fear of being parted from home or loved ones. These childhood disorders aren't tracked by the national surveys in any case.

What's the best way to discover how frequently psychological disorders occur in men and women? The answer is to look to the results of epidemiological surveys. But not all surveys will do; for a survey to be truly useful it must meet certain essential criteria. For a start, if

Table 2.1 Principal categories of psychological disorder

Childhood-onset disorders	Includes a wide range of problems, all of which are typically first diagnosed in childhood. These include autism, learning disorders, and attention deficit hyperactivity disorder (ADHD).
Dementia	Characterized by a gradual deterioration in the functioning of the brain. The most widespread form of dementia is Alzheimer's disease, though vascular dementia (caused by strokes) is also relatively common.
Substance-related disorders	Abuse of, or dependence on, everything from alcohol and nicotine to illegal drugs and gambling.
Schizophrenia and other psychotic disorders	Conditions involving hallucinations (perceptions without an obvious cause), delusions (unfounded and exaggerated beliefs), disorganized speech, and unusual, unpredictable, or inappropriate behaviour.
Mood (or affective) disorders	The main examples are depression and bipolar disorder.
Anxiety disorders	Including generalized anxiety disorder, social anxiety, fears and phobias, post-traumatic stress disorder, obsessive-compulsive disorder, and panic disorder.
Somatoform disorders	In which the person suffers from distressing physical symptoms that can't be traced to a medical condition.

(*continued*)

Table 2.1 (Continued)

Factitious disorders	Feigning physical or psychological illness.
Dissociative disorders	These disorders are characterized by disruption to normal functioning of consciousness, memory, sense of identity, or perception. For example, in depersonalization disorder the person feels as though they're detached from their thoughts or body.
Sexual and gender identity disorders	Sexual problems tend to involve difficulties becoming or staying aroused, achieving orgasm, or pain during sex. People with gender identity disorders, on the other hand, are sure that their biological sex is the 'wrong' one for them—that they are, for example, a woman locked in a man's body.
Eating disorders	Namely anorexia nervosa and bulimia nervosa.
Sleep disorders	The most common type is insomnia, but other sleep disorders include narcolepsy (which involves suddenly falling asleep no matter where you are or what you're doing), nightmare disorder, and sleepwalking disorder.
Impulse-control disorders	Characterized by 'the failure to resist an impulse, drive, or temptation to perform an act that is harmful to the person or to others'.[3] Examples are kleptomania (stealing) and pyromania (setting fires).

Table 2.1 (Continued)

Adjustment disorders	Adjustment disorders are triggered by stressful events. The person's reaction is either more extreme than would be expected or causes major disruption to their day-to-day functioning.
Personality disorders	Defined by the DSM as involving a personality that is 'inflexible or maladaptive, and causes[s] significant functional impairment or subjective distress.'[4] Examples include antisocial personality disorder and conduct disorder, both of which are characterized by wildly rebellious, aggressive, and deceitful behaviour; and borderline personality disorder, whose sufferers are emotionally fragile, very unsure of themselves and their identity, and fearful of abandonment.

American Psychiatric Association (2000). *Diagnostic and Statistical Manual of Mental Disorders*. Fourth Edition. Text Revision. Arlington: APA.

you want to know how prevalent these problems are in the general population it's no good simply counting the number of hospital admissions or attendances at clinics. What you need are large-scale, national surveys, with the participants picked at random and the resulting statistics weighted to ensure that the data is representative of the population in general. (For instance, a sample's gender mix might be a little different from that of the country as a whole; weighting will correct and compensate for that imbalance.)

Take the 2007 Adult Psychiatric Morbidity Survey (APMS), for example. This was 'designed to be representative of the population living in private households'[5] (98 per cent of the adult population) in England. The team began by selecting 519 Royal Mail postal sectors, each of which contains around 2,550 households. Although the sectors were chosen randomly, they'd first been screened to ensure a proper geographical and socio-economic spread—for example, by assessing the percentage of people in the area without a car or engaged in non-manual work. (Clearly, if your selected postal areas happen to be largely drawn from, say, the relatively affluent commuter belt of south-east England or the comparatively deprived former mill towns of the north, they're unlikely to be representative of the country as a whole.) From each of these 519 postal sectors, the team randomly selected twenty-eight addresses. All 14,532 addresses were then visited by interviewers to check that they were indeed private households (1,318 proved not to be), and to invite one adult from each address—once again chosen at random—to take part in the survey.

In phase one, a total of 7,461 people—57 per cent of those potentially eligible—were interviewed by trained researchers from the National Centre for Social Research. On average, these interviews lasted around ninety minutes, though some took as long as three hours. In addition to clinically validated assessments for a range of psychological disorders, participants were also questioned about a wide range of issues including their physical health, religious or spiritual beliefs, use of mental health services, social support networks, caring responsibilities, and experience of stressful life events. Around 850 participants who'd scored highly for possible psychosis (schizophrenia), certain personality disorders, or Asperger syndrome (a form of autism) were then asked to take part in a second interview. These conditions are particularly difficult to identify with any certainty, hence the need for additional assessments carried out by clinically trained interviewers, many of whom had worked on the previous APMS in 2000. Based upon information about the 7,461 participants, data on the general population, and taking into consideration the households that didn't respond, the survey results were then weighted statistically to ensure the sample was representative of adults in the country. It took around three years for the survey to move from its initial planning in the spring of 2006 to the two rounds of interview and data analysis and all the way through to publication in 2009. Given the volume of work involved, you probably won't be surprised at the time required.

For the purposes of our research, we needed surveys that could match the scope, rigour, and reliability of the APMS. Specifically, we were looking for studies that:

- Present data on a nationally representative sample of the adult population. Surveys that cover just a particular region or city, or that don't use bona fide sampling techniques, failed to make the cut.

- Assess several disorders, including at the very least drug-related disorders, alcohol problems, depression, and anxiety disorders (these being the archetypal 'gendered' disorders: the latter two are typically regarded as more common in women and the former as more prevalent in men). In fact, the studies that cover this bare minimum of disorders also tend to include many more conditions too.

- Use established, reliable, and valid psychiatric interviews—by which we mean that the assessments can be trusted to produce the sort of conclusions that a clinician might arrive at were they to assess the participant in person based on DSM or ICD criteria. In practice, these requirements limited us to surveys carried out since the 1980s.

- Give separate figures for men and women, both for individual disorders and, importantly, for psychological problems in general. Obviously, deducing anything about gender and mental health without this key information would be impossible.

As we saw with the APMS, the kind of studies that can meet these criteria are enormously time-consuming, labour-intensive projects. They are also expensive. As a result, such surveys tend to be fairly few and far between. In the remainder of this chapter, we'll consider the ones that do fit the bill; let you know about two major studies that—perhaps surprisingly—don't; and describe the results of a World Health Organization study that has combined several national surveys.

Before we begin, it's worth remembering that none of the surveys we discuss covers every single disorder in the DSM or ICD. Instead, they focus on the sort of problems that have historically been treated by psychiatrists, and generally only the most common of these. As we'll see, those psychological and emotional troubles that don't usually bring people into contact with psychiatrists—sleep problems, for example—are often excluded from these surveys. This doesn't, of course, mean that such problems are necessarily any less distressing or widespread, but rather that they're usually treated by GPs or, in the case of sleep problems, sometimes by specialist clinics. Such omissions mean that it's tricky to make judgements about the overall prevalence of mental health problems in men and women.

(The surveys also tend to exclude individuals who are in prison or homeless. Such people are much more likely to be male than female, and they're also much more likely to suffer from mental health problems. But they represent a very small proportion of the population; as such, their omission is unlikely to have a big effect on the overall picture.)

In fact, no one has set up a survey with the aim of comparing overall rates of disorder in men and women. So we decided to carefully analyse the epidemiological surveys that have been carried out in order to discover what they can tell us about gender and mental health. As we scrutinized each survey, we sought answers to four key questions:

- Which disorders were assessed?
- How common was each disorder in men and women?
- For psychological disorders as a whole, did men and women differ in their vulnerability?
- Which were the most comprehensive studies?

We found twelve national surveys that meet the criteria we set out above. They're listed in Table 2.2.

Each of the twelve surveys focuses on recent problems. Usually this means assessing a person's mental health over the previous year, though some of the surveys also provide estimates for lifetime incidence of disorders. We chose to concentrate on the figures for recent problems. This is because they tend to be much more reliable. After all, can you recall what your mood was like five years ago? How about ten or twenty years back? We might have an approximate sense of events and feelings, but most of us find it difficult to be absolutely sure. Specific details tend to disappear into the fog of time. And even when we *are* confident that we can recall a particular episode, the more distant it is from the present the greater the likelihood that our memory is playing tricks. This isn't to say that we should ignore data on lifetime rates of psychological disorder, but we're on firmer ground when dealing with figures from a comparatively recent time frame.

Which disorders do our surveys cover? Each of them, naturally, provides information on rates of anxiety, depression, and substance-related disorders (this was, after all, one of the criteria we used to select the studies). But arguably just as significant as the disorders they include are those they exclude. For instance, precisely *none* of

Table 2.2 National epidemiological surveys of mental health

UK

OPCS Survey of Psychiatric Morbidity 1993 (Number of people surveyed = 10,000)

Psychiatric Morbidity Among Adults Living in Private Households 2000 (N = 8,800)

Adult Psychiatric Morbidity Survey 2007 (N = 7,461)

Other European countries

Mental Health Supplement of the German National Health Interview and Examination Survey (N = 4,181)

Netherlands Mental Health Survey and Incidence Study (NEMESIS) (N = 7,076)

United States

National Comorbidity Survey (NCS) (N = 8,098)

National Comorbidity Survey Replication (NCS-R) (N = 9,282)

Australia and New Zealand

Australian National Mental Health Survey 1997 (N = 10,641)

National Survey of Mental Health and Wellbeing 2007 (N = 8,841)

New Zealand Mental Health Survey 2003 (N = 12,992)

Other countries

Chile Psychiatric Prevalence Study (N = 2,978)

South African Stress and Health Study (N = 4,351)

the surveys reported on the prevalence of sleep or sexual disorders. Yet as we saw in Chapter 1, research suggests that both these types of problem are more common in women than men. Historical artefact though it may be, the absence of these very widespread conditions from the surveys leaves a sizeable hole in the overall data on gender and mental health.

Also missing from all but two of the surveys—the German and Chilean studies—is another category of problem more commonly diagnosed in women: somatoform disorders (though people presenting with the symptoms are often also experiencing depression and/or anxiety, and thus would quite likely be captured in an overall figure for mental illness). As if that weren't sufficiently vexing for our review, the standard diagnostic interviews omit several problems that are seen *only* in women. These include conditions such as premenstrual syndrome (also known as premenstrual tension or PMT) and premenstrual dysphoric disorder (an especially severe form of premenstrual syndrome). In an attempt to rectify this situation, a new questionnaire was created in 2009: the Composite International Diagnostic Interview for Women, or CIDI-VENUS. It came too late, however, for the surveys we discuss here. It's worth bearing these omissions in mind as you read through the results of the surveys in the next pages.

Before we get to those results, however, a brief word about statistical terminology. When we describe a difference between male and female rates of psychological disorder as 'significant' we're referring to what's known as *statistical significance*. In essence, this denotes that the difference is sufficiently large to mean that it's unlikely to have occurred by chance. Statisticians have put a figure on chance and that figure is 5 per cent. For a difference between the sexes to be significant, therefore, the likelihood of that difference arising by accident must be less than 5 per cent. Because we're relying on probabilities here, for every hundred results five could be accidental and misleading. Anomalies are an inevitable feature of statistical research. So if five out of a hundred studies show that there are differences between men's and women's overall mental health, that could be pure chance. On the other hand, if several out of a dozen pick up on those differences, there's a much better chance that what we're seeing is the real deal.

One of the most striking results to emerge from the surveys is much more indicative of *similarity* between the sexes than difference. Again and again, these studies show a worryingly high rate of psychological problems across the population as a whole: that is, for both men and women. In the UK and United States, around one in four people meet the diagnostic criteria for a psychological disorder in the previous twelve months. In Australia things seem only slightly better: there, the figure is one in five. Across the surveys, that twelve-month figure varies between 20 and 30 per cent, depending on the number of problems assessed and the diagnostic criteria used. Extrapolating those percentages makes alarming reading. In the UK, for example, approximately ten million adults (aged 16 or above) will have experienced a clinical psychological problem in the previous year. In the United States, 58 million people over the age of 18 are affected. These kinds of figures have become commonplace in the news in recent years, but they still shock. Huge numbers of people are struggling with emotional and psychological problems, and from one perspective whether these individuals happen to be male or female is almost immaterial.

But if overall rates of psychological problems are alarmingly high in the population in general, our surveys agree that the sexes differ in the *type* of problem they're likely to develop. Every one of the twelve studies reports that women are more likely than men to suffer from anxiety and depression. Men, on the other hand, have a greater propensity for abuse of, and dependence on, alcohol and illegal substances.

For example, the US National Comorbidity Survey Replication (NCS-R) found that 23 per cent of women had experienced an anxiety disorder in the previous twelve months, as compared to 14 per cent of men. For depression, the figures were 9 per cent for women and 5 per cent for men. But when we look at the data for substance-related problems (including nicotine), the balance tilts in the opposite direction: 15.4 per cent of men are affected and 11.6 per cent of women. A similar story emerges from the Australian National Survey of Mental Health and Wellbeing (2007), which reported anxiety problems in 18 per cent of women and 11 per cent of men; depression in 7 per cent of women and 5 per cent of men; while the figures for alcohol- and drug-related disorders were 7 per cent in men and 'just' 3 per cent in women. Finally, the UK Adult Psychiatric Morbidity Survey 2007 put the current rate of mixed anxiety and depression disorder at 11 per cent in women and 7 per cent in men. Alcohol dependence, however, was more common in men than women (9 per cent compared to 3 per cent), and the same was true for drug dependence (5 per cent versus 2 per cent).

When it comes to other disorders, the surveys vary in their coverage. But it seems clear that women are more likely to develop borderline personality disorder and eating disorders, while rates of conduct disorder and antisocial personality disorder tend to be higher in men. Perhaps surprisingly, there aren't large differences between adult males and females in rates of ADHD. The NCS-R found that 3.9 per cent of women and 4.3 per cent of men had experienced the condition in the previous twelve months; in the APMS 7.7 per cent of women and 8.8 per cent of men were currently affected. (The situation is rather different for ADHD in children, as we'll see in Chapter 3.) Psychotic disorders such as schizophrenia appear to be fairly evenly distributed between the sexes.

To recap: so far we've discovered that our twelve surveys reveal a somewhat chilling landscape in which perhaps a quarter of people have experienced a recent psychological disorder. And they also show that the pattern of disorder varies: some problems are more prevalent in men, some are more common in women, and others are just as likely to develop in either sex. But here's the big question: what do the studies tell us about *overall* rates of psychological problems in men and women? Are women more at risk—or is it men? Alternatively, is the World Health Organization correct when it states that: 'Overall rates of psychiatric disorder are almost identical for men and women'?[6]

The results are striking. Eight of the twelve surveys indicate that rates of psychological disorder are significantly higher among women than men. Let's look at these eight studies in more detail, beginning with the most comprehensive in terms of disorders assessed: the Mental Health Supplement of the German National Health Interview and Examination Survey. Carried out between 1997 and 1999, the German study gathered data on more than sixty of the disorders listed in DSM-IV, including anxiety, depression, substance-related disorders (alcohol and illicit drugs), somatoform disorders, eating disorders, pain disorder, and psychosis.

One in four of the men interviewed (25 per cent) had experienced at least one of these disorders in the previous twelve months. This in itself is an eye-opening statistic, but it's dwarfed by the figure for women, which came in at a staggering 37 per cent. So the study that seems best equipped to answer our question produces an unequivocal result.

The US National Comorbidity Survey Replication (NCS-R) covered a smaller range of problems, but told a similar—albeit less dramatic—tale to the German study. Focusing on anxiety, depression, so-called impulse-control problems such as ADHD and conduct disorder, and substance-related disorders (alcohol, drugs, and nicotine), the NCS-R reported that 34.7 per cent of women had met the DSM-IV criteria during the previous year, as compared to 29.9 per cent of men. The forerunner of the NCS-R, the National Comorbidity Survey

(NCS), was carried out in the early 1990s and therefore based its assessments on the earlier psychiatric handbook, 1987's DSM-III-R. The NCS collected statistics on the prevalence of disorders including anxiety, depression, substance use, antisocial personality disorder, and psychosis. What it found was that twelve-month rates were higher in women than men (31 per cent versus 28 per cent). The odds on women reporting a disorder were 1.2 times those for men.

And here we need to take another statistical timeout. When we talk about odds—as we will repeatedly in the coming pages—we mean 'the probability of an event occurring divided by the probability of that event not occurring'.[7] When we compare the odds on women and men experiencing a problem—as we've just done—we use what's known as an *odds ratio*: that is, 'the ratio of the odds of an event occurring in one group compared to another'.[8] Imagine that a disorder affects 50 per cent of men and 25 per cent of women. Here's how we calculate the odds ratio. The odds on the disorder in men are 0.5/0.5. In other words, the probability that the event will happen is 0.5, and the probability that it will not happen is also 0.5. We can also express this as 1: that is, 0.5 divided by 0.5. For women the odds are 0.25/0.75, or 0.33. We divide the odds on men by the odds on women—that is, 1/0.33—and arrive at an odds ratio of 3. Now let's illustrate the idea using the figures above from the NCS. Thirty-one per cent of women surveyed had experienced a disorder, meaning that their odds were 0.31/0.69, which equals 0.45. For men the odds were 0.28/0.72, or 0.39. If we divide 0.45 by 0.39 we obtain an odds ratio of 1.2.

Travel several thousand miles south from the United States to Chile and the picture that emerges is essentially the same, with 25 per cent of women and 19 per cent of men having experienced a psychological disorder in the previous twelve months. The Chilean survey was conducted in the 1990s and, like the US NCS, used the criteria set out in DSM-III-R. As usual, the disorders assessed vary a little from the other surveys: in this case, participants were quizzed about their experience of anxiety, depression, substance use (including nicotine), antisocial personality disorder, psychosis, somatoform disorders, and eating disorders.

Across the Pacific, the Australian National Survey of Mental Health and Wellbeing (2007) assessed the prevalence of anxiety, depression, and problems with alcohol and illicit substances, using the rules set out in the tenth edition of the *International Classification of Diseases and Health Related Problems* (ICD-10). Once again, women were significantly more likely than men to have experienced a disorder in the previous year—22.3 per cent compared to 17.6 per cent. The New Zealand Mental Health Survey is entitled 'Te Rau Hinengaro' (the Māori term for 'the many minds', a reference to the huge variety of psychological states we all experience in our lives). Te Rau Hinengaro collected data on rates of anxiety disorders, mood disorders such as depression, alcohol and drug problems, and eating disorders. What it found was that women were not simply more vulnerable to psychological disorders: their symptoms were often more disruptive and distressing than those of men with the same problem. In the twelve months leading up to the survey, nearly one in four women (24 per cent) met the DSM-IV criteria for at least one of the disorders; for men the figure was significantly lower—albeit still high—at 17 per cent. Severe problems were likely to affect 5.4 per cent of women and 3.9 per cent of men.

The 1993 and 2007 UK surveys also indicate that women are more prone to psychological problems than men, but in both cases this is a finding that required a little spadework by us to unearth. The 1993 OPCS Survey of Psychiatric Morbidity, for example, doesn't actually provide a figure for total prevalence by gender. But when we analysed the original data, we found that 21.7 per cent of women had experienced anxiety, depression, psychosis, alcohol dependence, or drug dependence in the previous twelve months. The figure for men was 19.5 per cent: not a massive difference for sure, but it turned out to be a statistically significant one nevertheless. (Like the Australian survey, the OPCS study used the criteria set out in ICD-10.)

As for the 2007 Adult Psychiatric Morbidity Survey (APMS), if you were to take the official report at face value you'd conclude that, for several of the main psychological disorders, there was *no* significant overall difference between the sexes. For anxiety, post-traumatic stress disorder, depression, eating disorders, ADHD, and alcohol and drug problems, the overall rate for women is 27 per cent and for men 26 per cent. Yet the 2007 UK survey is a useful reminder of the need sometimes to scrutinize the detail of the data for oneself. Because when you do that, the picture can change.

For instance, the APMS asked participants about their alcohol use over the previous six months, and their consumption of drugs over the previous year. However, it employed a very different time frame for anxiety and depression, focusing on how people had been feeling during the previous *seven days*. Clearly, this makes it difficult to compare rates of, say, alcohol abuse and depression. And what might seem like just a methodological quirk turns out to have a direct bearing on the question of gender and mental health. Alcohol and drug problems, after all, are more usually seen in men. Anxiety and depression, on the other hand, tend to affect a greater number of women. Were anxiety and depression to be tracked over a longer period, we can be pretty sure not only that the figures for prevalence of these disorders given in the APMS would be significantly higher, but that the scales of mental illness could well tip decisively in the direction of women. Indeed, it's rather surprising that the APMS figures for overall psychological disorder are so similar for women and men given that typical male problems were assessed for at least twenty-six times as long as typical female problems! Even with the gauge skewed like this, the survey suggests women are (slightly) more likely to develop a psychological disorder.

There's more. The APMS report didn't address the prevalence of sleep disorders, but we knew from research we'd undertaken in the past that the participants had in fact been asked about their sleep habits. And so we returned to the data once again. We wanted to find out how many of those interviewed had reported symptoms of insomnia. Specifically, we were looking for individuals who had experienced all of the following:

- difficulty getting to sleep in the last month and on four nights in the previous week
- taking a minimum of an hour to get to sleep on at least one of these nights
- sleep problems lasting six months or more.

As we saw in the previous chapter, experts on sleep disorders have argued that insomnia tends to be more common in women than men. Our analysis of the APMS data bore this out: 12.7 per cent of the women interviewed had suffered from insomnia, compared to only 8.2 per cent of the men.

All it takes is the addition of the statistics for sleep problems for the impression created by the APMS to be transformed. No longer are overall rates of psychological disorder for men and women essentially identical. Now the odds on women developing problems are 1.2 times greater than those for men (an odds ratio of 1.2 in other words). When we include the data on insomnia, the figure for women jumps from 27 per cent to 32 per cent, and that for men from 26 per cent to 29 per cent. We see a distinct gap open up between the rates for the sexes, which were previously so close. You can imagine how that gap would widen were anxiety and depression to be assessed over twelve months rather than one week. And how it would probably grow still larger had the APMS collected data on another common set of disorders more frequently seen in women than men: sexual problems.

Incidentally, there are some other disorders that *were* covered by the APMS but that don't feature in the headline figure for overall rates of problems in each sex. As you might remember, autism spectrum disorders and certain personality disorders were assessed only in a specially selected subsample: some 850 people, or just 11 per cent of the 7,461 individuals interviewed. Including the data for these disorders in the total figure isn't straightforward because the participants didn't all receive the same kind of assessment. But it's doubtful whether it makes a great deal of difference, because both autism and personality disorders are relatively rare. Autism spectrum disorder (a catch-all term for a range of autistic conditions of varying severity) was found to affect 1.8 per cent of men and just 0.2 per cent of women. The personality disorders were even less common: 0.6 per cent of women and 0.3 per cent of men had experienced borderline personality disorder in the previous twelve months; for antisocial personality disorder the figures were 0.6 per cent for men and 0.1 per cent for women. Bear in mind too that autism spectrum and personality disorders are, to use the jargon, highly comorbid conditions. An individual with antisocial personality disorder, for instance, is very likely to be also struggling with other, much more common problems such as depression, anxiety, or alcohol or drug abuse. This means, of course, that they'll already have been counted among those with a psychological disorder.

In fact, although the APMS report suggests that there's little significant difference between the sexes in their overall vulnerability to certain common psychological disorders, a more sophisticated analysis carried out by the survey's authors tells a rather different story. The reasons for that analysis lie in the steady proliferation of disorders listed in successive versions of the DSM. The latest edition includes over 400: indeed, the DSM has more diagnoses than there are basic elements in the periodic table. But many of these conditions share very similar features. As a result, the DSM has been criticized for producing a taxonomy that's so minutely nuanced that it can sometimes be difficult for clinicians to decide exactly into which category—or categories—an individual's symptoms should be placed. For example, if I'm having trouble sleeping, worrying constantly, finding it difficult to concentrate, undereating, and constantly feeling down and on edge, am I suffering from depression, an anxiety disorder, an eating disorder—or all three? And how significant is the diagnostic label in any case? Isn't it better to focus on understanding and treating the symptoms themselves? An individual might end up being diagnosed with several, overlapping conditions; but the suspicion is that all we're doing is putting multiple names to the same basic problem.

This kind of classificatory conundrum presents issues for epidemiological surveys. Because if you focus your efforts on distinguishing between a plethora of rather similar conditions, you run the risk of missing the bigger picture of distress. That's to say, of not seeing the metaphorical wood for the trees. And so the APMS and the US National Comorbidity Survey Replication (NCS-R) both include a very clever statistical analysis designed to find the broader patterns of psychological ill health among the population. The idea is to identify groups of people with generally similar mental health profiles. The statistical technique used to do this is called 'latent class analysis'.

So into the pot the APMS put anxiety disorders, depression, alcohol and drug dependency, psychosis, borderline personality disorder, antisocial personality, ADHD, eating disorders, problem gambling, and suicide attempts. The NCS-R analysed anxiety disorders, depression, ADHD and related problems, bipolar disorder, and problems with alcohol and illicit substances. From this mass of diagnoses, the UK researchers identified six broad groups of people, and the US team seven. Both included a group comprising people with no significant symptoms, and we'll see why in a moment.

Now we have clusters of people, each representing a distinct profile of psychological disorders, plus one denoting an absence of psychological problems. What happens when we add in the issue of gender? When the NCS-R researchers analysed their data, they discovered that the odds on US men being in the symptom-free cluster were 1.4 times greater than those for US women. This finding was mirrored in the UK survey, which found that the odds on men ending up in the unaffected cluster were 1.3 times those for women. Fitting the pattern identified in other surveys, in both the NCS-R and APMS, men were more likely than women to experience disorders in the so-called 'externalizing' cluster, such as alcohol problems or ADHD, and less likely to suffer from 'internalizing' emotional problems like depression or anxiety. (Internalizing disorders are those which principally affect our feelings; externalizing disorders manifest themselves mainly in our behaviour.) The NCS-R researchers summarized their findings:

> The results regarding sociodemographic correlates are broadly consistent with previous surveys in finding that mental disorders...are associated with a general pattern of disadvantaged social status, including being female, unmarried, and having low socioeconomic status.[9]

Two-thirds of our twelve national surveys indicate that women are more likely than men to experience a psychological disorder. What do the other four tell us?

Three suggest that there are no major differences between the sexes.

The Australian National Mental Health Survey of 1997 assessed its participants using the ICD-10 criteria for anxiety, depression, substance use (alcohol, illicit drugs), psychosis, and personality disorders. The odds on women having experienced a disorder in the previous twelve months were 1.1 times greater than those for men. But the disparity in this survey didn't achieve statistical significance. The South African Stress and Health Study came up with an identical figure when it analysed twelve-month rates of anxiety, depression, alcohol and drug use, and impulse control disorders (using DSM-IV categories). That said, women in the South African survey were significantly more likely than men to experience *severe* problems. Participants in the Netherlands Mental Health Survey and Incidence Study (NEMESIS) were asked about their experience over the past year of anxiety, depression, eating disorders, psychosis, and substance use. When gauged against the criteria set out in DSM-III-R, the figures for men and women were all but identical: 23.5 per cent and 23.6 per cent respectively.

One of the twelve studies bucks the trend by reporting that it is men rather than women who are more likely to develop psychological problems. The UK survey of Psychiatric Morbidity Among Adults Living in Private Households (2000) assessed neurotic disorders (essentially anxiety and depression) over the previous week; psychosis and drug dependence during the previous year; and alcohol dependence in the past six months. One in four men (25 per cent) had experienced at least one of these problems, compared to 22 per cent of women. The report doesn't include a test of whether this difference is statistically meaningful. So we went back to the data ourselves, and discovered that the disparity was indeed statistically significant: the odds on women developing a disorder were markedly lower than those for men.

Now this might be the result of the big difference in male and female rates of alcohol dependence (11 per cent compared to just 3 per cent). Or it might be a product of the contrasting time frames—anything from seven days to a full twelve months—used to assess the various conditions. Because, just like the 2007 and 1993 surveys, the disorders that typically affect women (anxiety and depression) were measured over a much shorter period than those more often seen in men (drug and alcohol dependence). Clearly, when you're asking someone whether they've experienced a particular set of symptoms, the chances of obtaining a 'yes' are likely to be rather higher if you're referring to the previous year than to the past week. What happens when insomnia is added to the mix? When we did this, the statistically significant difference between the sexes disappeared.

The UK 2000 study assessed the same disorders, and used the same ICD criteria to do so, as the 1993 OPCS Survey of Psychiatric Morbidity. The latter, as we've seen, suggested that psychological problems are more common in women than men. So how might we account for the difference between the findings of the two surveys? What, if anything, changed over those seven years? In fact, the overall rate of disorder for women was more or less the same in both surveys. But the figure for men leaped up, overtaking that for women. That increase is due entirely to higher figures for male drug and alcohol dependence. However, there may be rather less going on here than meets the eye. It's probable that what seems like a rise in the number of men struggling with alcohol and drug problems is simply the result of different questionnaires being deployed to assess these disorders. At the very least, the fact that different assessments were used makes it difficult to compare the results directly. All of which leaves a large question mark beside the survey's finding that men are more at risk of psychological problems than women.

Two very big surveys didn't make the cut for our selection. One is the European Study of the Epidemiology of Mental Disorders (ESEMeD), which in the early 2000s assessed 21,425 people in nationally representative samples from Belgium, France, Germany, Italy, the Netherlands, and Spain. ESEMeD covered anxiety, depression, and alcohol disorders, using the schema set out in DSM-IV. But its main reporting paper didn't analyse problems with illicit substances—one of the common 'male' types of disorder—and so the survey didn't meet the criteria for inclusion in our review. The fact that illicit substances weren't covered no doubt partly explains why ESEMeD found such a big difference between male and female rates of disorder in the previous twelve months: 7 per cent for men and 12 per cent for women. The odds on women in the survey developing a disorder were fully 1.8 times greater than those for men.

The US Epidemiologic Catchment Area (ECA) study was historically important because it produced a reliable structured interview for the assessment of DSM disorders. The ECA interviewed 18,571 people in the early 1980s, but it wasn't nationally representative—which is why we excluded it from our analysis. The survey did, however, cover a wide range of conditions, including depression, anxiety, alcohol and drug problems, schizophrenia, antisocial personality disorder, and anorexia nervosa. The ECA assessed a number of different groups, with varying results. Among the participants drawn from the general population, women were significantly more likely than men to have experienced a psychological disorder in the previous month (17 per cent compared to 14 per cent). On the other hand, when this group was combined with people in residential accommodation (psychiatric hospitals, nursing homes, and prisons), there were no differences between the sexes for six- and twelve-month rates of disorder, and a much higher rate in men than women for lifetime rates (35 per cent compared to 30 per cent).

On balance, then, the major national epidemiological surveys suggest that women are more likely than men to develop psychological problems. The difference between the sexes isn't huge, and we should keep in mind that the rates for *both* men and women are worryingly high. Nevertheless, the data indicates that women experience something like 20–40 per cent more mental ill health than men. And remember that the surveys don't cover common conditions such as sleep and sexual problems, both of which are much more prevalent among women. We urgently require a more comprehensive study to substantiate what we think seems to be occurring. In our view, though, the current survey data indicates that gender is an important factor in a significant proportion of mental disorders as they are currently defined and classified by the medical profession.

As we've seen, not all of the surveys come to the same conclusion. But that's to be expected given the size of the difference. Were the disparity greater, it'd be easier to spot. But there's another way to obtain a more reliable picture of the situation and that's to survey larger numbers of people, or to combine the results of several studies. If we were to do that, we'd expect the difference between rates of mental illness in men and women to emerge with even greater clarity. As it happens, the World Health Organization (WHO) is running just such a project right now. Its World Mental Health Survey Initiative (WMH) 'aims to obtain accurate cross-national information about the prevalences and correlates of mental, substance, and behavioral disorders'.[10] (You can read more about the WMH at <www.hcp.med.harvard.edu/wmh>.)

Twenty-eight countries across the globe are participating in the WMH programme, including Brazil, Peru, Nigeria, South Africa, Iraq, Israel, France, Germany, Turkey, India, China, Japan, and New Zealand. Many of these studies have yet to report, but the eventual number of people surveyed is expected to be more than 154,000. In order to make valid comparisons between surveys of different countries, those surveys have to be run on the same lines. So, for example, each of the studies carried out under the auspices of the WMH project uses the same questionnaire: the WHO Composite International Diagnostic Interview (CIDI). Staff are trained centrally. And the data produced by each survey is analysed in the same place— Harvard Medical School—in collaboration with the respective national team.

What does the WMH programme have to tell us about gender and mental illness? Exactly this question was explored in a 2009 article published in the American Medical Association's *Archives of General Psychiatry*, one of the leading scientific journals. The article's authors analysed WMH surveys from fifteen countries, drawn from both the developed and developing worlds, and spanning Africa, the Americas, Asia, Europe, the Middle East, and the Pacific. All in all, the data covered more than 70,000 people, which adds up to a very considerable sample indeed. Among the fifteen studies were some that we included in our selected dozen surveys (for instance, the US National Comorbidity Survey Replication, the New Zealand Mental Health Survey, and the South African Stress and Health study). Others we excluded, either because they didn't cover the full range of substance problems (ESEMeD), or weren't fully national in scope (such as the Japanese and Mexican surveys), or didn't report a figure for total rates of disorder by gender (the studies from the Ukraine or Lebanon, for example). In total, the surveys provide information on the prevalence of eighteen disorders (though not every study reports on all eighteen). These conditions include anxiety; depression; bipolar disorder; externalizing disorders such as ADHD, conduct disorder, and intermittent explosive disorder; and substance problems—all of them assessed using the criteria set out in DSM-IV. Conspicuous by their absence, as ever, are sleep problems, sexual disorders, and somatoform disorders. As we've seen, these are conditions that tend to be more common among women than men.

The article looked at the lifetime risk of developing one of the eighteen disorders. By now you won't be surprised to learn that women reported higher rates of anxiety and depression whereas men were in the majority when it came to externalizing disorders and substance-related problems. How about overall rates of illness? Again, the picture is a familiar one. Across all age groups, women had a greater chance of developing a disorder than men. The difference between the sexes wasn't vast—the odds on women experiencing problems were 1.1 times greater than those for men—but it was statistically significant nonetheless. Given the number of people assessed, and the rigour with which these surveys were carried out, this is a finding it's difficult to discount. Add in the data for twelve-month rates of disorder in the surveys we've discussed earlier in this chapter, and the case for women's increased risk of psychological illness seems more persuasive than ever.

But if so many credible epidemiological surveys have come to this conclusion, how do we account for the view often put forward that men and women are equally likely to develop mental health problems? What's the evidence to support such a position? The answer can be found in two large US studies, the National Comorbidity Survey (NCS) of the early 1990s and its successor, the National Comorbidity Survey Replication (NCS-R), carried out a decade later. You might remember that both studies show that women had higher rates of illness over the previous twelve months. But they also report that, over the course of a lifetime, there's no real difference between the sexes. (The Dutch NEMESIS survey found much the same thing, though in that case men seemed to have a slightly higher—if statistically insignificant—rate of disorder than women.)

What might be going on here? Why is it that women in these US surveys report more problems over the previous year, only for the figures to even out over the longer time frame? There are at least three possible explanations.

Theory number one is that the lifetime rate isn't reliable. It's because the average human memory grows increasingly fallible as time passes that we decided to focus on twelve-month measurements of disorder. Here's an example of how the NCS-R interviewers attempted to compensate for the tricks and inadequacies of memory:

> 'Can you remember your exact age the very first time you (HAD THE SYNDROME)?' Respondents who answered 'no' were probed for a bound of uncertainty by moving up the age range incrementally (e.g. 'Was it before you first started school?' 'Was it before you became a teenager?').[11]

Even with this kind of prompting, remembering how we felt five or ten years ago can be tricky. But some of the participants in the US surveys were in their sixties or older: that's a very long time to recall with a high degree of accuracy. Logically, of course, one would expect lifetime rates of disorder to increase with age: the longer you live, the more time you have in which to develop a problem. Yet the NCS and NCS-R found the opposite. Perhaps the reason why rates actually declined with age in the US surveys was simply that the participants had forgotten past difficulties. Other research has also shown that if you ask a group of elderly people about the number of psychological problems they've experienced over the course of their life, they'll tend to give a lower estimate than people in middle age—presumably because they struggle to recall events in the distant past. (Less plausibly, perhaps older generations have actually experienced fewer problems over the course of their lives.)

The second possibility is that the statistics are correct and that, over the course of a lifetime, men and women really do experience very similar levels of mental illness. Why then do men show lower rates of disorder over a twelve-month period? Well, it may be that their problems tend not to last as long as women's—that's to say, men generally recover more quickly. As a result, it's less likely that a disorder will show up in a survey of recent and current problems. Let's imagine, for example, that in January a man and a woman both visit their GP seeking treatment for depression. By April, the man is feeling much better; but it takes until July for the woman to recover. The following June, both individuals are asked about their mental health in the previous twelve months. And though they each developed the same problem at the same time, only the woman would be categorized as having suffered from a disorder. However, this theory is difficult to square with the finding of longitudinal studies (which follow a group of people over a number of months or years) that the number of women reporting a first experience of depression or anxiety is higher than that for men. In other words, when you look at the new incidence of problems (when time to recovery is not an issue), the disparity between male and female rates of the most common psychological disorders remains intact.

The third potential explanation is that men are usually more comfortable discussing psychological problems in the distant past than they are owning up to difficulties they've experienced recently. But although the US surveys found that the gap between male and female lifetime rates of psychological disorder is closing, it isn't because the incidence of anxiety and depression is gradually evening out. Women are still more prone to these sorts of emotional problem. Instead, men catch up with women due to the big difference in their vulnerability to substance disorders (a typical male problem throughout adulthood).

The findings of the NCS and NCS-R have been hugely influential in shaping the view that overall rates of mental illness in men and women are identical. As we've seen, gathering data on people's experiences over the course of their entire life is fraught with difficulty. But even if the US figures are reliable, higher lifetime rates of disorder in *women* have been reported by several surveys, including the most comprehensive of the lot, the German National Health Interview and Examination Survey, as well as the New Zealand Mental Health Survey and the Chile Psychiatric Prevalence Study. Remember too that the analysis of fifteen WHO studies we discussed earlier in this chapter focused on lifetime figures. It found that the odds on women developing a disorder were 1.1 times greater than those for men. All of which suggests that, at the very least, we should be wary of leaping to conclusions based on the two US studies. Perhaps lifetime rates of disorder for men and women are indeed very similar. But when you take a comprehensive look at the current evidence, it seems unlikely.

Until now, no one has sought to pin down what the national epidemiological surveys carried out since the 1980s tell us about male and female experience of psychological problems. Our analysis reveals three key points. First, rates of disorder are alarmingly high in both men and women. Second, certain disorders are more common in men, others are more frequently seen in women, and still others occur equally in the sexes. Third, women generally show higher total rates of disorder. As we've seen, you don't have to look very far to find the view that men and women are equally likely to develop psychological problems. Yet the results of these large-scale national surveys leave this argument looking distinctly precarious. On the basis of this data, we conclude that rates of psychological disorder are not the same for both sexes. And it's women who bear the brunt of the burden.

3

Digging Deeper into the Data

In the previous chapter we discovered that a series of national epidemiological surveys suggests that women experience a greater total burden of psychological disorders than men. Not that men are miraculously spared these kinds of problem—far from it. Rates of disorder for both sexes are much higher than is often assumed. And there are some disorders that are more often seen in men, just as some conditions are more common among women. Nevertheless, when you look at the data for overall prevalence, the rates for women tend to be significantly higher. In a race that no one wants to win, women are currently leading.

In this chapter we're going to dig a little deeper, exploring beyond the basic diagnostic approach to mental health. Behind every dataset lies a number of sometimes knotty interpretative issues, and it's no different with these surveys. So we'll highlight some of the key areas of debate and assess their impact on the question of gender and mental health. And because the national studies we discuss in Chapter 2 focus exclusively on adults, we'll also investigate the situation with children: is the pattern we see in adults replicated in this younger age group? Throughout the chapter we'll be drawing on a variety of research data. But this material isn't plentiful. So until that situation is rectified, any conclusions we might draw can only be provisional.

Each of the twelve surveys we looked at in the previous chapter uses the classificatory system, and the criteria for disorders, set out in either the American Psychiatric Association's *Diagnostic and Statistical Manual of Mental Disorders* (DSM) or in the similar *International Classification of Diseases and Health Related Problems* (ICD), published by the World Health Organization. This makes perfect sense: these are, after all, the standard reference works for all mental health professionals. They summarize and define our current understanding of psychological illness. Nevertheless, this is still contested territory. The DSM, for example, has changed dramatically since its first incarnation in 1952. And its contents are always the subject of intense debate.

Publication of the fifth edition of the DSM—'one of the most anticipated events in the mental health field',[1] as the American Psychiatric Association put it, with no little justification—is scheduled for 2013. Yet planning for the volume began back in 1999, shortly before a revised version of the *fourth* edition appeared. Project leaders have certainly been mindful of the need to think seriously about the way in which the DSM handles the issue of gender. (As we saw in Chapter 1, the manual has drawn criticism from some feminist writers.) In a bid to stimulate debate on the topic, in 2007 key figures in DSM-V—including Michael First, editor of DSM-IV and director of the DSM-V Prelude Project, and Darrel Regier, DSM-V Task Force Vice-Chair—edited a collection of papers on *Age and Gender Considerations in Psychiatric Diagnosis: A Research Agenda for DSM-V*.

'Let us designate a "decade of the gendered brain"!'[2] went the rallying cry from the authors of one of the chapters. Yet none of the contributors tackled the question of overall rates of disorder in each sex, not even the authors of the chapter on 'Gender and the Prevalence of Psychiatric Disorders'. (Unfortunately, since this would have saved us a lot of work.)

Instead the focus was on issues such as understanding the role gender plays in the categorization of psychological disorders. Should diagnostic criteria remain overwhelmingly 'gender neutral'—in other words, identical for men and women? This assumes, of course, that the problems express themselves in the same way in both sexes. Or should different thresholds be used for men and women? Would it be better to develop more gender-specific diagnoses? (This is an approach already—and understandably—employed for several sexual problems, such as male erectile disorder and vaginismus.) These are questions without easy answers, at least at present. The authors conclude:

> there is a need for more research concerned specifically with how each of the disorders is manifested in males and females. Increased understanding of phenomenology [that is, the precise nature of the experiences constituting the disorder] and whether symptom expression differs in males and females is needed to inform the development of valid diagnostic criteria. Of course this is an iterative process, because research on phenomenology is usually based on the DSM criteria sets and vice versa.[3]

In other words, we don't yet know enough to be sure about the role gender should play in the diagnosis of psychological disorders. We need a much clearer sense of exactly how those disorders affect people, and especially the form they take for each sex. But the task is made more complicated by the fact that we're working with existing classifications and definitions—and perhaps therefore biases too. Researchers tend to study the disorders set out in the DSM and ICD, so the parameters of the investigation have to some degree already been set. The board isn't about to be swept clean; the manual isn't going to be ripped up and rewritten from scratch. Instead we can expect a gradual process in which our understanding of a particular condition is modified little by little.

Part of the problem here is that producing a set of criteria for a psychological disorder is necessarily an exercise in interpretation (by committee). Matters would be far more straightforward if mental illnesses were entities possessing constant and easily recognizable properties, like some chemical compound. But when drawing up those criteria, the experts responsible for the DSM and ICD must make judgements about the number, type, and severity of symptoms that are sufficient to warrant a diagnosis. As a result, those criteria can sometimes seem a little arbitrary (as we'll see in a moment, they can certainly shift over time). For example, you might feel as low as a dog, but unless you're experiencing the exact number and type of symptoms set out in the DSM, you wouldn't currently be classified as suffering from 'major depressive disorder' (though different criteria have been used in the past and things will doubtless change again in the future). Fall short by one symptom and you wouldn't get a diagnosis, for all the misery you might be enduring.

This interpretative aspect to the classification of disorders means that it can be tricky to know how to handle differences between the sexes. What does it mean if men's and women's experience of a particular condition isn't identical? Should the criteria for that disorder be tweaked to accommodate the differences? Are men and women undergoing the same thing in diverse ways, or are they suffering from qualitatively distinct problems? As the article's authors put it:

> In the absence of an independent, objective gold standard for the valid diagnosis of a respective mental disorder, it is not clear how gender differences in etiology [the causes of the condition], pathology [the form of the illness], and symptomatology should impact diagnostic criteria sets.[4]

Their recommendation is to focus first on understanding those gender differences and then to decide whether the criteria for disorders should be modified in the light of that research:

> studies could compare across males and females the relationship of criteria sets to external validators (e.g. course, level of impairment, treatment responsivity, and family history). As disorders' etiopathology [i.e. their causes] is increasingly elucidated, criteria sets could be examined in relationship to various etiopathological variables.[5]

Yet gender is just one of several contentious issues circling the DSM and ICD. One of those issues concerns the highly changeable nature of these classificatory systems: set in stone they are not. The first two editions of the DSM, for example, were heavily influenced by psychoanalysis, which dominated US psychotherapy in the middle of the 20th century. The number of disorders listed in the DSM trebled in just forty years. And it's not simply a question of categories and conditions being added: others are dropped (homosexuality, notoriously, was removed from the DSM only when the third edition was published in 1980). Society's view of what constitutes normal and abnormal behaviour shifts over time and, as if they were dancing some pas de deux, the psychiatric classifications move accordingly.

Given the mutability of these classificatory systems, and the proliferation of conditions (almost 300 in the revised version of DSM-IV), it's hardly surprising that some diagnostic criteria are perhaps rather more sound than others. Then there's the practical problem for health professionals of trying to distinguish between several very similar conditions to decide which, if any, their client is dealing with. So it makes more sense to concentrate on *clusters* of related problems. This is the thinking behind recent proposals from a number of researchers for a 'meta-structure' of psychiatric disorders. Such a meta-structure typically comprises five groups of conditions:

- Neurocognitive disorders (that is, problems such as dementia which are caused by damage to, or deterioration of, the brain)
- Neurodevelopmental disorders (cognitive problems that first occur in childhood: for example, learning disabilities)
- Psychoses (like schizophrenia)
- Emotional disorders (depression, anxiety)
- Externalizing disorders (for example, antisocial personality disorder and substance-related problems)

The problems inherent in the current system, and the possible benefits of the cluster approach, have been encapsulated by Gavin Andrews and colleagues:

> DSM-III/IV and ICD-10 were designed to facilitate clinical care as the first priority but the classifications and their thresholds are too complex for many clinicians to use. Could grouping disorders into clinically meaningful clusters facilitate both patient care and research?[6]

Of course in Chapter 2 we saw that two of our national surveys—the US National Comorbidity Survey Replication and the English Adult Psychiatric Morbidity Survey 2007—adopted a very similar approach in order to get around the problem of multiple diagnoses. They looked at clusters of problems. And both studies found the total rate of psychological disorder was higher for women than for men.

The second major criticism levelled at current psychiatric systems is that they aren't sensitive to *dimensions of severity*. The DSM and ICD are essentially binary in their approach: either you meet the criteria for a particular condition, or you don't. Just as you can't be a little bit pregnant, no one is going to receive a formal diagnosis of 'slight depression'. But many would argue that this kind of all-or-nothing attitude, with hundreds of separate conditions, doesn't fit well with people's real-life experience of psychological problems. Better instead to think of psychological experience as being dimensional—that is, encompassing a wide variety of experiences, from the unproblematic to the severely distressing. The further a person is along that dimension, the more symptoms they're likely to have and the more upsetting and disruptive those symptoms will be. Robert Kendall and Assen Jablensky put it neatly:

> Despite historical and recent assumptions to the contrary, there is little evidence that most currently recognised mental disorders are separated by natural boundaries. Researchers are increasingly assuming that variation in symptoms is continuous and therefore questioning the validity of contemporary classifications.[7]

The eminent behavioural geneticist Robert Plomin talks in terms of 'quantitative traits':

> thinking quantitatively will be aided by speaking quantitatively—a shift in vocabulary is required so that we start talking about 'dimensions' rather than 'disorders' and about genetic 'variability' rather than genetic 'risk'.[8]

There is no binary opposition between disorder and 'normality', no radical divide between the two states. Plomin argues that we should see common psychological disorders instead as simply the extreme manifestation of traits that we all possess to varying degrees. So, for example, almost everyone experiences feelings of anxiety from time to time. Those individuals who develop an anxiety disorder aren't experiencing something qualitatively different. They're simply going through a more intense version of the same thing. In other words, they're at a different, more advanced point along the anxiety dimension. And this dimensionality is reflected at a genetic level. It seems pretty clear that there's a genetic element to most psychological disorders. But we aren't born with, say, a 'panic disorder' gene. Instead, panic disorder is partly the product of a large number of genes, each of which may exert only a small effect, in combination of course with the things that happen to us in our life. Therefore even the genetic risk is quantitative, spread out over the general population in a bell-shaped curve. Some people will be at low risk of disorder; some will be at high risk; and a lot will be somewhere in the middle. (This is what Plomin means by 'genetic variability'.)

Such a dramatic shift in approach has potentially far-reaching implications for the questions we're exploring in this book. Perhaps the gender differences in mental health are predominately a product of where the threshold for a diagnosis happens to have been placed for each disorder. Imagine, for instance, that in some hypothetical assessment you have to score 100 to be classified as suffering from an anxiety disorder. Scoring 90 means you're still pretty anxious, but isn't enough to get you a diagnosis. And then you end up in the same group as those who've scored zero. The threshold, or cut-off point, skews the data. Perhaps women score slightly higher than men for certain disorders, and vice versa. But actually, if you think dimensionally, maybe there isn't a great deal of difference between the sexes. (Later in this chapter, we'll try to discover whether this might really be the case.)

What's implicit here, of course, is a debate about the very nature of mental illness. Derek Bolton, a philosopher and clinical psychologist, highlights three models. First is the *psychiatric/medical*, which thinks in terms of separate, discrete disorders, just like physical medicine. This is the approach taken by the DSM and ICD. The second, *psychological*, model embodies a dimensional approach. (The eminent psychiatrist David Goldberg calls these two respectively the categorical or Platonic and dimensional or Aristotelian approaches.

Plato believed that abstract concepts or forms exist beyond human perception. Thus the Platonic approach to psychological disorder 'endows diagnoses with a mysterious independent existence but holds that they are, at least for the time being, unobservable. We can acquire information about them only indirectly, by observing symptoms.'[9] By contrast, 'Aristotle asserted that the only reality resides in the evidence of our senses, so followers of this school assert that all we have are the symptoms.'[10]) Finally, the *sociological* model argues that psychological disorders aren't illnesses at all. Instead, they're a label used to stigmatize and control behaviour society deems objectionable.

Our view is that psychological problems aren't illusory. They are real expressions of distress, manifested by individuals, and for which most people understandably want help. But we think it's wisest not to focus on particular diagnoses. Better instead to adopt a dimensional approach, and to concentrate on the key experiences characterizing certain broad types of problems. How do we judge what these key experiences might be? First of all, we can look at epidemiological information to see which experiences occur together. This is called a data-driven approach.

Second, we can be informed by our knowledge of how the brain works. For example, basic emotions such as fear or unhappiness are powered by distinct circuits in the brain. So we can understand certain psychological problems as what follow when these emotional circuits don't function properly. We can match up the emotion and the problem: sadness and depression, fear and anxiety disorders, for example. This is what we might call a theory-driven approach. It may also be an optimistic one, given the complexity of the interactions that occur in the brain.

We should bear in mind too that the bar has been set differently for some emotions. Anger, for instance, is regarded as a basic emotion.

We all feel it from time to time, right from the first few months of life. But there's no such thing as 'anger disorder'. Extreme anger tends to be seen as a symptom of other problems or, when it spills over into violence, as a matter for the police. The contrasting attitudes to anger and, say, anxiety serve as another reminder that psychiatric classifications are constructed, rather than merely revealed by research. Who knows whether, if anger disorder were recognized as a psychological condition, one sex would be more likely to be diagnosed than the other? If we look at the data for externalizing disorders, it seems likely that men would show higher rates of a putative anger disorder than women. And what effect might that have on the overall figures for psychological problems?

What do those national surveys that have taken a dimensional approach tell us about gender and mental health? Some of the studies we discussed in the previous chapter adopted just such a method, alongside their focus on particular DSM-specified disorders. Were the results different? Did these dimensional analyses also find that women were at greater risk than men of developing psychological problems?

The Adult Psychiatric Morbidity Survey (2007) provides dimensional scores for emotional and alcohol problems. Women had significantly higher scores on the measure of anxiety and depression problems, and lower scores on the alcohol assessment—a result that will have surprised nobody familiar with the mass of epidemiological data on these disorders. What we're seeing here is confirmation that a dimensional analysis is likely to reveal the same gender differences as the diagnostic approach.

The UK survey also produced figures for mental well-being, which is perhaps a way of gauging overall psychological health. By analysing responses to nine questions in the survey, the APMS researchers measured two types of well-being: the *hedonic* (being happy, calm, and peaceful; feeling full of life; having lots of energy) and the *eudaemonic* (getting on well with family and friends; feeling a sense of belonging; enjoying one's spare time; being able to complete tasks). Women scored significantly lower than men for hedonic well-being—which suggests that they tend to feel less content than men. On the other hand, the sexes were roughly equal for eudaemonic well-being. Interestingly, when these scores were adjusted for the presence of anxiety and depression disorders (that is, when the researchers stripped out the influence of these problems on the scores), women still scored lower than men for hedonic well-being, but they ranked higher on the eudaemonic measures.

As part of the Australian National Mental Health Survey (1997), participants were asked to complete the General Health Questionnaire (GHQ-12). The GHQ is used to screen for common mental health problems such as anxiety and depression. Six of its twelve questions are positively worded:

Have you recently:

1. Been able to concentrate on whatever you are doing?
2. Felt that you are playing a useful part in things?
3. Felt capable of making decisions about things?
4. Been able to enjoy your normal day to day activities?
5. Been able to face up to your problems?
6. Been feeling reasonably happy, all things considered?[11]

The other six questions are negatively worded:

Have you recently:

1. Lost much sleep over worry?
2. Felt constantly under strain?

3. Felt you couldn't overcome your difficulties?

4. Been feeling unhappy and depressed?

5. Been losing confidence in yourself?

6. Been thinking of yourself as a worthless person?[12]

What we have here in the GHQ is a measure of psychological well-being, though ideally it'd be more wide-ranging: it focuses on emotional problems and doesn't ask about externalizing behaviours (such as alcohol and drug problems and aggressive or disruptive conduct). We saw in Chapter 2 that emotional problems tend to be more common in women and externalizing disorders more prevalent in men. And the results of the Australian GHQ bear that out again, with women reporting poorer mental health than men.

The New Zealand Mental Health Survey, 'Te Rau Hinengaro', also included a dimensional measure. Its ten questions asked people about their experience of feeling tired, nervous, hopeless, restless or fidgety, and worthless. These kinds of feelings are very much associated with depression and anxiety, and so it's no surprise that women reported significantly more problems than men.

What we really need, though, is an assessment that covers all the key areas of psychological well-being, and that provides a total score for each sex. Such an assessment would go against the idea that there are several dimensions of disorder. But it would give us an overall picture of mental health—and one that's more nuanced than simply counting the number of people who meet DSM criteria for a particular set of disorders (useful though that undoubtedly is). This kind of analysis hasn't been done before, so we decided to carry it out for this book.

To do so, we investigated the dataset produced by the National Comorbidity Survey Replication (NCS-R), the main US psychiatric survey. It turns out that the NCS-R dataset includes a wide-ranging dimensional assessment for symptoms in the previous month (and we've seen already that these kinds of short-term assessments are likely to be more reliable than those that quiz people about, say, their mental health over the course of their entire life). To our knowledge, the results of this assessment have never been examined. Participants in the survey were asked how often they'd experienced thirty-three separate problems. Those problems included:

- Feeling psychological distress
- Feeling lonely
- Feeling frightened
- Feeling blue
- Worrying too much
- Having trouble concentrating
- Feeling as though everything is an effort
- Feeling irritable or grumpy
- Feeling angry
- Experiencing the urge to hit, push, or hurt someone
- Feeling the urge to break or smash something
- Feeling that objects, people, or the world aren't real
- Hearing voices in your head.

The questions mainly focus on emotional problems, which will skew the results a little (because women are more likely than men to experience these kinds of difficulties). But externalizing problems—which are more common in men—also get a look in, for instance in the questions that ask about anger and aggression. The assessment even touches upon psychosis (for example, hearing voices), which other studies have suggested tends to affect men and women in equal numbers. All in all, it's the widest dimensional screen we've come across in a national survey. And when you add up the total scores, what does it reveal? Well, only 4,000 of the NCS-R's original sample of 9,282 actually completed all the items. But we made this reduced number of respondents representative by applying the appropriate statistical weights. Then we compared the mean scores of men and women. This showed that women experienced significantly more of these problems than men.

The NCS-R dataset also includes four questions assessing happiness. They ask participants how often over the previous thirty days they've felt confident; optimistic; happy; and full of life. Again, we've not found any previous analysis of these items. We added up the totals for the four items, applied weighting to ensure the results are applicable to the general population, and discovered that men reported significantly greater amounts of happiness than women. Given what we found with the thirty-three-question assessment of psychological problems, this result doesn't come as a shock. After all, if women are on average experiencing more mental health issues, it's likely that they're going to be unhappier than men too. And it's a finding that fits with work done by social scientists. Betsey Stevenson and Justin Wolfers, in a 2009 article in the *American Economic Journal*, describe what they see as 'the paradox of declining female happiness':

> The gender wage gap has partly closed. Educational attainment has risen and is now surpassing that of men. Women have gained an unprecedented level of control over fertility. Technological change, in the form of new domestic appliances, has freed women from domestic drudgery. In short, women's freedoms within both the family and market sphere have expanded.... [Yet] measures of women's subjective well-being have fallen both absolutely and relatively to that of men.[13]

Despite all these positive changes, survey after survey in a variety of Western nations has found that women's level of happiness has been decreasing. (These aren't studies of mental health like the ones we've been discussing so far in this book, but general social surveys of attitudes, behaviour, and life satisfaction.) Back in the 1970s, women's reported happiness exceeded that of men. These days there's still a happiness gap between the sexes. However, it's now women that are trailing behind.

So it seems that whichever approach we take to the data, the outcome is more or less identical. Whether we focus on specific diagnoses, or analyse the figures dimensionally, the same gender differences crop up. The dimensional assessments emerging from the national surveys tend to concentrate on emotional problems— though as we've seen with the NCS-R they don't entirely ignore other areas. Perhaps it's no surprise given their emphasis on emotional difficulties. But, like the diagnostic surveys we discussed in Chapter 2, these dimensional assessments suggest that women experience more psychological problems than men. Clearly, the gender differences are unlikely to be due to quirks of the traditional diagnostic systems.

But could it be that these differences aren't real at all? Perhaps all they show is that women are more willing to recognize and report symptoms. Or that they have better memories for psychological problems. Maybe men are reluctant to admit that something might be wrong. We're reminded of an interview with the rock band Pink Floyd at the height of their success in the 1970s. By this point, relationships within the all-male group were reputed to have become somewhat strained. 'Are there some difficult moments?' asked guitarist David Gilmour rhetorically. 'Yes.' 'How do you get around them?' asked the journalist. 'We pretend they're not there,' responded bassist Roger Waters. 'We certainly don't face up to them in an adult way, if that's what you mean.'[14]

There's undoubtedly something to this argument. We know, for example, that men are less likely than women to go to the doctor for treatment of physical and psychological problems. The difficulty, though, lies in gauging exactly how much truth the theory contains. Can it really account for the entirety of gender differences revealed by national surveys? Is this truly all there is to it? Some writers have argued that it is. But that can only be speculation: it's impossible to be sure. We can never, after all, know exactly how many men are *not* reporting psychological problems (nor, for that matter, how many women are keeping difficulties to themselves). We think it's plausible that men's reticence, or their reluctance to admit even to themselves that they may have a problem, explains some of the difference between men's and women's rates of mental illness. But, as we'll see in Part 2 of this book, it's likely that there are other factors at work too.

There is some data to suggest that women are better than men at recalling depressive episodes several years in the past. This is partly why we've opted to focus our attention on shorter time frames—that's to say, problems in the past month or year. But men and women alike tend to be fairly poor at retrospective recall: other studies show that both sexes tend to underestimate the extent of their psychological problems when they look back over an extended period of time. Research that interviews participants at frequent, regular intervals (so-called *prospective* studies) shows a higher rate of symptoms than surveys that ask people to cast their minds back over their entire lifetime. Perhaps we tend to forget the bad times. Maybe our troubles seem less severe in retrospect. Or possibly, for whatever reason, our reluctance to admit to psychological problems increases with the passing of time.

We have to remember too that attitudes toward emotion are strongly gendered. For example, in many societies children learn that it's less acceptable for a boy to show fear than a girl. These lessons may not be spelled out explicitly by our parents. Yet research suggests that even parents who strive to bring up their children without sexist attitudes often end up unconsciously reinforcing the very biases they're trying so hard to avoid. And gendered attitudes towards emotion are certainly embedded in our culture. One study, for example, looked at forty-one best-selling children's books published between 1984 and 1994. Girls were typically described as (among other things) *frightened, weak,* and *scared,* while boys were *fierce, brave,* and *proud.* Or take your pick of Hollywood blockbusters featuring a courageous and intrepid male hero calming a weeping, frightened woman. While girls may be indulged in their fears, boys are encouraged to overcome them. And this isn't simply a presentational issue. As we'll discuss later in this book, the way we're taught to handle our emotions can have profound and long-lasting consequences for our psychological make-up. Men, for example, may not merely have learned to keep silent about their fears. Their upbringing may actually have made it less likely that they'll experience anxiety. This is because research has shown that if you confront your fears, you'll suffer fewer of them.

Very few scientific studies have attempted to measure men's reluctance to admit to 'unmasculine' feelings or experiences. In fact, we've come across just one. It was small, involving twenty-three women and seventeen men. Moreover, the participants were all college students and thus not especially representative of the population as a whole. Nonetheless, the study provides a neat illustration of some of the tendencies at work here. Kent Pierce and Dwight Kirkpatrick, two behavioural scientists at Purdue University in Indiana, set out to answer the question: 'Do men lie on fear surveys?' To do so, they asked a group of college students how much they feared a number of objects and situations, including rats, mice, and roller-coaster rides. A month later, the participants were asked to retake the survey. But this time there was a crucial difference. The students were informed that before filling in the questionnaire they were going to see a video of these objects and situations. During the video, it was explained, their heart rate would be monitored, allowing the researchers to determine just how scared the students *really* were:

> During the viewing of this video, your finger will be connected to a light sensor which will provide a measure of your heart rate. Heart rate is one of the measures often used in a lie detector test because it changes with your emotions. This makes it important to rate the items on this fear questionnaire as accurately as possible, because we will compare your answers with changes in your heart rate.[15]

In fact, the heart rate readings proved not to correlate with the students' reported fears. But the participants could not have predicted this. Anyone who'd faked a response on the previous questionnaire would have assumed that the game was up—that the time for false bravado had passed. As it happened, only one sex had been telling fibs on the first survey. On the second, the men scored significantly higher for fear, while the women's ratings remained unchanged. Yet although this experiment provides some evidence that men really do play down their anxieties, it also found that women experienced more fear than men, even after the temptation to lie had been removed. There's more going on here, then, than men simply being loath to confess their supposed frailties. But clearly it's difficult to draw too many conclusions from a single study: more are needed. And not just on emotional problems. It'd be fascinating to explore whether women, for example, are more likely than men to *under-report* their alcohol intake, given that drinking has traditionally been regarded as a distinctively male pursuit.

No one who saw it can forget the sight of England footballer Paul Gascoigne breaking into tears during the 1990 World Cup semi-final against Germany. (Gascoigne had just been booked, meaning that he could not have played in the final, had England made it that far. As it turned out, he need not have worried.) But even more remarkable than the picture of a macho sportsman weeping uncontrollably was the public reaction. Rather than being mocked as a 'cry-baby', Gascoigne's grief triggered an unexpected wave of empathy. It may be fanciful to imagine that this marked the moment when attitudes towards male vulnerability began to alter. But certainly mental health professionals are now encouraging men to ditch the stiff upper lip and face up to their emotional problems. It's a trend reinforced by the increasing number of male public figures who have talked openly about their depression, among them Alastair Campbell, Stephen Fry, Jon Hamm (Don Draper in the hit TV show *Mad Men*), and Kevan Jones, one of several MPs to speak candidly about their personal struggles during a 2012 parliamentary debate on mental health. And the issue was given added urgency by the apparent suicide in 2011 of the handsome, charismatic, and youthful manager of the Wales football team, Gary Speed. (Speed's death came just two years after Robert Enke, the German international goalkeeper, had walked in front of a train near his home in Hannover. Enke had suffered from depression for several years.) But will these cultural shifts result in more men being prepared to admit to emotional problems? Will the gap between male and female rates of reported depression and anxiety begin to close?

So far, at least, there's been very little sign of any change. The Adult Psychiatric Morbidity Survey of 2007, for example, showed large gender differences in rates of anxiety and depression across the age groups from 16 upwards (with women, of course, affected much more than men). When the results of the 2007 survey were compared with those of the OPCS Survey of Psychiatric Morbidity, which was published in 1993, it was found that one sex is indeed now reporting more emotional disorders. But, as you may have guessed, it's women who seem to be experiencing greater problems. The figures for men haven't altered.

So much for the UK. Is the situation any different elsewhere? The World Health Organization (WHO) has examined lifetime rates of disorder in fifteen countries (excluding the UK, but including nations as diverse as Colombia, Lebanon, South Africa, Ukraine, Italy, Japan, and the United States) and in four separate age groups: 18 to 34, 35 to 49, 50 to 64, and 65 years and older. For the majority of disorders, where there was a gender difference it was similar in each of the age groups. Interestingly, however, that wasn't so in the case of depression and substance problems. For these disorders, the gap between men and women was significantly smaller for the younger cohorts. Why is this? The authors of the WHO study speculate that it may be due to changes in traditional gender roles:

> increases in female opportunities in the domains of employment, birth control, and other indicators of increasing gender role equality promote improvements in female mental health by reducing exposure to stressors that can lead to depression and by increasing access to effective stress-buffering resources... [On the other hand] opportunities for female substance use and attitudes about the appropriateness of female substance use both change as female roles become more similar to male roles, resulting in an increase in female substance use.[16]

We'll return to these possible explanations in Part 2. But for now we should bear in mind that the WHO study has some methodological drawbacks. It's what's known as a 'cross-sectional' survey: it analyses several different groups at one particular moment in time. But a cross-sectional survey isn't dynamic. It doesn't change with the passing of time. It won't, for instance, tell us how the youngest group will be affected when they're older. Perhaps the reduced gap between male and female rates of depression and substance disorder is only temporary; maybe it'll widen as the years go by. Longitudinal studies, on the other hand, follow the same group of people over time. Which means they're a much better way of tracing the influence of age on mental health. Unfortunately, this kind of study hasn't yet been carried out. Moreover, neither the WHO study nor the UK surveys attempted to deal with the elephant in the corner—that is, the willingness of participants to tell researchers how they've really been feeling. Are men readier these days to admit to emotional problems? It doesn't seem as though they are, but that's only speculation; we can't know for sure.

Popular wisdom (and a mass of pop psychology books to boot) holds that men, unlike women, prefer not to discuss their problems. Doubtless this stereotyping contains a kernel of truth, and may account for some of the difference between male and female rates of emotional disorder. On the other hand, as so often with stereotypes, we tend to notice the evidence that supports our preconception and overlook that which doesn't. Moreover, lacking the ability to read people's minds, it's rather difficult to know whether or not someone is struggling with a psychological problem. How, then, can we judge how many men—or women—aren't being candid about these kinds of difficulties? Overall, there's a clear consensus in the academic literature that the disparity between male and female rates of depression and anxiety is real, and not simply—or predominately—a consequence of under-reporting by men. There may be slight reporting biases, but the difference is too large to be explained away by this alone. To really get to the bottom of what's going on, we need to look elsewhere.

Our focus is on psychological problems in adults. But what about children? Are the same gender differences evident in this younger age group?

You know you're on to an important topic when you discover that Michael Rutter has devoted his attention to it. Rutter was the first person in the UK to be appointed as a consultant of child psychiatry and he has been a hugely influential figure in child psychology for many decades. In Rutter's view, the fact that rates of psychological disorder vary between the sexes isn't a secondary issue. It's not merely an interesting gloss on the data. Instead it goes right to the heart of mental illness. Because if we can work out what lies behind these differences we're going to be a lot clearer about what causes such problems in the first place.

And those differences set in early. Here's how Rutter and co-authors Avshalom Caspi and Terrie Moffitt (both leading research-ers in their own right) summarize what's known about the childhood occurrence of psychological disorders:

> On the face of it, sex differences in mental disorder fall into two main groups. First, there are the early-onset neuropsychiatric disor-ders, such as autism, developmental language disorders, attention deficit disorder with hyperactivity (ADHD), and dyslexia. All of these show a marked male preponderance, as well as childhood onset. Second, there are the adolescent-onset emotional disorders, such as depressive conditions and eating disorders like anorexia and bulimia nervosa, which show a marked female preponderance. Antisocial disorders appear to constitute an anomaly in that they are substantially commoner in males despite the fact that their onset peaks in adolescence. The paradox is, however, more apparent than real

because the early-onset variety associated with neurodevelopmental impairment shows a male preponderance, whereas females commonly evidence adolescent-onset antisocial behaviour.[17]

It's a view echoed by two leading US developmental psychologists, Nicki Crick and Carolyn Zahn-Waxler:

> During early childhood (i.e. prior to approximately age 4), girls and boys are equally likely to exhibit adjustment difficulties [that is, problems coping with stressful situations]...After the toddler years, the picture of gender and psychopathology changes substantially. Specifically, boys have been overwhelmingly identified as exhibiting more significant adjustment problems than girls during the pre-school and elementary school years. These are primarily of an externalizing nature and include such difficulties as oppositional defiant disorder, conduct disorder, physical aggression, and ADHD...Starting in adolescence, some research suggests that adjustment problems are more equally distributed across the sexes. However, adolescent boys continue to outnumber girls in physical aggression and violence and also show more criminal behavior. At this time in development there also is a marked shift toward a preponderance of females showing internalizing disorders (e.g. depression, anxiety, eating disorders).[18]

It's a picture that we've become familiar with when looking at the data on adults. Males are more prone to externalizing problems, while females show higher rates of emotional and eating disorders. And yet perhaps things aren't quite so straightforward. Crick and Zahn-Waxler argue that female conduct problems are actually 'underestimated and underidentified.'[19] Girls, they suggest, are in fact far more aggressive than is commonly supposed. It's just that the *type* of aggressive behaviour they tend to favour isn't usually picked up by adults. When a boy thumps someone in the play-ground, everyone notices. Torn clothes, bruises, and bloody noses: it's pretty difficult not to spot those. But girls of all ages tend to use rather more subtle—though arguably even more damaging—methods to hurt other people. They employ what Crick has termed 'relational aggression': for example, 'threatening to end a friendship unless a peer complies with a request, using social exclusion as a retaliatory behaviour, and spreading false rumours to encourage peers to reject a classmate'.[20]

Aggression, then, takes different forms in boys and girls. And if we focus solely on physical aggression, Crick and Zahn-Waxler argue, we'll overlook over 80 per cent of aggressive girls. Of course that's exactly what the current diagnostic categories do. Perhaps this is because physical aggression is so much easier to identify. (Not only is relational aggression much less obvious in general, Crick and her team have shown that men are less adept than women at identifying it in preschool children.) If the criteria for conduct disorders were revised to include relational aggression, the gap between male and female rates would instantly narrow.

On the other hand, there's much less reason to believe that internalizing problems like anxiety and depression are being underestimated in boys. Interesting research by Amanda Rose suggests that the development of these sorts of emotional disorder in girls may be linked to the nature of their friendships. We know that the deepest friendships are built on self-disclosure: to get close to another person, we have to be prepared to share our innermost thoughts and feelings. And we also know that constantly dwelling on the negative can help cause emotional problems. Rose and her team interviewed 600 children, aged between 8 and 15, from the US Midwest. She discovered that the girls were more prone than the boys to something she terms 'co-rumination': that is, 'extensively discussing and re-visiting problems, speculating about problems, and focusing on negative feelings'[21] with a friend. So there's lots of disclosure going on, which is a proven method of building strong friendships. But also a great deal of worrying about problems, which is a similarly reliable means of feeling worse about life.

Sure enough, Rose found that the girls who co-ruminated enjoyed closer relationships with their friends, but were also more susceptible to anxiety and depression. And this was the case for all age groups; it was strongest for the adolescent girls in the survey, but present nonetheless in the younger children. Perhaps it's this tendency towards co-rumination that partly explains the apparent contradiction between girls' stronger relationships (normally an important factor in positive mental health) and their higher rates of emotional problems.

What do diagnostic surveys reveal about gender and childhood disorders? In 1999 the UK government carried out a study of *The Mental Health of Children and Adolescents in Great Britain*. A representative group of more than 10,000 children from England, Scotland and Wales, aged between 5 and 15, was interviewed, and parents and teachers were also invited to give their views. The survey found that 5 per cent of the children currently met DSM or ICD criteria for conduct disorder; 4 per cent for emotional disorders (anxiety and depression); and 1 per cent were rated as hyperactive. Autism, tics, and eating disorders were present in 0.5 per cent of the children. Interestingly, and in sharp contrast to the data on adults, boys were more likely to be suffering from a disorder than girls (11 per cent compared to 8 per cent). Emotional disorders were evenly distributed between boys and girls, though boys had higher levels of conduct disorder and hyperactivity. And again in contrast to the situation among adults, boys with a problem were more likely than girls to receive professional help. These results bear witness to the fact that boys tend to develop problems earlier than girls. As children approach adulthood, however, the balance shifts. If the UK survey had included older teenagers, the results would probably have been markedly different.

In the United States the 'Adolescent Supplement' (NCS-A) to the NCS-R assessed a nationally representative sample of 10,000 young people aged between 13 and 18. Rather like the UK survey, parents in the NCS-A were asked to provide feedback on their child's mental health. But unlike in the UK, diagnosis was made on the basis of *either* the child's or the parent's report. If one of those assessments met the criteria for a disorder, that was sufficient. (The UK survey reached its diagnostic decisions after weighing up all the available information on each child: the so-called 'case vignette' approach.) The NCS-A set out to discover lifetime rates of disorder, using the criteria set out in DSM-IV. What it found was remarkable: 50 per cent of the teenagers had experienced at least one disorder at some stage of their life.

Remarkable and also, if you bear in mind the results of the NCS-R, a little puzzling. According to the adult survey, lifetime prevalence was 46 per cent—that is, 4 per cent lower than the figures for children. Logically, one would expect the rate to increase as people age: the more years you've lived, the greater the likelihood that you'll eventually experience a psychological problem. It's true that many disorders first crop up during adolescence, but of course lots emerge later in life. Perhaps that astonishingly high figure of 50 per cent and the fact that the lifetime prevalence rates for children and adults don't really add up explain why the NCS-A researchers chose to lead with a different statistic in their published report. 'Approximately one in every four to five youths in the U.S.,' they wrote, 'meets criteria for a mental disorder with severe impairment across their lifetime.'[22]

But this emphasis on the severe end of the spectrum only highlights another surprisingly high figure. Is the data plausible? Well, remember that the NCS-A could classify a teenager as suffering from a disorder based solely on information provided by the young person's parent. Now you might think that every parent sometimes suspects their teenager is psychologically disturbed. It can take an awful lot of perspective to remember that all that mystifying moodiness, aggression, and rebellion is a perfectly normal part of growing up. Certainly basing a diagnosis on information from a third party— parent or not—seems to leave ample room for potential misunderstandings. And who knows what kind of jump we'd see in adult rates of disorder if parents and/or partners were asked to comment.

In terms of gender difference, the pattern we saw in the majority of the adult surveys is also evident in the NCS-A. Teenage girls report higher rates of anxiety than teenage boys (38 per cent and 26 per cent respectively). Ditto for depression (18 per cent compared to 11 per cent). On the other hand, 23.5 per cent of boys and only 15.5 per cent of girls met the criteria for behaviour disorders such as ADHD, conduct disorder, and oppositional-defiant disorder. In the case of substance disorders, the NCS-A found little difference between the sexes: 12.5 per cent for males and 10.2 per cent for females. The rates are higher for drug abuse and dependence (9 per cent of boys and 8 per cent of girls) than for alcohol problems (7 per cent and 5.8 per cent respectively). In adults, as we've seen, substance problems are usually more common among men.

Overall, 51 per cent of girls and 48 per cent of boys in the NCS-A survey had already experienced at least one disorder during their lifetime. The difference isn't statistically significant, but it does point to the emergence of the sort of trend we see among adults. In the youngest children, problems are more often seen in boys; by the teenage years, girls are beginning to catch up and overtake; in adulthood, the transformation is complete and the positions well and truly reversed. Later we'll explore the potential reasons for this turnaround.

And this brings us on to the next stage of our journey. In Part 1 of this book we've discovered that, in either childhood or adulthood, there seem to be important gender differences in mental health. Whether you look at children or adults, whether you think in terms of dimensions of disorder or opt for the diagnostic approach, survey after survey produces very similar results. What the data tells us is unmistakeable: certain problems are more prevalent in women; others are more common in men. And, though not everyone seems to want to acknowledge it, the national adult surveys appear to point towards the conclusion that women are more likely in general to experience a disorder. Now it's time to investigate why.

PART 2

*Differences between Men & Women
in Mental Health*

What Are the Reasons?

4

Emotional Disorders

'The only immediate utility of all sciences,' wrote the 18th-century philosopher David Hume, 'is to teach us how to control and regulate future events by their causes.'[1] He had a point. Understanding why something occurs gives us a chance of influencing the likelihood of it happening again. Of course, it's not always enough. Being au fait with the gravitational forces determining tidal flows would not have kept Cnut the Great's feet dry. But without knowledge of causes we're operating on the proverbial wing and prayer.

In the first part of this book we explored the data on gender and mental health. We were mapping the terrain, charting the lay of the land. Now it's time to move from the 'what' to the 'why'. And, though establishing the data was a complex business, getting to the bottom of the factors that have combined to produce those statistics—and the tale of human distress to which they attest—is an even more ambitious task.

The Gendered Brain?

This isn't to say that the topic has been ignored by researchers. In recent years it has received increasing attention from scholars. And increasing funding too, notably through the US National Institutes of Health (NIH), which in 2003 issued a call for research into gender and mental health:

> The epidemiology and disability burden of mental disorders provide clear evidence of the value of a focus on sex and gender differences research. There are differences in both the prevalence and clinical course of mental disorders between men and women.... This pattern of disparities in the epidemiology of mental disorders in males and females provides indirect evidence of genetic, hormonal, biological, social, cultural and developmental factors in etiology and course. An increasing body of basic and clinical research also provides evidence of neurobiological sex differences that may predispose to clinical differences in mental disorders.[2]

The research studies funded under the NIH programme tend to focus on sex differences in specific disorders (why women are more likely than men to develop depression, for example). They don't directly tackle the issue of why women are more likely to experience psychological problems in general. And as the final sentence of the paragraph we've just quoted suggests, there's an emphasis on the neurobiological factors that may underlie those differences. That emphasis was heavily influenced by a report published in 2001 by the US Institute of Medicine (IOM) entitled: *Exploring the Biological Contributions to Human Health: Does Sex Matter?* The short answer, according to the IOM report, was that: 'Sex does matter. It matters in ways that we did not expect.'[3] And, perhaps rather obliquely: 'Undoubtedly, it matters in ways that we have not yet begun to imagine.'[4]

The debate about women's mental health, argues the psychologist Mary Blehar, has moved decisively into the realm of the biomedical: 'To a great extent, this evolution reflects the ascendancy of a disease model of mental illness as well as the ascendancy of a model of mental illness as a "brain disorder".[5] (It's this 'disease model' that underpins the principal psychiatric reference works, such as the *Diagnostic and Statistical Manual of Mental Disorders*.) Psychological disorders, according to these models, aren't extreme versions of normal thoughts and feelings. They are illnesses, as diverse and distinct from one another as physical ailments. Like physical problems, mental illnesses occur when the body (the brain in this case) becomes damaged or diseased in some way. So, the argument runs, if we want to understand why the sexes differ in their mental health we need to look at their neurological make-up.

Scientists have been saying for centuries that men's and women's brains aren't the same. Many of their pronouncements have proved so absurd that the idea has become pretty disreputable. Nicolas Malebranche (1638–1715), for example, argued that women were physically incapable of grasping abstract concepts because of the 'delicacy of the brain fibres'.[6] And it was taken for granted by many Victorian scientists that women could not be as intelligent as men because their brains were smaller. But in fact, as the neurobiologist Larry Cahill noted in an article published in 2006 in *Nature Reviews Neuroscience*, there are 'copious sex influences on brain anatomy, chemistry and function'.[7] Those influences mean that men and women differ neurologically. The extent of those differences has been summarized in a review by scientists at Yale Medical School:

> The literature suggests that while there are many similarities in brain structure, function and neurotransmission in healthy men and women, there are important differences that distinguish the male from the female brain. Overall brain volume is greater in men than women, yet, when controlling for total volume, women have a higher percentage of gray matter and men a higher percentage of white matter. Regional volume differences are less consistent. Global cerebral blood flow is higher in women than in men. Sex-specific differences

in dopaminergic, serotonergic and GABAergic markers indicate that male and female brains are neurochemically distinct.[8]

Male and female brains, for example, develop at varying rates during childhood and adolescence. And you may not be surprised to learn that boys tend to lag behind girls. Take the frontal cortex: this is the part of the brain responsible for planning, decision-making, language, and conscious thought: the kind of complex thought processes we humans like to think separates us from the rest of the animal world. When it comes to development of the frontal cortex, girls may be as much as twenty months ahead of boys.

The two key factors causing these gender differences are *hormones* and *genes*. Hormones are essentially chemicals released by cells, and some of them—the so-called 'sex hormones'—play a crucial role in our development into boys and girls. The process begins in the womb, continues shortly after we're born, and surges back into life during puberty. Most research has focused on the role of testosterone. Though this hormone is present in females, it is much more abundant in males. Indeed, it's the hormone considered to 'masculinize' brain and body.

Sex hormones are activated by our genes. In fact, sexual identity is primarily and originally determined by our genetic make-up. From the moment of conception, a foetus with two X chromosomes (one each from the mother and father) will be female; a foetus with an X and a Y chromosome (the former from the mother and the latter from the father) will develop as a male. But it's not simply a question of the development (or not) of testes, caused by the expression of a Y-linked gene (Sry), and the subsequent release of testosterone. It has been suggested that 'genes residing on the sex chromosomes can directly influence brain phenotype in a gonadal hormone-independent manner'.[9] In other words, the structure of our brains may also be partly influenced by certain sex-linked genes independent of the sex hormones.

Does all this mean that it's useful to think in terms of the 'male' or 'female' brain? It's certainly the kind of thing you often see in popular books on gender. But though it makes for good copy (and frequently enviable sales figures), it's an overstatement: the similarities far outweigh the differences. Men and women are not, at least from a neurological point of view, creatures from different planets.

And yet men's and women's brains are clearly not identical either. This has led to some pretty heated debate about the effects of those differences. Does this, for example, mean that men and women are best suited to different sorts of cognitive activity? Are men innately superior at mathematics, perhaps? Are women biologically predisposed to excel at communication?

Given the complexity of the brain, and our still relatively limited ability to decipher what's going on in it, making links between sex differences and human behaviour is fraught with difficulty. Later in this chapter, and throughout Part 2, we'll see what current research has to say about the possible impact of brain differences on psychological disorder. But for cognitive ability, the evidence is patchy at best. Many experiments have detected little or no difference between male and female performance on a variety of verbal and mathematical tests. On the other hand, although men and women may be equally adept at these kinds of task, studies suggest that they may sometimes use different parts of the brain to accomplish them. As Cahill writes: 'The picture of brain organization that emerges is of two complex mosaics—one male and one female—that are similar in many respects but very different in others. The way that information is processed through the two mosaics, and the behaviours that each produce, could be identical or strikingly different, depending on a host of parameters.'[10]

We'll hear much more about the influence of biological and neuro-logical factors in the following chapters, because now it's time to begin our exploration of the causes that may explain why men's and women's experience of mental illness is often so different. As we've mentioned, researchers haven't really looked at overall rates of psy-chological disorder in relation to gender. No one has tried to explain why women are in general more prone to problems than men. Instead, the work that has been done focuses on individual disorders. Of these disorders, some have received more attention from researchers than others. The disorder that has received the most attention is depres-sion, which makes it the logical point at which to begin our explora-tion of the causes of gender differences in mental health.

Depression

Depression, as we saw in Part 1, affects roughly twice as many women as men. Rates are pretty similar in childhood, but from the age of 13 or so girls rapidly overtake boys—which suggests that there's some-thing significant happening during adolescence. But though women are more likely than men to develop depression, it's a problem that is common in both sexes. The US National Comorbidity Survey Repli-cation (NCS-R), for example, found that 9 per cent of women and 5 per cent of men had experienced depression in the previous twelve months. The UK Adult Psychiatric Morbidity Survey estimated that 11 per cent of women and 7 per cent of men met the criteria for mixed anxiety and depression disorder over the previous week. So depres-sion is emphatically not simply a female disorder.

Scientists have identified a number of factors that may explain the statistics on gender and depression. Over the next few pages, we'll explore their research, moving from the influence of genes to the role of hormones and the nature of the brain, and then to psychological and social factors. As we'll see, what comes across very forcefully from this work is that depression is most likely to occur when a person who is vulnerable to the disorder finds themselves going through a stressful period in their life. Janet Shibley Hyde and colleagues put it like this:

> Vulnerability factors are interactive; that is, the vulnerability factor, by itself, is not hypothesized to increase depression. Rather, vulnerability factors, combined with negative life events, increase the chance of depression.[11]

Those vulnerability factors may be biological, psychological, or social (we'll explore them in detail in the following pages). But they don't come into play until we hit a rough patch. It's known as the stress-vulnerability or diathesis-stress model (diathesis means predisposition). Depression isn't inevitable, even if your genes or the way you typically think about yourself and the world make you vulnerable to the illness. Neither is it inevitable if you lose your job or fall out with your best friend. After all, many people experience difficult times without developing depression. It's the combination of the two, predisposition and stress, which causes depression. But there's a sliding scale here: the greater the vulnerability, the less unpleasant the event needs to be in order to trigger problems; equally, the worse the event, the less important the degree of vulnerability.

Genes

How can we judge what influence, if any, genes have on depression—or indeed anything else? Family history can offer a clue. Imagine, for example, that Jo suffers from depression, and that her father and sister are also prone to the disorder: we may suspect that Jo carries a genetic susceptibility to depression. But we can't be sure. Families certainly share a lot of genes, but they also tend to share a lot of experiences. And perhaps it's these experiences that explain why several members of Jo's family have developed depression at some point.

This is why studies involving twins are so useful. Fraternal (or 'dizygotic') twins develop from separate eggs that have been fertilized by separate sperm. Like all siblings, fraternal twins share 50 per cent of their genes. Identical (or 'monozygotic') twins, on the other hand, result from the fertilization by a single sperm of one egg that subsequently splits into two. This means that their genetic make-up is exactly the same. So if rates of depression are more alike in identical twins than fraternal twins, we can be fairly sure that this is the result of their genes.

Twin studies suggest that depression is moderately heritable—somewhere in the region of 40 per cent. It's important to be clear about the meaning of the term 'heritability'. What it *doesn't* mean is that 40 per cent of a person's level of depression is necessarily the result of their genes. What it signifies is that around 40 per cent of the *differences* in levels of depression *across the population* are likely to be genetic in origin. So heritability tells us nothing about individual cases: it's relevant only to populations. The remainder of the differences between people are the product of environmental factors—by which scientists mean everything except our DNA, including the mass of experiences a person has in their lifetime, though also taking in some biological influences. And clearly when it comes to depression, environment is more significant than genes. Right away then we have a potential pointer as to where sex differences in mental illness may come from. Given that the environment is most influential for depression, perhaps it is pressures arising from this source that explain the discrepancy in male and female rates of the illness.

But is depression equally heritable in the sexes? Is women's increased vulnerability to depression at least partly genetic in origin? Perhaps. Some surveys have found no difference in estimates of heritability between men and women. Others suggest that women show higher heritability than men. The largest study was led by the influential US psychiatrist Kenneth Kendler, who interviewed 15,000 pairs of twins in Sweden (plus another 12,000 single twins). Overall heritability of major depression—defined using a version of the criteria set out in DSM-IV—was estimated to be 38 per cent. But the figure for women was considerably higher than that for men: 42 per cent compared to 29 per cent.

Perhaps the genes that help cause a vulnerability to depression are different in men or women, or maybe the same genes function in different ways in each sex:

> These results imply the existence of genes that have different impacts on the risk for major depression in men and women. For example, genes may exist that would alter the risk for depression in women in response to the variable hormonal environment of the menstrual cycle and pregnancy. Such genes would affect genetic risk for major depression in women but not in men. These twin findings are of particular interest in light of results from three genome scans for major depression, all of which detected genomic regions that appear to have different effects on the risk of illness in men and women.[12]

Whether or not genetic transmission functions differently in men and women has yet to be conclusively established, but the current evidence suggests that it's likely. However, genes seldom produce an effect on their own. Instead, they usually work in tandem with environmental influences. A fascinating example of this gene–environment interaction in relation to depression emerged from a study by Thalia Eley and colleagues at the Medical Research Council (MRC) Social Genetic and Developmental Psychiatry Centre in London. They analysed DNA from adolescents, focusing specifically on certain genes known to be involved in serotonin transmission.

Now serotonin is one of the select number of neurotransmitters (brain chemicals) whose name is well known to non-scientists. Serotonin seems to help produce feelings of contentment; when we're short of it, our mood dips. This is the (hotly debated) theory behind the latest generation of antidepressants, SSRIs (selective serotonin reuptake inhibitors)—the hypothesis being that they somehow boost the levels of serotonin in the brain. Many scientists have suspected for some time that people possessing a variant form (a 'functional polymorphism') of 5-HTT, the serotonin transporter gene, are at increased risk of major depression. That vulnerability remains only that—a vulnerability— until the individual finds themselves having to cope with a particularly stressful situation: say, a bereavement, health problems, or money worries. But if that happens, so the theory goes, the person has an above-average chance of developing depression.

The link between the variant form of 5-HTT (known as 5-HTTLPR) and depression was first suggested in an article written by the eminent psychologist Avshalom Caspi and colleagues. Published in 1993, the paper has gone on to become one of the most discussed in psychiatry. One way of gauging a scientific article's impact is to check out the number of times it's been referred to in other papers: this one has been cited an enviable 2,500 times. But Caspi and co didn't tackle the issue of gender. Eley's team, on the other hand, made it the focus of their research—and with intriguing results. The presence of certain serotonin genes ($HTR2A$ and TPH) was associated with an elevated risk of depression, regardless of sex or environmental factors. Yet the link between stressful events and the 5-HTT polymorphism was only evident for female participants.

Could part of the explanation for women's greater experience of depression lie in the way their genes interact with their life experiences?

It's possible, though as yet scientists haven't even agreed that there is an established link between a particular gene, the environment, and depression, let alone a connection with gender. A robust debate is taking place over what the sum total of relevant studies tells us on the topic. So far in the battle of meta-analyses, Caspi's theory is holding its own. But studies that connect specific genes with psychological disorders are notoriously difficult to replicate. All too often, what team A finds, team B doesn't. We're still some way from knowing exactly what role genes play in depression, or how genetic influences play out in each sex.

The brain

Few psychological experiments are as gruelling as the Trier Social Stress Test. First, the participant is given a few minutes to relax. Then they're shown into another room, where they find three people they've never met before sitting behind a table, plus a tape recorder and video camera. The participant is asked to go away and devise a five-minute speech, as if they were giving a presentation at a job interview. They're informed that a behavioural expert will analyse the video and sound recordings of their performance. After ten minutes' preparation time, the participant is invited back in front of the fictitious company 'managers' to give their talk. Having done so, the fun isn't over (though the participant must dearly wish it was). Now they have to field questions from the 'managers'. And then they're asked to count backwards from a very large number—in thirteens. If they make a mistake, they must start counting all over again. Twenty minutes after arriving in front of the panel, the ordeal is over. The participant is taken back to the room where they prepared their speech, and the purpose of the experiment is explained.

As its name suggests, the Trier Social Stress Test is designed to induce stress in the participants: an objective it normally achieves in spades (though it can also be pretty draining for those on the other side of the interview table ...). But of course it's not just about triggering stress; the idea is to do so in a laboratory setting where that stress can be measured. This is done by monitoring key physiological indicators, such as heart rate and the presence of various stress-related hormones, notably cortisol. The more worried you are by the Trier test, the greater the quantity of cortisol circulating around your body (it can be measured by analysing your saliva).

Cortisol is one of the products of the hypothalamic pituitary adrenal (HPA) axis, the body's principal system for regulating the reaction to stressful situations. All mammals possess an HPA axis. It comprises a series of interactions between the hypothalamus, which is located just above the brainstem, the most ancient part of the brain; the pituitary gland, situated close to the hypothalamus; and the adrenal glands, which can be found just above the kidneys. When we experience stress—that's to say, when we fear that we can't cope with the situation confronting us—the HPA axis helps prepare us for immediate emergency action. It can do this because it's well connected to the amygdala and hippocampus, two areas of the brain that play a key role in identifying threats.

In essence, the HPA axis activates what's known as the sympathetic nervous system (SNS), which prepares the body for 'fight or flight'. Meanwhile it suppresses the parasympathetic nervous system, which controls and counterbalances the frenzied activity of the SNS, and helps us 'rest and digest'. The adrenal glands release cortisol, which increases blood sugar (thereby keeping us well stocked with energy), subdues the immune system so that the physiological resources usually devoted to maintenance and repair can be switched to dealing with the short-term emergency, and helps the body process fat, protein, and carbohydrate (thus ensuring we obtain a timely energy boost). Helping to regulate the HPA axis are a number of neurotransmitters, including oxytocin and our old friend serotonin (chemical name: 5-hydroxytryptamine, or 5-HT).

Research has demonstrated that in depressed people the HPA axis doesn't function properly. Usually it's overactive, meaning that depression involves being very stressed, pretty much all of the time: in other words, it's a chronic stress reaction. How do we know? Well, we can measure the amount of cortisol in a person's saliva. If you do so after a depressed person has undertaken the Trier Social Stress Test, you generally find that their cortisol level is significantly higher than that of a non-depressed participant. And it stays at this elevated level for much longer than normal. Their HPA axis is working overtime. Certainly there are more relaxing ways to spend a couple of hours than taking the Trier test. But the depressed person's HPA axis overreacts, repeatedly sounding the alarm for a catastrophe that hasn't occurred.

Not all depressed people react in this way, though. Older people, and those who've suffered from depression for a long time, often don't have much of an HPA reaction to specific stressful situations like the Trier test. It's normal for cortisol to spike when we're in a challenging situation, and then to diminish relatively swiftly as that stress passes. But cortisol levels in these older depressed people don't seem to fluctuate in response to events. Their HPA reactions are blunted. And when their cortisol level is high, as it generally is, it takes a long time to fall away again. It's as if the alarm's on/off switch has broken, leaving the person feeling continually on edge.

The HPA axis, then, plays a central role in depression. And if depression follows when the HPA axis is out of kilter, perhaps antidepressant drugs work by pulling it back into line. Because although SSRIs are now the standard pharmaceutical treatment for mild to moderate depression, scientists still don't really know how they work. (In fact, some experts dispute whether they're actually effective at all.

But that's another debate, for another book.) One theory is that SSRIs increase the quantity of serotonin in the brain, which serves to dampen down HPA activity.

Does the HPA axis operate differently in males and females? Might this help explain why depression is more prevalent in women than men? It certainly seems plausible when you bear in mind that boys and girls have similar rates of depression until they reach adolescence (roughly age 13). As we'll see later in this chapter, a number of changes happen at puberty that seem to have a bearing on depression: changes in the amount of body fat, for example, or in the way boys and girls think about themselves. But aside from these indirect effects, puberty is essentially a massive hormonal upheaval—and one which may affect the way in which we respond to stress.

The first true marker of puberty is something called *gonadarche*: the maturing of the gonads (ovaries in females; testes in males). This is accompanied by a huge increase in the production of sex hormones. Boys experience a surge of testosterone; and girls a flood of estrogen and progestrogene. Of course, puberty isn't the first time these hormones make their presence felt: as we have seen, they have very significant effects both prenatally and in early infancy. Scientists classify the impact of sex hormones as *organizational* or *activational*. Organizational changes occur early in life and help determine brain structure. Activational effects, on the other hand, tend to be more transient, and they are often dependent on prior organizational changes. But whether their impact is organizational or activational, permanent or temporary, sex hormones change the way the brain functions. And it turns out that they may influence our neurological reaction to stress too.

A number of studies of both animals and humans have suggested that the HPA axis is strongly affected by female sex hormones. In particular, estrogen has a big impact on the parts of the axis that are important for the experience of emotion. These hormones are present in males too (just as testosterone occurs naturally in girls and women). But they're much more plentiful in females, hence their label. Puberty, of course, brings with it a surge of these hormones—which may explain why differences in male and female HPA reactivity emerge for the first time during adolescence. When you consider how sex hormones influence the HPA axis, the idea that women's increased vulnerability to depression may be at least partly due to abnormalities in the way the brain processes stress seems increasingly plausible.

Sure enough, studies have shown that men and women do indeed differ in HPA responsiveness. (This is typically assessed by asking people to perform a stressful task—such as the Trier test—and then measuring their salival cortisol levels.) But this is where things become complicated. Because the difference is not what we might expect. The most obvious prediction would be that women are at greater risk of depression because their HPA axis is hyperactive. As a result, they're more likely to detect threats in safe situations and experience unnecessary stress and anxiety. This is clearly a pretty exhausting and demoralizing way to live, and it's what scientists commonly find when they test younger people with depression. In studies of rats, females do indeed tend to show greater HPA responsiveness than males. But research with humans has typically produced very different results. Between puberty and menopause, it's *men* who generally react most strongly to stress.

Is the HPA axis innately different in men and women? Or might sex hormones be influencing stress reactivity? This was a question that a research team in the United States sought to answer by suppressing sex hormones in groups of men and women aged 18 to 45 (they did this by injecting the participants with hormone-inhibiting drugs). In effect, they created a level playing field for HPA function, free from any distortions potentially created by sex hormones like testosterone and estrogen. The participants were subjected to both physical stress (running on a treadmill) and chemically induced stress (being injected with the hormone CRH, which triggers a stress response). The results mirrored those of other studies: 'With both pharmacological and physiological stressors, we observed greater HPA axis response in young to middle-aged men compared with women.'[13] Whatever is making the male HPA axis more reactive, it isn't just sex hormones.

How do we explain these results? If men are neurologically more sensitive to stress, why isn't it they and not women who are experiencing greater levels of depression? Well, when we look at studies of HPA reactivity we need to bear in mind three potentially very significant caveats.

First is the fact that possessing a less reactive HPA axis can actually be an indicator of problems, rather than the reverse. As already stated, people with a history of depression tend to show blunted reactions to stressful events. Their cortisol levels may be high, but they're consistently high: they don't ebb and flow as events unfold. When our stress system is working properly, the HPA axis swiftly picks up on the emergence of a threat in the environment and prepares us physiologically to deal with that possible danger. Among those physiological changes is the release of the hormone cortisol. The brain registers that there's been a rush of cortisol, and gives the HPA axis the signal to calm down—thereby turning off the cortisol tap. But for chronically depressed people this doesn't seem to happen. The HPA axis is sluggish in its reaction to sudden stresses. Because there's no sudden elevation in the amount of cortisol produced, the brain is less able to spot that the HPA axis is active and so can't quickly contain the stress reaction. And long-term stress has a nasty habit of causing depression. So perhaps what we're seeing in the data is indirect evidence of the blunted reactions typical of chronic depression.

Then there's the possibility that the studies have been skewed by the type of task used to generate stress. Usually participants are asked to make a speech, or tackle a difficult arithmetical problem (the Trier test, somewhat sadistically, does both). It's generally assumed that, broadly speaking, men attach more importance to this kind of challenge than women: mastering a tricky task in front of an audience can provide a huge boost to the male ego. If giving a presentation matters more to men, it's reasonable to suppose that they'll experience greater stress when asked to do so. Women, on the other hand, tend to derive more of their self-esteem from social interaction. So you'd expect that women would show a more pronounced stress reaction than men if they were, say, increasingly ignored and excluded from a conversation between two other people. And indeed this is what researchers have found. The problem is, relatively few studies have been conducted using these kinds of socially oriented stressful tasks. Maybe women are more vulnerable to depression because their stress system reacts so vigorously when things aren't working out with other people. But right now the evidence is too scant for it to be any more than an intriguing theory.

And finally, it's possible that stress reactions in men and women are qualitatively—rather than simply quantitatively—different. The standard view of what happens when we're stressed was developed a century ago by Walter Cannon, a professor of physiology at Harvard. Stress alerts us to a potential threat, and prepares us to deal with it—for either 'fight or flight' (literally or metaphorically). But according to Shelley Taylor, a psychologist based at the University of California, Los Angeles, 'fight or flight' isn't our only reaction to stress:

under conditions of stress, tending to offspring and affiliating with others ('befriending') are at least as common responses to stress in humans as fight-or-flight.[14]

'Fight or flight', Taylor suggests, may be a better description of the male response to stress than it is of the female. Women, on the other hand, are more likely to 'tend and befriend'.

'Fight or flight' and 'tend and befriend' aren't simply contrasting behavioural reactions: they involve two very different hormones. Fight or flight is all about cortisol: the stress hormone, pumping us up for action. Fuelling the tend and befriend response, on the other hand, is oxytocin which, Taylor notes, 'has been implicated in a broad array of social relationships and social activities, including peer bonding, sexual activity, and affiliative preferences under non-stressful circumstances'[15] (this is why oxytocin has achieved a modicum of media celebrity as the 'love hormone'). We know that the effects of oxytocin are boosted by the female sex hormone estrogen. And that oxytocin calms the HPA response to stress. Moreover, when scientists use a scanner to observe neurological activity during a stressful task, they find that different regions are busy in men's and women's brains. What all this means is that attempting to differentiate between male and female reactions to stress simply by comparing levels of HPA activity isn't going to cut it: things are more complex than that.

To sum up: there do seem to be differences in HPA activity between males and females. What this means, on the other hand, is far from clear.

However, what we can say with certainty is that the events that befall us when we're young can produce long-lasting changes in the HPA axis. Studies of both animals and humans have shown that early exposure to stress can make the HPA axis acutely hyperactive. We become especially sensitive to stress, liable to react in a way that's out of proportion to the reality of the situation. In the long run, as we encounter the inevitable trials and tribulations of adulthood, this sensitivity to stress can cause significant psychological problems: such as depression.

Perhaps, then, depression is more common in females because they experience greater stress when young. Certainly girls are at least ten times more likely to be a victim of childhood sexual abuse than boys. Could this trauma instigate changes in the HPA axis—changes that would leave the affected individual susceptible to later depression? Well, research has shown that adults who have been sexually abused as children tend to possess an overactive HPA axis. Moreover, early stress doesn't just alter the HPA axis: it also shrinks the hippocampus—by up to 15 per cent in one study. The hippocampus is part of the brain's limbic system (it gets its name from the Latin word for 'seahorse', which early anatomists thought it resembled). The hippocampus helps form and store contextual memories: where we were and what we were doing when an event occurred. But it's also involved in regulating the HPA axis, quietening it down when its message has been delivered. Probably the hippocampus is damaged by prolonged exposure to cortisol, which doubtless flooded out in reaction to the childhood trauma. The net result is the removal of a key brake on the HPA axis, making it much harder to rein in during later times of stress, and thereby exposing the affected person to anxiety, distress, and eventually perhaps depression. All this seems highly plausible, but it's important to remember that it's the early trauma that's primarily responsible for the later depression. What happens in the brain—fascinating though it undoubtedly is—is just the biological effect of these stressful events.

Is there a link between the genetic contribution to depression and the role of the HPA axis? If Thalia Eley's findings are correct, one possible pathway to the illness runs like this: a woman with the variant form of the serotonin gene who experiences stressful events will show an elevated risk of depression. We can slot in the HPA axis too, because women with the *5-HTT* polymorphism also seem to show an overactive stress response. Of course, all this assumes that the *5-HTT* variant isn't a red herring. In a recent review of research on the topic, the renowned psychiatric geneticist Peter McGuffin concluded that 'there probably is a real, if small, effect of 5-HTLPR' on response to environmental adversity. He noted: 'The truth is that there are just too many straws travelling in the same direction for us not to know which way the wind is blowing.'[16] However, Eley's suggestion that women are particularly at risk is less well established.

Perhaps the genetic and neurological influences on depression are connected via the personality trait of neuroticism. Psychologists generally agree that there are five fundamental personality traits: extraversion, agreeableness, conscientiousness, openness, and neuroticism. We all have greater or lesser amounts of each of these so-called Big Five. People high in neuroticism are acutely sensitive to the negative—or potentially negative—aspects of existence. Even when things are going well, disaster seems to lurk just around the corner: any silver lining is obscured by the huge black cloud. As a result, the highly neurotic person tends to feel pretty anxious or low much of the time. Individuals low in neuroticism, on the other hand, are easy-going, calm, and self-confident.

You won't be surprised to learn that neuroticism is a risk factor for clinical depression. It seems to be partly genetic in origin, with heritability estimated at a moderate 40 per cent (that is, 40 per cent of the variation in levels of neuroticism in the population are the result of genetic factors). Indeed it's been suggested that the variant form of the *5-HTT* gene is one of those involved in transmitting neuroticism from parent to child. But the web of connections is about to become still more elaborate. For one thing, neuroticism is associated with HPA hyperactivity. This makes sense: if you're temperamentally inclined always to fear the worst, it's almost inevitable that you'll experience more stress. And then there's the fact that women tend to show higher levels of neuroticism than men. (As ever, we're talking about very general statistical patterns; individuals may—and of course very frequently do—diverge significantly from these abstractions.) Indeed, the difference between male and female levels of neuroticism partly accounts for the difference between male and female rates of depression.

So if we're looking for an insight into women's greater vulnerability to depression, perhaps it lies at least partly in this combination of genetic factors, neuroticism, and HPA activity. It seems plausible, but as we've seen several times already in the course of this book, things are rarely straightforward. One complication is the fact that though neuroticism and depression appear to be genetically linked, that link is no stronger for women than it is for men. In particular, some experts doubt whether there's any difference between the sexes when it comes to the connection between the variant form of *5-HTT* and neuroticism. So if there is a link between women's higher rates of neuroticism and of depression, it looks as though it's not these particular genetic factors that lie behind it.

But the most significant caveat in our view centres on the usefulness of neuroticism as an explanation for depression. Remember our description of neuroticism: the worrying, nervousness, low mood? It sounds a lot like a low-level type of depression or anxiety disorder (and we know that people's neuroticism increases when they're going through depression). Perhaps neuroticism can't tell us a great deal about why depression develops because it is itself a mild form of depression.

It's getting complicated! So let's recap what we have so far. We've discovered that the increased rate of depression in women may be the result of a combination of factors: namely, genetic influences; traumatic early life experiences, such as sexual abuse; personality (and specifically neuroticism); HPA axis overactivity; and finally the stressful later events that actually trigger the depressive episode. However, this may seem a more coherent account than it actually is. We've put together disparate pieces of the puzzle to make a picture. But what's needed is studies that focus on this bigger picture rather than simply concentrating on the individual elements: studies that try to determine whether and how these factors combine to cause depression. That research has yet to happen.

Psychological factors

We're on firmer ground when it comes to the way in which psychological processes interact with gender to produce depression. There's been a great deal of theorizing on the topic, and more experiments putting those theories to the test.

One approach centres on two particular styles of thinking that seem to make individuals more vulnerable to depression: a pessimistic way of explaining events; and something called 'ruminative coping'.

At the heart of the pessimistic (or optimistic) style of thinking is a distinctive way of explaining negative and positive events, particularly in situations where the true cause isn't obvious.

When something bad happens to a pessimist, they tend to assume it's down to them. Let's take a trivial example, drawn from this very morning: a broken mug, dropped while drying up. If we're prone to pessimism, we'll see this minor accident not as the sort of thing that happens to everyone once in while but as yet another indication of our clumsiness and misfortune: one more in a long line of calamities that will stretch far into the future. We glance glumly at our favourite crockery in the cupboard and reflect that it's only a matter of time before we break that too. Warming to our gloomy theme, we may conclude that life is essentially a sequence of disasters. Thus an apparently insignificant slip actually seems to tell us something very important—and the news is not good. Bad things happen to us because we are somehow bad or innately unlucky. And the future will only bring more of the same. To use the psychological jargon, the pessimist explains unpleasant events as internal (their fault), global (typical of their life in general), and stable (permanent).

How does the pessimist react to a positive event—let's say, encouraging feedback from their manager at work? Does the praise make them happy? Does it boost their self-esteem? Not really, or at least not for long. They look at good news in exactly the opposite way they look at negative news. Their boss may have paid them a compliment, but actually it was nothing to do with them. Doubtless the manager was just being cheery because she's about to go on holiday. Perhaps she's been instructed by her boss to be more encouraging and is simply ticking that box for the day. Or, worst of all, she's being ironic. And because the praise cannot be a well-deserved reflection of their effort and ability, the pessimist assumes it's a short-lived one-off. In other words, happy events are regarded as external in origin, specific to that one moment, and unstable (that is, temporary).

The concept of ruminative coping was developed by Susan Nolen-Hoeksema, a professor of psychology at Yale:

> Rumination involves passively and repetitively focusing on one's symptoms of distress ('I'm so tired,' 'I'm so unmotivated') and on the meanings and consequences of the distress ('What's wrong with my life?', 'My

boss is going to get annoyed if I keep missing deadlines')....[People under stress] search for some understanding of why their lives are not going as they wish, why they feel frustrated and distressed so much of the time.[17]

We may ruminate in an effort to improve our situation, to find some way out of the hole we believe we're in. But we end up trapped in a loop of despondency, endlessly thinking negative thoughts about negative feelings.

As you might guess, rumination and pessimism aren't great for improving mood. People who tend to think in this way will probably feel anxious and down more often than people who don't. And when life gets tough, their habitual reasoning style leaves them especially vulnerable to depression. Nolen-Hoeksema provided a compelling illustration of how this works in a study she carried out with Jannay Morrow. At the beginning of October 1989, Nolen-Hoeksema and Morrow had interviewed 137 Stanford University students to gauge how they tended to think about negative events. Then on 17 October the Loma Prieta earthquake struck:

This was the largest earthquake in the Bay Area since 1906 and meas-ured 7.1 on the Richter scale....62 people were killed, 3,757 were injured, and 12,000 were left homeless. Over 18,000 homes and 2,575 businesses were damaged. For days, the local and national news media played and replayed horrifying scenes of damage caused by the earthquake: In the city of Oakland, the upper deck of a major highway collapsed onto the lower deck, crushing and killing people. A fire in the Marina district of San Francisco raged for hours. A sec-tion of the Bay Bridge, the major link between San Francisco and the East Bay, collapsed, rendering the bridge unusable.[18]

Ten days after the disaster, Nolen-Hoeksema and Morrow met with the students once more. They did so again six weeks later. They dis-covered that the students who'd been prone to rumination before the earthquake were most likely to be depressed (and show symptoms of post-traumatic stress disorder) afterwards.

Are women more likely than men to adopt these negative cognitive styles, thereby increasing their risk of depression when they encounter stressful life events? There is evidence that, from adolescence onwards, women are more prone both to pessimistic thoughts and to ruminative coping. It also appears that women might have a greater chance of experiencing negative events (as we shall see later in this chapter). For example, in the late 1990s Susan Nolen-Hoeksema and colleagues followed 1,100 Californians aged 25 to 75 over the course of a year. Just like so many researchers before and since, they found that women reported more depression than men. But where the study broke new ground was in its identification of the reasons underlying this difference between the sexes. The women in the study reported more stressful life experiences, more ruminative coping, and a lower sense of control over their life than the men. And when Nolen-Hoeksema and co crunched the numbers, these three factors were sufficient to explain the higher rate of depression in women (to use the technical term, these variables 'fully mediated' the relationship between depression and gender). The researchers concluded:

> The results of this study suggest that women carry a triad of vulnerabilities to depressive symptoms compared to men: more chronic strain, a greater tendency to ruminate when distressed, and a lower sense of their mastery over their lives. In turn, these variables contribute to each other.[19]

But it's not simply the way in which people habitually think (their cognitive styles) that may help account for the different rates of depression between men and women. It's also the things we tend to think *about*. Two topics in particular have been suggested as prime candidates in fostering depression in women: body image and relationships.

Until adolescence, depression is no more likely to strike girls than it is boys. But the advent of puberty signals a decisive shift: females overtake males and the balance is never redressed. As we've seen already in this chapter, the hormonal upheaval that puberty involves—and specifically its effect on the body's stress system—may partly explain why teenage girls show higher rates of depression than teenage boys. But of course puberty also brings dramatic changes to body shape. Before puberty, lean body mass, bone mass and body fat are about equal in males and females. After puberty, boys possess one and a half times the lean body mass and bone mass of girls, while girls have twice as much body fat. For boys, these changes are relatively positive: they shift their body shape further towards what society expects in men. Not so for girls, however. Contemporary popular culture typically celebrates a female form that is lithe, angular, and above all slim. It's a body shape that is, in some ways, essentially juvenile. And puberty drags the majority of women ever further from this idealized body shape—just at the moment when the way one looks seems to matter more than ever.

Anxiety and shame about body shape are regarded by specialists as a major factor in eating disorders. But arguably it hasn't received the prominence it merits in relation to depression. And yet there's plenty of evidence that worries about body image can contribute to depression in women. One study, for example, found that women with concerns about their body image were more likely to develop depression when teased about their weight. This was true regardless of the women's actual appearance. How an individual looked to other people—the objective details of their height and weight and shape—had no bearing on their susceptibility to depression; what really mattered was how they perceived themselves.

Much of the time, of course, worries about body image are likely to be stoked by far less direct means than outright teasing. But if a person is anxious about the way they look, chances are they'll be confronted with difficult moments on a regular basis. This negative view of one's body feeds into lower self-esteem. Indeed, research suggests that appearance is a more significant factor in self-esteem for women than it is for men—perhaps because women, unlike men, are frequently judged on the basis of how they look rather than, say, how they behave. There's good evidence to suggest that, on the whole, women have slightly lower self-esteem than men. And low self-esteem is a proven risk factor for depression. Having a negative opinion of yourself doesn't mean that you're depressed. But when people with low self-esteem experience stressful life events, they're more likely to develop depression.

Much of the ground-breaking work in this area has been done by the British psychologists George Brown and Tirril Harris, who found that depression was most likely to occur when those stressful events involved humiliation or entrapment, and when social support was lacking. (For humiliation, Brown and Harris give the real-life examples of the discovery of a partner's infidelity; 'a woman being told by her husband that she is abnormal (because of her epilepsy) and not fit to be a mother, in a row that later led to a marital separation; a single mother criticized by a magistrate for failing to keep up payments for a fine incurred by her teenage son and told she could in future be sent to prison; a 9-year-old daughter who said she wanted to leave her mother and go back to live in the West Indies'.[20] Being told that your partner has an incurable illness that requires you to become their full-time carer is an example of entrapment.)

Worries about body image may play a significant role in female self-esteem, but perhaps even more crucial is the way in which women view their relationships. There's plenty of evidence that, right from childhood, girls attach more importance than boys to their friendships—their 'affiliative need' is stronger. Even among preschoolers, the average girl performs better at tasks that measure empathy; she is more accomplished at reading other people's intentions; and her social skills are more sophisticated. As if all that weren't enough, linguistic ability tends to develop faster in girls than in boys. Indeed, some scientists have suggested that you can detect girls' greater interest in other people in newborn babies, arguing that they're more responsive to social stimuli (such as the sound of a person's voice) and better able to maintain eye contact with an adult. From their earliest days in the world, perhaps, girls give the impression of being more adept at dealing with other people. It's exactly the skill set you need if relationships are destined to be among the most important elements in your life.

Our relationships can be a rich source of strength and happiness. But of course they can also bring anxiety and sadness. Perhaps women's greater affiliative need leaves them especially vulnerable to these stresses, thereby increasing their risk of depression. Jill Cyranowski and colleagues have argued that girls' need for close relationships intensifies during puberty (which is precisely the moment, as you'll recall, when girls begin to suffer more depression than boys). This increased emphasis on relationships happens for two reasons. One is hormonal, and specifically a surge in the sex hormone oxytocin. The other is sociocultural: the pressure to conform to stereotypically gendered behaviour—such as developing intense and devoted friendships with other girls—ratchets up in adolescence.

Clearly, if your well-being is inextricably linked to your closest relationships, you're placing an awful lot of power over your happiness in the hands of other people. That's a risk we're all used to taking. But the perils can be especially acute during adolescence when we generally look less to our parents to satisfy our affiliative needs and much more to peers and romantic partners. Thus adolescent girls are peculiarly vulnerable. Their need for intimacy is stronger than ever, yet they must learn to build an entirely new type of relationship in order to meet that need. For some girls—those who are prone to anxiety, who don't enjoy a strong relationship with their parents, or who aren't good at coping with setbacks—that transition can be especially difficult. When they encounter stressful times (and especially if their problems involve relationships) these girls are more likely to develop depression.

Further support for the idea that women's vulnerability to depression may be linked to the importance they attach to relationships comes from research into interpersonal dependency (IPD). IPD has been defined as 'a reliance on other valued people for emotional and social support'.[21] There's good evidence that people with high levels of IPD are more at risk of depression, particularly after they've experienced separation, loss, or rejection. Visant Sanathara and colleagues followed more than 7,000 US adults for several years. They found that women tended to score more highly for IPD than men. The link between IPD and depression was strongest for men, though still significant for women. Indeed, once you take IPD level into account, the difference between male and female rates of depression narrows.

Social factors 1: Stressful life events

At one level, why people develop depression is pretty simple: bad things happen to them. To put it in psychological terms, negative life events trigger depressive episodes. One large study showed that stressful events such as assault, relationship break-up, financial problems, serious illness or injury, job loss, big problems at work, and legal difficulties increase the risk of depression in the following month by almost six times. If the event is particularly unpleasant, that risk period can elongate.

Some negative events are more damaging than others when it comes to depression. Especially toxic—for men and women alike—are those that involve:

- loss—perhaps of a loved one, through bereavement, relationship breakdown, or relocation; one's health or material possessions; or one's job or a cherished ideal
- humiliation—feeling that you've lost status, either in the eyes of others or one's view of oneself; often involves a sense of rejection and/or failure
- entrapment—defined by psychologists as a long-running stressful situation that looks like it won't improve and from which it seems impossible to escape.

Worst of all are situations that involve a combination of loss and humiliation—being fired from your job, for instance, or having to come to terms with a partner's infidelity. In cases like this, the risk of depression is significantly higher.

All of which probably won't seem very surprising. Undergoing the kind of experiences we've just mentioned is bound to get anyone down. But though most of us will feel low for a time after a significant setback, in some people the reaction is more severe and long-lasting. Depression intensifies; it takes root. And this is why some experts have proposed the 'differential activation' hypothesis, arguing that it's how we respond to the initial, normal feelings of depression that determines how severe and persistent the episode will be. One factor that's been proven to influence our reaction to negative events is childhood adversity—and we'll come back to this issue.

(It's worth mentioning, incidentally, that the odds on bad things occurring in one's life are not the same for everyone. Some people are genetically vulnerable to setbacks, presumably because their personality leads them to behave in certain ways. And these same genetic factors also seem to make the person susceptible to depression. As Kenneth Kendler and colleagues have written: 'a genetically influenced set of traits both increases individuals' probability of selecting themselves into high-risk environments likely to produce stressful life events and increases their vulnerability to major depression'.[22] Kendler's research suggests that these genetic factors account for around a third of the association between stressful events and depression.)

Are women more likely to develop depression because they experience a greater number of stressful life events? Perhaps the problems that confront women tend to be more severe than those facing men. Or do women react more negatively to setbacks?

On first inspection, the data tells a rather mixed story. It's certainly true that men and women differ in the *kind* of negative event they're likely to encounter. Broadly speaking, the evidence suggests that men experience more work-related problems; women's stresses tend to revolve around relationships. And this pattern is reproduced when it comes to sensitivity to depression: job stuff seems to affect men more acutely than it does women, and the situation is reversed when it comes to interpersonal problems. All of which seems like a plausible reflection of current gender roles and expectations. You can see this difference in sensitivity operating in a study by James Nazroo, Angela Edwards, and George Brown. They assessed 100 heterosexual couples in London, all of whom had recently experienced the kind of event that frequently leads to depression. Where those events involved children, housing, or reproductive problems—stereotypically female concerns—women were five times more likely than their partners to develop depression. But this difference was only found in those couples that had adopted conventional gender roles, with domestic duties falling largely to the woman. Perhaps, the authors speculated, this was because in these cases women felt that the problems were primarily their responsibility. (Nazroo and colleagues also analysed the couples' response to other difficulties, such as crime, health, or finances. In these cases, however, the differences between the sexes weren't statistically significant.)

But what about the overall picture? Some research suggests that women experience slightly more negative life events than men; other studies, however, have found no such thing. There's more evidence that women show greater sensitivity to stressful situations. But here too the data is contradictory. One large US study, for instance, found no evidence that women experience a greater number of difficult life events or that they react to these events more negatively than men. This seems curious. Given that depression seems to be largely caused by environmental factors, one might assume that men and women would differ markedly in their exposure to stressful events. On the other hand, perhaps women are more vulnerable to depression partly as a result of genetic factors and HPA axis reactivity. If so, this environmental difference might not need to be particularly significant to produce a disparity in rates of depression (though one might still expect to see this greater sensitivity reflected in the data). So let's take a closer look at these studies.

What about, for example, the *timing* of negative events? Does that have a bearing on gender and depression? A recent study by George Slavich and colleagues analysed the case histories of 375 people who'd been diagnosed with the disorder. Women reported many more negative events prior to the onset of their depression—but only between the ages of 18 and 29. So it looks as though these kinds of events do indeed play a more important part in depression among women than among men (though why that should be the case is unclear). Moreover, they seem to be especially powerful in early depressive episodes. And this fits with a general finding that negative events are less influential in triggering *repeated* bouts of depression.

It's known as the 'kindling hypothesis': the first depression might be brought on by a traumatic event, but external influences become less significant with each successive episode. The mind grows progressively sensitive to the negative, spiralling into depression in response to the slightest of setbacks—and sometimes with no clear trigger at all. As the path becomes increasingly well trodden, we need ever fewer signposts in order to find it. Perhaps negative life events exert their greatest influence early in women's lives, sparking a depression that then recurs down the years, sometimes set off by stressful situations but often needing little outside provocation. And indeed, a 1999 meta-analysis of 119 studies covering more than 80,000 people found that women reported greater exposure to stress than men, and *especially* in adolescence, though the size of the effect was small.

We also need to consider the way in which negative events are measured. As we've already seen, the type of difficulty experienced makes a big difference to the likelihood of subsequent depression in men and women, as does the gender role adopted by an individual. But when, and how often, we assess people's experience of problems is also important. And then there's the question of where we set the cut-off point for a negative life event: how serious must a problem be in order for it to be included in the analysis?

Most studies are cross-sectional: on a given day, the participant is assessed for their experience of depression in the preceding months, and asked about any setbacks that might have occurred during that period. Because they're retrospective, cross-sectional studies rely on the accuracy of the participant's memory. This is partly why they typically cover a relatively restricted time span. But research can also be prospective, following individuals over a number of months and even years. These kinds of studies can offer a much more nuanced view of why an illness such as depression occurs and its relation to other factors. You can see a sophisticated example of this approach in a study carried out by Benjamin Hanklin, Robin Mermelstein, and Linda Roesch. They asked 538 teenagers in Chicago to keep a daily diary for seven days, first at the start of the project, and then after six and twelve months. Shortly before the diary weeks, Hanklin and colleagues assessed the participants' emotional and psychological well-being.

In their diaries, the teenagers were advised, they should:

> write down the 'worst event' that occurred to them that day and then explain 'what made it the worst event.' Examples of events written by the adolescents include, 'got kicked out of school,' 'dropped all my books in the hallway,' 'got an F on my quiz,' 'got in argument with my mother,' 'girlfriend got mad at me,' 'brother got arrested,' and 'my best friend's mother passed away,' and 'my football team lost the game.'[23]

The research team then assessed the severity of these 'worst events', and sorted them into types depending on whether they were interpersonal (involving family, peers, or romantic relationships) or achievement related (involving school or sports).

We should keep in mind that the Hankin study included some relatively minor stressors that wouldn't have made the cut in other research. Nevertheless, it showed that girls experienced more problems than boys, with the difference being especially marked in the case of interpersonal difficulties. And that extra stress helped explain why girls suffered more depression.

So when we're scrutinizing the evidence on the relationship between negative life events and depression, we must look beyond the headline figures. Age seems to make a difference. So too does the type of event, and how it interacts with an individual's role in life. If, for instance, you're the one doing most of the childcare and running the family home, domestic problems are likely to cause you greater stress—and ultimately, perhaps, depression—than if you tend to leave these kinds of issue to your partner. If your primary focus in life is your work, or your relationships, difficulties in that area are probably going to affect you most.

When we apply this kind of fine-grained analysis to the data, it seems that part of the difference between the sexes when it comes to depression can be explained by negative events that involve interpersonal relationships, with the biggest damage often caused by problems during adolescence. These interpersonal difficulties are so potent because, in general, women have learned to regard relationships as a priority (and often perhaps the overriding priority) in their life. And the social pressure to adopt an accepted gender role is never more intense than during the teenage years. Friendships, infatuations, love affairs: suddenly nothing seems more important. Consequently, when things go wrong the distress can be profound. For a proportion of young people—predominately, the data suggests, girls—it can be severe enough to trigger depression. And in so doing, it readies the ground for additional depressive episodes in the future.

But there's another category of negative life event that the studies we've discussed so far omit: childhood sexual abuse. There's a very simple reason for its exclusion. These studies focus on problems that occur close in time to the depressive episode—say, within the previous month. When psychologists talk about 'life events', by definition it's this restricted time frame that they have in mind. And so these research projects aren't going to pick up on trauma experienced years before (though recent rape is included in the adult studies).

There's very strong evidence linking childhood sexual abuse to later depression (not to mention a host of other psychological disorders). And we saw earlier that this may partly happen through the effects of stress on the brain's HPA axis. Not only is sexual abuse a major risk factor for depression, it's one that largely affects girls, typically during early adolescence. The legacy of this trauma is frightening. The UK survey of Psychiatric Morbidity Among Adults Living in Private

Households, published in 2000, found that 5.2 per cent of the 4,701 women interviewed reported sexual abuse, as compared to 1.6 per cent of the 3,848 men. Women were more likely than men to have tried to commit suicide. The link between sexual abuse (at any point in life) and suicide attempts was stronger for women than men. And a greater proportion of suicide attempts in women could be explained by sexual abuse than in men. As Paul Bebbington and colleagues have noted in relation to the survey's findings: 'in the absence of sexual abuse the female rate of suicide attempts over a lifetime would fall by 28 per cent, relative to 7 per cent in men.'[24]

Social factors 2: Chronic strain

So far the social factors we've focused on have been time limited: an unpleasant event takes place and depression follows, normally quite rapidly. But what about long-term stresses? Is there any evidence to suggest that women might be prone to depression simply because of the social pressures attached to being female? Are the roles women are taught to play putting them at greater risk of psychological illness?

We learn our roles early, with the most influential teachers usually being our parents. But it's a complicated issue. For a start, the process isn't one-way. Children are not merely passive receptacles of parental wisdom (*if only*, you may be thinking, *if only*...). Instead, it's likely that the way parents behave towards their child is partly determined by the personality of the little one herself. Second, it's unwise to assume that mothers and fathers will parent in the same way: a child may be exposed to a broader range of messages about gender roles than we might expect. A father, for example, might present his daughter with a fairly stereotyped view of acceptable female behaviour. But the mother—battle-hardened by experience perhaps—might encourage the kind of tough and single-minded determination typically valued in boys. Ultimately, the only truly effective way to discover what's going on is to study parent–child interactions in minute detail. That's time-consuming, labour-intensive work.

On the whole, the evidence suggests that parents do help socialize their children into gender roles, either through overt instruction or more subtle means. For instance, girls are encouraged more often than boys to feel empathy, to share, and to help the people around them. Girls are more likely to be praised for obedience; female assertiveness, on the other hand, is less valued. And girls and boys may be taught differing attitudes towards emotion. One study, for example, found that preschool girls drew more attention from their fathers when they showed 'submissive' emotions such as sadness and anxiety. The researchers noted:

> Parents use more anger-related words with boys than with girls and refer more to sadness and happiness...with girls than with boys...Sadness and anxiety communicate personal vulnerability; they signal a need for soothing and comfort from others that reflects a willingness to submit oneself to the care of another...Submissive emotions are consistent with the stereotype for female role sociali-zation, that is, helping a child become motivated to take care of others and to avoid selfishness or overt aggression that might threaten relationships.[25]

Certainly there's some evidence that parents put more pressure on boys to control their crying—and indeed to control their emotions in general (the 'stiff upper lip' school of child-rearing). Children seem to get the message. Girls and boys, for example, differ in how they expect adults to respond to their emotions, with boys expecting more parental disapproval of sadness than girls.

Much of the time, parents may be oblivious to the lessons they're imparting. Hence the surprise of so many parents who have sought to raise their kids in a 'gender-neutral' fashion and yet find themselves with a toy gun-toting son or doll's home-making daughter. We demonstrate gender roles as unconsciously as we inhabit them ourselves. Many studies have shown this tendency at work, though perhaps the most famous was carried out in the mid-1970s by John and Sandra Condry. They showed adults a video of a baby staring and then bursting into tears as a jack-in-the-box sprang open. Half the participants were told that the baby was a boy while the other half were led to believe it was a girl. Those who thought the child was male described its reaction to the jack-in-the-box as 'anger'; the others labelled the emotion 'fear'.

So children begin to learn their gender roles at a very young age. But as we've seen already in this chapter, the process cranks up another gear (or several) during adolescence. It's known as the 'gender intensification hypothesis': social pressure sees male and female roles become increasingly differentiated during the teenage years. And the female role is, arguably, not a great one. Boys are often encouraged to pursue influence and achievement in the outside world—to go out and 'make something' of themselves. Girls, on the other hand, are still frequently expected to prioritize the domestic realm, marrying well and building a home and family. (It sounds like a Jane Austen novel, doesn't it? Jane Austen, incidentally, died in 1817.) In many cases, boys are given licence to put their own interests first; girls' primary responsibility is to care for other people: partner, children, parents, friends . . . and male and female roles are not valued equally. What matters is building a career, acquiring influence, and amassing wealth—not running a household and raising children. Designating an activity as 'women's work' is not a form of praise.

Many women do of course hold paid jobs outside the home, but there's a good chance that their employment will be part time and low status. Their career aspirations may be hampered by their family responsibilities (or by their employer's assumption that such responsibilities will limit their commitment). Even when both part-ners work full time, women still do the bulk of the housework and childcare. The time available for women to build a career can be squeezed, in the early years, by the need to look after young chil-dren and, in later years, by the need to care for elderly parents. Even when women are actually doing the same job as men, they are typi-cally paid less.

If you feel as though you have limited control over your own life, and that society doesn't value who you are and what you do, your self-esteem is probably going to take a hit. As we know, there's a proven link between low self-esteem and depression. Indeed there's evidence that the demands of the female role can have a negative effect on women's happiness from a very early age. Lars Wichstrøm, a psychologist at the Norwegian University of Science and Technol-ogy, collected data on a representative sample of more than 12,000 Norwegian young people, aged 12 to 20. Among the 12-year-olds, there was no difference in rates of depression between boys and girls. But over the next couple of years, girls overtook boys. Why was this? Wichstrøm found that:

> the gender difference could be explained, in part, by increased devel-opmental changes for girls—pubertal development, dissatisfaction with weight and attainment of a mature female body, and increased importance of feminine sex role identification.[26]

Puberty takes the average female body ever further from the 'ideal' of slimness. And it happens just at the time when girls are increas-ingly conscious of both their femininity and the expectations that go with it—notably, of course, the importance of looking attractive. Can you be attractive unless you're pencil-thin? To judge by the rep-resentations of women in the media, one might assume not. Hence many young women, dissatisfied with their new body shape, will feel that they don't measure up to the required standard. It's hard to imagine anything, at this age especially, more damaging to one's self-esteem—and thus more conducive to depression. (Wichstrøm also found that there was a direct correlation between girls' increased sense of their own femininity and depression. This was less influential, though, than a more inclusive picture involving unhappiness with body shape and consequent lower self-esteem.)

In the Norwegian study, pretty much the entire difference between male and female rates of depression could be accounted for by these two factors: the effect of the physical changes associated with puberty and the increased identification with gender stereotype. But it was a cross-sectional analysis and, though these kinds of study are good at showing that factors A and B (for example, depression and dissatisfaction with one's appearance) are linked in some way, they can't tell us much about the specific nature of that link—most importantly, whether A is produced by B. To really pin down causation what we need are longitudinal studies, which follow a group of people over time, or experimental research, in which one makes something happen in order to observe the consequences.

We can see more evidence—albeit indirect—of the possible connection between gender roles and depression in a study by Soraya Seedat and colleagues. You might remember from Chapter 2 that the World Health Organization has set up the World Mental Health Survey Initiative, covering more than 150,000 people in twenty-eight countries. In their analysis of preliminary results from the programme (data collected from over 72,000 people across the world), Seedat's team discovered that women of all ages were more likely than men to suffer from depression. This finding is unlikely to have surprised anyone, given the weight of data from other studies. But Seedat and co also found that the gap was narrower in younger age groups, a phenomenon they were able to attribute to changes in traditional gender roles. Better education; greater access to the job market; more say over whether, when, and who they marry; and greater control over their own fertility through contraception—all, the researchers found, may have improved women's mental health. Were equality between the sexes ever to be achieved, presumably the disparity between male and female rates of depression would shrink even further. (Seedat's analysis isn't without its problems, however, as we saw.)

What effect does marriage have on mental health? (You may insert your own joke here.) Quite a bit of research has been done on this issue, and the bottom line seems to be that it depends on whether you're male or female. Marriage seems, on the whole, to be rather more beneficial for men than it is for women. Interestingly, a study of data collected by the World Mental Health Survey Initiative on 34,000 people in fifteen countries found that marriage helped prevent a first episode of almost all psychological disorders in both sexes. But not so in the case of depression (and panic disorder): here, only men benefited. Judging by the results of numerous surveys, marriage certainly appears to be less rewarding for many women than it is for men. Perhaps this is because—and we're talking broad generalizations here—a married man becomes cared for, while a married women becomes, alongside her existing responsibilities, a carer. Understandably, the latter role may not suit everyone. In fact, it may have a direct impact on women's happiness, thereby increasing their vulnerability to depression. (There is some evidence, however, that the gender gap in marital satisfaction reduces over time.)

Marital dissatisfaction increases for both partners with the arrival of children, and the more children, the greater the parental discontent. The effect is especially acute where the children are young, as anyone who has spent extended time looking after little ones will understand. For all the joy that children bring to their parents, they may not make everyday life any easier. Adapting to the role of mother or father can be difficult; no matter how many books you may have read on the topic before the little one arrives, nothing can prepare you for the reality of your permanently altered existence. Parents find that what was once free time is now largely spent on childcare. And there may be financial pressures too: quite how much it costs to raise a child is hotly disputed, but one thing's for sure—it isn't free. However, parenthood has a more negative effect on women's view of marriage than it does on men's. This is probably because it's women who, generally speaking, are primarily responsible for childcare—alongside running the home and, quite possibly, holding down a paid job too. As such, mothers shoulder most of the burden that having children typically involves.

Childbirth itself can trigger postpartum depression, of course, but this doesn't explain why women experience more depression than men. The gender difference, after all, spans early adolescence to menopause. And it's not only women who can develop depression after the birth of a child. Men are at risk too, though the figures are lower than for women. Most studies of postpartum depression focus on women, but a few also include men. One study of parents in Spain, for example, found that three months after birth 9.3 per cent of mothers and 3.4 per cent of fathers had been newly diagnosed with depression. After twelve months the gap had closed, with 4.4 per cent of women and 4 per cent of men suffering from depression (though in both cases we can't be certain that it was the arrival of the child that caused the illness).

Let's summarize what current research tells us about why women are more prone to depression than men.

We know that low self-esteem is a proven risk factor for depression. We've seen that women's self-esteem is lower than men's, and may be especially affected by:

- worries about appearance
- the conventional female role, with its unequal distribution of burden and rewards
- negative cognitive styles, specifically a tendency to dwell on problems ('ruminative coping') and a pessimistic way of explaining events
- negative life events, and particularly those that involve relationships (most potently during adolescence).

Depression is usually triggered by stress, typically interacting with self-esteem. Women may experience more stress than men. And because of differences between the sexes in the HPA axis, it seems likely that women are either more sensitive to certain stresses, or at least respond differently, depending on the kind of problem they're facing.

Certainly, if people are sexually abused as children they usually suffer significant damage to their self-esteem, and become much more sensitive to stress. Girls, as we've seen, are much more likely than boys to experience this kind of trauma.

Finally—and here the evidence is weakest—it may be that women have a slightly greater genetic vulnerability to depression than men, though it might take prolonged or severe stress to activate that genetic influence. This vulnerability perhaps explains why men and women differ in HPA axis reactivity.

Clearly, we're some way from a unified theory. It's not yet clear which factors are most important, nor how they might be linked and interact. The ideal research project would assess a representative sample of people, ideally catching them at an early age, and then following them closely over many years, collecting a wide range of data on their life experiences—not to mention their genetic make-up and neurological function—at regular intervals. Several studies currently under way may have the potential to clarify the picture.

Anxiety

Like depression, anxiety seems to be primarily a female disorder (which is not to say, of course, that large numbers of men aren't also affected). Why is this?

Unfortunately, there's much less research on gender differences in anxiety disorders than in depression. But what there is suggests that many of the same factors are involved. This is unsurprising, given that anxiety and depression are so closely linked. In fact, it's probably more common for people to suffer from both disorders simultaneously than one alone.

The list of similarities is a long one. Let's start with genetic factors. As we saw, heritability of depression is estimated to be approximately 40 per cent; it's the same for anxiety problems. Indeed, research suggests that the same genes may be involved in both disorders (such as 5-HTT, the serotonin transporter gene). Are women more likely than men to inherit a genetic vulnerability to anxiety? As with the data on depression, the evidence here is mixed. Remember the link between depression and the personality trait of neuroticism? Well, people prone to neuroticism—and women generally show higher levels than men—are also vulnerable to anxiety problems. And it's the same with the HPA axis: the hyperreactivity (and sometimes hyporeactivity) found in people suffering from depression tends also to be present in those with anxiety disorders. Again, HPA irregularities may be more prevalent among women than men.

Then there are the psychological similarities between the two conditions. Rumination, worry, pessimism—all increase the chances of developing both depression and anxiety problems. At the risk of sounding like the proverbial scratched record, these are ways of thinking that seem to be more common in women. Ditto for the role of traumatic or stressful events: heavily involved in causing depression, they generally also play a major role in anxiety disorders. Certainly girls are far more likely to be victims of childhood sexual abuse—a trauma whose legacy is, all too frequently, depression and anxiety problems (not to mention a panoply of other psychological disorders) later in life.

So much for the similarities. There are, though, a few differences in emphasis when it comes to the attempt to explain gender differences in anxiety. Two areas that have received some attention are *disgust sensitivity* and *anxiety sensitivity*.

The first term is used to describe how easily the emotion of disgust can be triggered. Research has shown that people with certain phobias—specifically, spider phobias and blood-injection-injury phobias, such as the fear of seeing blood or an injury, or of having an injection or similarly invasive medical procedure—are particularly susceptible in general to feelings of disgust. (Phobias are defined by the *Diagnostic and Statistical Manual* as a 'marked and persistent fear that is excessive or unreasonable, cued by the presence or anticipation of a specific object or situation',[27] and are classified as an anxiety disorder.) There is a logic here. Physical disgust is designed to prevent us coming into contact with substances that could cause illness. So a blood phobia might be based on a fear of infection; spiders may be seen as possible sources of contamination. Women tend to score higher than men for disgust sensitivity, though it's not clear why. And there's some evidence that this may partly explain why these phobias are more common in women. But stringent testing is required before we know for sure.

Anxiety sensitivity denotes the extent to which a person believes that the physical sensations experienced when they're excited or anxious are harmful. It's anxiety about anxiety, in other words. People high in anxiety sensitivity mistake the signs of normal, everyday anxiety (faster heart rate or breathlessness, for instance) for something far more sinister (heart attack, say, or imminent collapse). Naturally, this misinterpretation only serves to increase their anxiety—and on it goes. Because they're worried about what these sensations might mean, they're often on the alert for the slightest physical change. It can be a stressful habit, and one that often presages the development of clinical anxiety disorders (and depression too). Anxiety sensitivity is higher in women, which perhaps helps explain why they're more likely to develop anxiety problems.

Then again, perhaps it doesn't explain anything very much. This is because it's possible that anxiety sensitivity signifies not so much a vulnerability to future anxiety disorders but the symptoms of *current* low-level anxiety. If the concept of anxiety sensitivity merely amounts to the insight that anxious people are prone to anxiety disorders, then we aren't any further forward.

It may be that our best chance of explaining gender differences in anxiety—at least on current evidence—lies in social factors. Girls only overtake boys in rates of depression during adolescence. But for many anxiety disorders it happens much sooner, at around the age of 6. This seems to fit with the idea that, to a large extent, we learn our fears early in life, either from our own experiences or from how others behave and what they tell us. (In depression, learning seems to be less of a factor.) In many cultures, it's less acceptable for a man to display fear than it is for a woman. So while girls may be indulged in their fears, boys are taught to overcome them. Big boys, as we know, don't cry. On the other hand, as we saw earlier in this chapter, encouraging girls to acknowledge their anxiety may actually suit the conventional female gender role, with its emphasis on feelings (rather than action) and relationships (rather than autonomy).

It's not simply a case of boys learning to mask their feelings, though doubtless that happens too: they may actually *feel* less anxiety. When we avoid what we fear, we deprive ourselves of the opportunity to discover that, in fact, we can handle the situation. And thus our fear is maintained. But if we put our anxiety to the test, if we face up to our fear, it will dwindle and die—and often amazingly quickly. (This insight is the basis of much very successful cognitive behavioural therapy for anxiety.) And so a child who always sleeps with a night light, for example, will take longer to realize that they have nothing to fear in the dark, and to experience the confidence boost that conquering anxiety brings. Do we as parents tend to spare our daughters the short-term anxiety that confronting one's fears involves, at the cost of making them more susceptible to anxiety problems in the long term?

Similarly, parents who attempt to control their child's behaviour too rigidly—quite possibly because of a desire to protect them—may unwittingly send out a signal that the world is a dangerous place. And the child doesn't have the chance to discover that, by and large, she can cope with the problems she encounters. When anxious and non-anxious adults are asked by psychologists to recall their childhood, the anxious individuals are more likely to describe their parents as overprotective or controlling. Memories are not always reliable, of course. But there is some observational research with children that backs up these findings. What it doesn't show, however, is that this kind of parenting is more likely to be used with girls than boys.

Perhaps girls, with their more sophisticated social skills, are just more skilled than boys at picking up on the messages their parents are sending. The psychologists Friederike Gerull and Ronald Rapee showed thirty Australian toddlers (aged 15 to 20 months) a green rubber snake and then a purple rubber spider, and studied their reactions. While the toys were on display, the children's mothers were asked to react in a happy and encouraging way or in a frightened or disgusted manner. Later, the snake and the spider were shown to the toddlers a couple more times, though on these occasions their mothers' reactions were strictly neutral. Gerull and Rapee noticed that you could predict how a child would react to the toy when they saw it again, because they mimicked the initial response of their mother. If the mother had feigned fear, the child was frightened. On the other hand, if the mother had appeared calm and happy, the toddler reacted in the same way. (This phenomenon is known as 'modelling' and it's believed to play a big role in our acquisition of fears.)

What Gerull and Rapee also found, however, was that a mother pretending to be frightened had more of an impact on girls than boys. The girls showed more fear, and were much more likely to avoid the snake and spider:

> when mothers reacted positively toward the toy, both males and females showed similar levels of approach/avoidance. However, in response to mothers' expressions of fear/disgust, girls showed greater avoidance of the toy than did boys. These data might suggest that girls actually learn greater degrees of avoidance from modelling of their mothers rather than having a greater basic avoidance of all stimuli.[28]

So maybe girls experience more anxiety, not because they're more apprehensive in general but because they are so adept at learning fear from their mother or father. It's an intriguing idea, but studying parenting is complicated work. Inevitably you're looking at micro-behaviours in response to specific events, and extrapolating out from these to general insights is risky. Then there's the fact that the way a parent behaves is influenced by the personality of the child. And research that looks at gender differences in parenting—either in general or in relation to anxiety—is fairly rare.

Sleep

When it comes to psychological disorders, sleep problems are very much the poor relation. Such is their lowly status that none of the major national surveys of mental health reports on them. Instead, they're usually regarded as a symptom of other psychological disorders. And it's certainly true that people with anxiety and depression often also report sleep-related problems. So although women are more likely than men to experience a sleep disorder, no concerted attempt has been made to explain why. Instead it's assumed that it's merely a reflection of the gender difference in rates of anxiety and depression.

But such a view does little justice to the importance of sleep problems, and the very significant distress they can cause. For one thing, it's clear that sleep problems aren't just a by-product. Longitudinal studies (which follow a group of people over time) have shown that the most common sleep disorder, insomnia, can actually help create anxiety and depression. ('Insomnia' is a general term for a number of problems including finding it difficult to fall asleep or to stay asleep and not enjoying enough good-quality sleep. It's exceptionally common: on any given night, roughly a third of adults are thought to be affected.)

If you think back to the last time you endured a wretched night's sleep, and then imagine how you'd feel after weeks of the same, you'll probably need little convincing of the dramatic effect sleeplessness can have on mood. F. Scott Fitzgerald reportedly claimed that the worst thing in the world is to try to sleep and not be able to—which may be putting it a little strongly but certainly captures the misery of insomnia.

When we look at primary insomnia—that is, sleeplessness without any other psychological disorders—we find that it's more common in women than men. The difference between the sexes is perhaps a little smaller than it is for comorbid insomnia, but it's there nonetheless. As with depression, sleep problems first become more common in girls during adolescence.

Why might women be more prone to sleep problems than men? Our sleep is controlled by two complementary systems. The *circadian rhythm* system tells us when to sleep and when to be awake. Most people become gradually more alert from around 6.00 a.m., reaching a plateau at around 9.30 a.m. We dip in the early afternoon, before building to a daily peak of alertness between 6 and 8 p.m. Then we steadily wind down, bottoming out between 2 and 6 a.m. (which is why it's unwise to drive in the small hours). The *homeostatic* system determines our need for sleep based on how long it's been since we last got our head down. If you've spent a delightful afternoon dozing on the sofa, for instance, you're going to find it difficult to fall asleep at night, despite what your circadian rhythm might be telling you. Some scientists have argued that both the circadian rhythm and the homeostatic sleep systems are affected by an individual's sex, principally through the influence of sex hormones. But no one has yet attempted to discover whether this might help account for gender differences in rates of insomnia.

One of the very few studies to seek to explain these differences focused on the possible contribution of sociodemographic factors. In a very large cross-sectional Taiwanese study (40,000 adults), only a small proportion of the discrepancy between male and female rates of insomnia could be traced to some basic social influences:

> While the sex discrepancy narrowed after controlling for marital status, employment conditions, and number of children in the household, women's sleep quality remained significantly worse than men's sleep quality. Even though women were over-represented

among the less educated and economically deprived, these disadvantaged socioeconomic conditions did not translate into more sleep disturbance.[29]

Divorce and unemployment seem, at least in the Taiwanese study, to lead more frequently to sleep problems for women than they do for men. And married women in the sample experienced more insomnia than married men, or indeed single women. (The more children in a household, the greater the likelihood of sleep problems, though the impact was the same for both sexes.) But if you strip all of these sociodemographic factors out of the data you still end up with a sizeable discrepancy between the sexes in levels of insomnia.

The most plausible explanation may lie in the idea of stress reactivity, which as we've seen is controlled by the brain's HPA axis. Sleep inhibits HPA activity. This makes sense: it's very difficult to rest with, for example, high levels of the stress hormone cortisol washing around our system. Sleep requires that our stress responses are calmed, allowing physiological and psychological relaxation. On the other hand, if we're not getting sufficient good-quality sleep our HPA goes into overdrive. There's evidence, for instance, that people with insomnia secrete more cortisol, especially in the evening.

Not only does sleeplessness increase our level of stress, there's plenty of evidence that the process can work the other way around too. Just as insomnia triggers the body's stress responses, stressful situations cause insomnia. And there's more: insomnia may cause people to react more strongly to potentially stressful situations. This is no surprise: it's tough to stay calm when you're dog-tired. All in all, it's easy to see how a debilitating cycle of sleeplessness can take shape, with an overwrought HPA axis working at full tilt, the body flooded with stress hormones, and rest seemingly a million miles away.

What we may be seeing in insomnia then—though admittedly there's very little research on the topic—is an interaction between stress, HPA activity, and disturbed sleep. And the result is a person so hyperalert that they're unable to get to sleep—or, if they do drop off, to stay asleep for long. What does this mean for the gender difference in insomnia? Well, there's evidence that each component in the interaction may affect women more than men. As we saw earlier in this chapter, women may be more likely to experience certain stressful events—such as childhood sexual abuse—and perhaps also stressful events in general. They may also react more strongly to some types of problems, for example those involving relationships. HPA axis irregularities may be more common in women. And women are more likely to experience disturbed sleep. All of which may leave them particularly exposed to the risk of clinical insomnia. Moreover, it's likely that worry and rumination often play a part in sleep problems—and women, as we know, are more prone than men to both. But these are early days: the effects of sleep and sleeplessness, in men and women alike, require a lot more attention before we really understand what's going on.

Another Look at the Data

What we've done in this chapter—and what we'll do in the two that follow—is to present the current evidence on gender and mental health. How, we want to know, does the best research explain why women are more prone to depression, anxiety, and sleep problems? But when you have access to the data from the 2007 UK Adult Psychiatric Morbidity Survey, it's impossible to resist testing out some of these hypotheses yourself. We do, and we have. Here's what we found.

The survey's dataset includes a variable termed 'any neurotic disorder'. Participants who reported mixed anxiety/depressive disorder, depression, generalized anxiety disorder, phobias, OCD, or panic disorder in the week prior to the survey were classified under this heading. Predictably, women far outnumbered men; of the almost 7,500 people questioned, 19.8 per cent of women had experienced 'any neurotic disorder', compared to 12.5 per cent of men. Indeed the odds on women reporting this kind of problem were 1.7 times greater than those for men. (For a reminder about the meaning of odds ratios, have a look back at Chapter 2.)

We set out to discover how much of this difference could be explained very simply by social factors—and specifically negative life events and gender roles. First of all, we analysed the data on childhood sexual abuse. As we've seen already in this chapter, there's good evidence linking sexual abuse to later psychological problems. And it's a trauma that typically affects girls rather than boys. Sure enough, the women in the UK survey were more likely to report that someone had touched them in a sexual way, and without their consent, before the age of 16 (11 per cent versus 5 per cent). Three per cent of women said that they'd experienced non-consensual sexual intercourse before age 16, compared to 1 per cent of men. The effect of this abuse on adult mental health is sobering. Being touched in a sexual way increases the chance of developing a neurotic disorder by three times; sexual intercourse without consent raises the odds sixfold. And yet reports of childhood sexual abuse alone can't explain why women are so prone to neurotic problems. If you control for it in the analysis, the odds on women experiencing these disorders are still 1.6 times those for men.

What about sexual abuse during adulthood? Again, rates are higher for women than men. From the age of 16, 8 per cent of women reported being touched in a sexual way without their consent and 5 per cent had experienced non-consensual intercourse; the figures for men were 2 per cent and 1 per cent respectively. This kind of trauma does increase the risk of later neurotic disorders. But, like childhood sexual abuse, on its own it's a relatively small element in the overall gender difference for these disorders, lowering the odds ratio from 1.7 to 1.6. Stripping out both child and adult sexual abuse leaves us with an odds ratio of 1.5. We can look at this in another way, by sorting the survey participants into two groups, one of which comprises people who have experienced sexual abuse at some point in their life, and one made up of individuals who've never been abused. In the first group, the odds on women developing a neurotic disorder are 1.6 times greater than they are for men; in the second group, the odds ratio is 1.5. So removing sexual abuse has only a small effect in reducing the gender difference in depression. Clearly there's much more behind this difference than simply sexual abuse.

We then looked at the impact of abusive relationships. Women in the 2007 UK survey were more likely than men to report that a partner had attempted to prevent them seeing friends or relatives (12 per cent versus 9 per cent). Fourteen per cent of women, and just 3 per cent of men, admitted that a partner had threatened to hurt them or someone close to them. And fully one in five women said that they'd been pushed, held or pinned down, or slapped by a partner (the figure for men was 9 per cent: much lower clearly but perhaps surprisingly high nonetheless). All these experiences were associated with higher rates of neurotic disorder. But, once again, taken in isolation they don't seem to be a hugely significant factor in the gender difference for this type of disorder. Even for women who have never been in an abusive relationship, the odds ratio is 1.5. If we also take out those individuals who've suffered sexual abuse, either as a child or adult, the ratio dips a little below 1.5—which suggests that these experiences tend to affect the same people.

And one might argue that this is a somewhat skewed way of approaching the data. After all, some negative life events are more likely to happen to men than women. If we take those into account, how does it affect the odds ratio for neurotic disorders? Take the example of being severely beaten by a parent before the age of 16. When we also control for this type of childhood physical abuse—plus sexual abuse or physical abuse from a partner—the difference between male and female rates of neurotic disorder widens again. And if we also control for any major trauma (that is, an event that made the person fear for their own or a loved one's life and safety), the odds ratio is back up to 1.6.

In other words, when these types of negative life event are considered in isolation they explain only a small proportion of the gender difference in emotional disorders.

What does the UK data tell us about the contribution of gender roles to mental health? One way of getting at this is to look at how much time individuals spend caring for other people. Traditionally this is a female responsibility. The survey asked people about their involvement in caring for family members, friends, or others due to ill health or disability. As we'd expect, women did more of this than men. And the more hours a person devoted to this kind of activity, the greater the chance that they'd report a neurotic disorder. Yet if we take this variable out of the data, the difference between male and female rates of emotional disorder remains unchanged. The fact that women do the bulk of this kind of caring doesn't explain why they're more susceptible to anxiety and depression.

Obviously we haven't been able to conduct a thorough test of all the possible factors behind the gender difference. This national survey wasn't conducted with that in mind. But we aren't the only ones to have had difficulty accounting for the gender difference by looking at some basic social factors. Here's what experts who analysed data from the Mental Health Supplement of the German National Health Interview and Examination Survey concluded:

Overall the emotional advantages or disadvantages of marital status, employment status, number of children, parenthood and social class apply equally to men and women. We cannot explain the female preponderance in most mental disorders by detecting specific unfavourable patterns of sociodemographic correlates.[30]

These sociodemographic factors don't seem to account for gender differences in mental illness at all. Controlling for them in the analyses, the odds on women reporting a psychological disorder were still 1.6 times those for men.

It's worth remembering though that both the UK and German surveys were cross-sectional studies. They present a snapshot of a situation and often rely on participants' longer-term memory to piece together what might have led up to that moment. Moreover, they don't capture any interaction between social factors and psychological and biological influences. This is a significant omission, because this interaction often magnifies the negative effects of the social factors (it's the stress-vulnerability model we discussed in the section on depression). And as we've seen, a much more effective way to observe the development of mental illness is to adopt a longitudinal approach, following participants over an extended period of time and checking in with them at regular intervals. That way, we're better able to see how events and influences play out, to track the subtle interplay of cause and effect.

Bear in mind too that it's not necessary to explain fully the difference between male and female rates of emotional disorder in order to remove the overall disparity in psychological problems. Imagine, for example, that we include only emotional and externalizing disorders. Imagine too that women outscore men for emotional disorders by ten percentage points, and men outscore women for externalizing disorders by five percentage points. If we account for just half of women's lead in emotional disorders, the overall totals will be the same for both sexes.

Having reached the end of this chapter, one might be forgiven for assuming that psychological disorders are predominately a female problem. Anxiety, depression, sleep problems—all are seen more often in women than men. We shouldn't forget, however, that large numbers of men are also affected by these disorders. Moreover, for some problems rates are significantly higher in men than women. Perhaps the most common of these 'male' disorders is substance abuse—alcohol and drugs—and it's to this that we turn our attention now.

5

Alcohol and Drug Problems

Girls not long from school were to be seen drinking cocktails, champagne, and liqueurs, while in time whiskies and sodas were added to the list of stimulants required to keep them going. Scarcely had the age of twenty been reached before the lines that rightly belonged to the woman of middle-age had become evident in such girls. Was it to be supposed that when girls of this kind reached womanhood and became mothers they could produce men and women with anything but the most miserable physique and of the neurotic type?

Lifestyle of the Modern Girl Condemned,
Manchester Guardian, 18 February 1926[1]

It may seem like a statement of the obvious, but given that we've just devoted so much attention to exploring why depression, anxiety, and sleep disorders are so prevalent among women, it bears repeating: psychological disorders affect men too, and in large numbers.

Indeed, certain problems are more common in men than in women. Of these, substance disorders are by far the most widespread. But what exactly is a 'substance disorder'? And what criteria will a health professional use in order to judge whether an individual may be suffering from one? Let's start by defining what counts as a problematic substance. It's a pretty wide range, encompassing alcohol, caffeine, nicotine, legal medications, and the gamut of illicit drugs from cannabis and cocaine to amphetamines and heroin and all points in between. As for the disorders, there are two types: abuse and dependence. If a substance is causing a person regular problems in their personal or professional lives—missing work because of yet another hangover, for example, or constantly arguing with their partner over their drug habit—they probably meet the criteria for substance abuse. To qualify for a diagnosis of dependency, an individual would need to meet at least three of the following criteria:

- Increased tolerance for the substance, so a person needs to use a greater quantity in order to achieve the same high
- Physical and psychological problems when consumption is reduced (also known as *withdrawal*)
- Taking more of the substance, or taking it over a longer period, than intended
- Repeatedly trying, but failing, to cut down or give up
- Spending lots of time planning how to get hold of the substance, taking it, or recovering
- Prioritizing the substance over other parts of life
- Carrying on taking the substance despite being aware of the harm it's causing.

Although the psychiatric category of substance disorders includes both alcohol and drugs (licit and illicit), problems with drink dwarf all others. The US National Comorbidity Survey Replication, for example, found that 3.1 per cent of those questioned had experienced alcohol abuse, with or without dependence, during the previous twelve months. For drugs, on the other hand, the figure was 1.4 per cent. (That figure includes abuse of illegal and prescription drugs, though it doesn't cover nicotine.)

Given that alcohol abuse and dependency are so much more widespread than drug problems, and because the gender difference is very similar for both substances, we're going to concentrate in this chapter on alcohol disorders. There's another good reason: researchers have spent a lot more time trying to account for the discrepancy between male and female rates of alcohol problems than they have for other substances. But choosing to focus on one substance rather than another may close fewer doors than we might think. Alcohol and drug disorders are strongly linked, and people often suffer from both. The US National Epidemiological Survey on Alcohol Related Conditions (NESARC), for example, collected data on a nationally representative sample of more than 40,000 individuals. It found that the odds for members of the general population with a drug dependency problem to also be dependent on alcohol were twenty times greater than they were for other people. This statistic isn't surprising: similar genetic and environmental factors have been implicated for all substance disorders. Though the drug may vary, the causes of abuse and dependence are essentially the same. (To be absolutely accurate, difficulties with alcohol and nicotine seem to have more in common with one another, genetically speaking, than they do with disorders involving cannabis and cocaine, and vice versa. Problems with legal and illegal drugs don't have absolutely identical genetic roots—though there is a lot of overlap.)

Cultural factors clearly play a big part in alcohol and drug disorders. And perhaps the most basic of those cultural determinants is simply whether or not you live in a place where you're likely to encounter a problematic substance. An individual might, for example, be born with a genetic vulnerability to alcohol abuse. But if alcohol isn't freely available, the risk of that person developing a problem is likely to be much reduced. In the United States, 92 per cent of adults have drunk alcohol at some point; 42 per cent have tried cannabis, and 16 per cent cocaine. In China, by contrast, 65 per cent have tasted alcohol, 0.3 per cent have experimented with cannabis, and 0 per cent (that is, too few to register) have taken cocaine. In Nigeria, the figures are 57 per cent for alcohol, 3 per cent for cannabis, and 0.1 per cent for cocaine. And the greater the number of people who try a drug, the higher the incidence of disorder. In the United States, 14.6 per cent of people will develop a substance disorder at some stage in their life; in China the figure is 5 per cent and in Nigeria 4 per cent. But though national statistics may wax and wane in line with the local availability of drugs and alcohol, one finding remains unaltered across the range of countries: it is men who consistently show higher rates of substance disorders.

Genetic Factors

Why are men more likely than women to develop problems with alcohol? Inevitably, a number of factors seem to be involved. Let's begin by looking at the part played by genetics.

Alcohol disorders tend to run in families. If, say, a person's parent and grandparent have been dependent on drink, there's an above-average chance that the individual will develop the same problem. In itself, of course, this doesn't prove that genes are responsible. Theoretically, the elevated risk of disorder might be entirely a consequence of the way the child was raised: for example, by being given the impression that it's normal to drink alcohol regularly and to excess. But in fact the data indicates that heritability of alcohol disorders is moderate to high, at around 50–60 per cent. (Heritability can be a tricky concept. In this case, it doesn't mean that 50–60 per cent of the causes of alcohol problems are genetic. What it tells us is that 50–60 per cent of the *differences* in rates of alcohol disorders across the population may be linked to genes, with the remainder caused by environmental factors.)

So genes play a significant part in alcohol problems. But does this help explain why men are more prone to abuse or dependence? Are men more likely to hit the bottle because of their genetic make-up? Some small twin studies have suggested that this might be the case, but larger surveys (from Finland, Sweden, Australia, the United States, and the UK) have not. The current consensus is that there are no differences between men and women in genetic heritability of alcohol dependence.

Things are more ambiguous, incidentally, when it comes to current data on heritability of illicit substance disorders, for example involving cannabis. Genetic differences between men and women haven't been ruled out, though they've not been clearly demonstrated either. This is because obtaining an accurate picture of what's going on is difficult. You need to assess an awful lot of people before you can draw any firm conclusions about genetic (and environmental) causes for any psychological phenomenon. And many of the drug studies have worked with small samples. This is understandable given that drug disorders are relatively uncommon (certainly much less prevalent than alcohol problems) and are especially rare in women, but it puts a significant spoke in the wheel of studies that focus on teasing out gender differences. Moreover, there's a distinction to be made between trying a drug (so-called 'initiation') and developing a problem with that substance. What leads some people to experiment with cannabis or cocaine, while others opt never to touch the stuff? And why do a proportion of those that do try these drugs slip into dependence? Genetic factors may well be involved in both initiation and problematic drug taking, but the nature and scale of their contribution are likely to differ.

It's worth noting, by the way, that framing a discussion of causes in terms of genes versus environment is an increasingly outdated approach. What we know now is that genetic and environmental factors interact, in a complex and highly dynamic way. We saw in the previous chapter, for instance, how individuals with a variant form of the serotonin transporter gene are at greater risk of developing depression when they experience a negative life event. This is a classic example of what's known as a gene × environment interaction: a person may carry a genetic vulnerability to a condition, but that vulnerability is only activated by events. Similarly, you may be genetically susceptible to heart disease. But if you eat well and take plenty of exercise your odds on developing a problem are likely to be substantially lower than for many people without those risky genes. As Avshalom Caspi and Terrie Moffitt have written:

> the gene–environment interaction approach assumes that environmental pathogens cause disorder, and that genes influence susceptibility to pathogens.[2]

The way we live our life and the events that befall us combine with our genetic inheritance to determine who we become.

As well as gene × environment interactions, we also have the so-called 'developmental dance'. What this means is that the influence of genetic and environmental factors varies according to age. Research indicates, for example, that in early adolescence our drinking habits have almost nothing to do with our genetic make-up. The average 14-year-old's alcohol consumption is very largely determined by environmental factors, such as the friends they hang out with. From this point onwards, genetic factors become increasingly important. But even so it's only when we reach our mid-30s that heritability for alcohol use reaches moderate levels.

And then there's the emerging field of *epigenetics* (literally, 'above genetics'). Every cell in our body contains our genetic blueprint, formed from extended molecules of DNA (deoxyribonucleic acid). But how those genes express themselves—and most importantly, whether they are turned on or off—is partly determined by the 'epigenome', a set of instructions located above the DNA sequence. The epigenome can change during the course of a person's life in response to environmental factors. One of those environmental factors is ethanol; in other words, alcohol can affect the way our genes operate. What does this mean for the gender difference in alcohol disorders? It's too early to know; this level of complexity is new in genetic research. But it's another indication that the interplay of genetic and environmental factors producing these disorders is likely to be far more sophisticated than we might once have imagined.

Physiological Factors

As you may have observed, alcohol doesn't appear to have the same effect on men and women. By which we don't mean that it's men that tend to fall asleep, or start a fight, or witter on about sport for hours: that's clearly far-fetched...No, what we're getting at here is the fact that women seem to become intoxicated more quickly than men. Or, as the stereotype has it, women can't handle their drink.

Is this true, or simply anecdotal conjecture: the sort of thing one might come up with after, well, a few drinks? Alcohol undoubtedly has more of an effect on women's physiology. To use the jargon, women show greater 'alcohol sensitivity'. If a man and woman drink an identical glass of wine, for example, the level of alcohol (ethanol) in the woman's blood will be higher. Why is this? Susan Nolen-Hoeksema and Lori Hilt suggest:

This may occur because women are generally smaller than men, because women's body-water content is smaller than men's per kilogram of body weight, or because activity of the enzyme gastric alcohol dehydrogenase is lower in women than in men, all of which lead to greater amounts of alcohol being passed through the stomach and into the blood stream in women compared with men.[3]

Women may feel increasing social pressure to keep up with men's level of alcohol consumption. But, physiologically at least, the playing field is not level.

What are the consequences of this greater alcohol sensitivity in women? Research in this area isn't without its methodological limitations: the samples are often small; the tasks used to measure intoxication, and the amount of alcohol consumed, vary; and the level of alcohol in the bloodstream isn't always measured. Even with these caveats, the evidence does seem to suggest that alcohol causes more problems for women than it does for men.

Women's thought processes—memory, for example—take a greater hit from drink. Some studies also suggest that women report *feeling* more intoxicated than men. But the results here are mixed, and may depend on whether what is being measured is alcohol's capacity to stimulate or to calm. Women who drink the same amount as men may be at greater risk of passing out, blacking out (that is, being unable to remember what happened after they started drinking), or suffering injury. Presumably this is because the level of alcohol in their bloodstream is higher. But it's striking that some of the same effects have been found even when the blood-alcohol concentration (BAC) is the same for both sexes. What this means is that women aren't simply suffering more ill effects because a greater amount of ethanol is reaching their system: it may be that alcohol *in itself* is more toxic for them.

There's certainly a good deal of evidence that women who drink regularly are more vulnerable to physical health problems. Thirty-four studies of the relationship between alcohol and mortality, covering more than a million people and 95,000 deaths, were analysed by researchers in Italy. The news for drinkers is both good and bad. The Italian team found that a 'J-shaped relationship' existed between alcohol intake and mortality. That is, daily consumption of a small quantity of alcohol was associated with lower mortality, while drinking a greater amount led to higher mortality rates. But the protective dose of alcohol was much smaller for women (1–2 drinks per day) than it was for men (2–4 drinks). The researchers concluded:

> Women are more exposed than men to death for any cause at moderate to high levels of alcohol consumption, probably owing to increasing risk of cancer.[4]

So there may be a very good reason why women feel the effects of alcohol more than men do: it is more dangerous for them. And perhaps rapid intoxication functions as a kind of early warning system to stop drinking before serious damage is done.

In fact, it is well established that the greater your response to alcohol, the less likely it is that you'll develop a disorder. Researchers have compared the responses of people with, and without, a family history of alcohol dependency. What they found was that the individuals with such a history reported less of a feeling of intoxication after a set dose of alcohol than those without. As we've seen, alcohol problems tend to be passed down from parent to child. (Research suggests that as many as 33 per cent of men and 18 per cent of women with this kind of background develop an alcohol disorder.) And perhaps this is partly because these individuals inherit a reduced sensitivity to alcohol. For many people, of course, drinking is a hugely pleasurable experience. But if you must consume larger amounts of alcohol in order to experience those positive feelings, you elevate your risk of slipping into abuse and dependence.

Something very similar may lie behind the gender difference in alcohol disorders. With a relatively high tolerance for alcohol, men tend to drink more. Women, on the other hand, have a very clear disincentive to consume large amounts of alcohol. Because their physiology is so sensitive to alcohol, the negative effects kick in quickly. And not only does this help protect women from physical health problems, it may also reduce the risk of them developing alcohol disorders.

Psychological Factors

1. Impulsivity

Do you often act on impulse? Does your will weaken at the thought of a drink or two? Does it shrug its shoulders when you sense you've had enough? Of course, almost everyone has moments of impulsivity, and life would surely be duller if we didn't occasionally succumb to temptation. But certain individuals are much more impulsive than others. And in some cases that can lead to substance abuse and dependence.

The psychological process of impulsivity is essentially a failure to control one's behaviour. It's the tendency to act first and consider the consequences later, if at all. But impulsivity is a complex phenomenon, and thus one that can be measured in several different ways. Indeed psychologists have identified five different forms, summarized here by Danielle Dick and colleagues:

> Two of the five dispositions are emotion-based: *positive urgency* is the tendency to act rashly when experiencing extremely positive mood, and *negative urgency* is the tendency to act rashly when experiencing extremely negative mood. Two are based on deficits in conscientiousness: *lack of planning* is the tendency to act without forethought, and *lack of perseverance* reflects a failure to tolerate boredom or to remain focused despite distraction. The fifth is *sensation seeking*, or the tendency to seek out novel or thrilling stimulation.[5]

It's not hard to imagine the part each of these types of impulsivity might play in problem drinking: the quick pint or four with friends to celebrate the weekend; the consoling bottle of wine at the end of a horrible day; joining a mate for a lunchtime beer without considering the effect it'll have on your afternoon's work; drifting to the pub on a free afternoon because you can't settle to anything else; or getting drunk just to see what happens this time...

Impulsivity means that we're much more likely to start drinking. The first drink usually feels pretty good, which can make it harder for very impulsive people to stop. Research backs up this theory: there's a strong link between impulsivity and substance disorders of all types. High levels of impulsivity increase the chances of a person developing a problem, and then help keep that problem going. And some experts believe that impulsivity is a big part of the reason why alcohol problems are often inherited: it's a personality trait passed down via our genes.

So maybe men are prone to substance disorders because they're more impulsive than women? Some experts certainly think so, and indeed it has been suggested that genes play a bigger role in impulsivity in men than in women. Perhaps, the argument goes, evolutionary pressures have resulted in men being genetically programmed for impulsivity. Our male ancestors needed to be risk takers: to hunt and to compete for mates. And risk taking is very closely related to impulsivity. For prehistoric women, the priority was raising children. Impulsivity would not have been an asset: danger had to be avoided; caution became instinctive.

Catherine Cross and colleagues at Durham University recently analysed the findings from 277 studies of impulsivity and gender. They found that men tended to show higher levels of both risk taking and sensation seeking. Women, on the hand, were better at 'effortful control', defined as the 'ability to choose a course of action under conditions of conflict, to plan for the future, and to detect errors'.[6] And women also proved more sensitive to punishment: that is, to the potentially negative consequences of an action. As you might imagine, neither of these female strengths is particularly compatible with high impulsivity: they require careful, measured consideration. And this is presumably why women generally outperform men in these areas.

Yet the picture that emerges from Cross's meta-analysis isn't straightforward. Certainly men score higher than women on some measures of impulsivity. But impulsivity takes several forms and men and women seem equally adept at both delay discounting (the ability to resist immediate rewards in favour of longer-term gain) and executive function (the term for a range of cognitive skills such as being able to maintain attention, to formulate and carry out a plan, and to handle more than one task at the same time). Perhaps, Cross and colleagues argue, 'impulsivity may be both hot and cool'.[7] Men are more likely than women to be carried away by their emotions, to act impulsively when they're angry, or anxious, or excited. Give the average man a logical problem to solve, on the other hand, and he'll be no more impulsive than the average woman.

Do these findings help explain the gender difference in alcohol disorders? Is there a link between men's greater impulsivity and their vulnerability to alcohol abuse and dependence? Our reading of current evidence is that it's very hard to tell. A few small-scale studies suggest that impulsivity may be a factor, but much more research is needed before we know for sure.

2. Stress

When it comes to dealing with stress, received wisdom holds that 'women worry and men drink'. But is this true?

Not for the first time in this book, we have to report that the evidence is mixed. Certainly there do seem to be differences in men's and women's use of alcohol in response to stress. But those differences vary between studies, with some data suggesting that it's women who drink more and other, larger surveys finding that men are more likely to reach for the bottle when times are tough. As Katherine Keyes at Columbia University and colleagues concluded in a 2011 review: 'research has been inconsistent as to whether stressful experiences are more predictive of alcohol disorders in men or women'.[8]

Let's take a look at some of the most significant of those studies. Deborah Dawson and colleagues analysed data on more than 27,000 adult drinkers in the United States, who'd been interviewed as part of the 2001–2002 National Epidemiologic Survey on Alcohol and Related Conditions (NESARC). They looked at the effects of four categories of stress:

(i) health-related stress (death of someone close, serious illness of self or someone close)

(ii) social stress (change in living situation, trouble with boss/co-worker, change of job responsibilities, separation/divorce/break-up, problems with neighbour/friend/relative)

(iii) job stress (job loss, sustained unemployment)

(iv) legal stress (major financial crisis, own or family member's trouble with police/arrest, criminal victimization of self or family member).[9]

Dawson and colleagues focused on the relationship between these types of stress and heavy drinking days (five or more drinks for men and four or more drinks for women). You may not be astonished to learn that, in general, the more stress a person experienced the greater their alcohol consumption. But some significant differences between the sexes emerged. For each stressful event reported by a woman, the frequency of heavy drinking days rose by 13 per cent. For men, however, the rate was almost double this, with each stressor upping their heavy drinking days by 24 per cent. Certain forms of stress seemed to have a greater effect than others. Job-related problems, and legal issues, triggered the heaviest drinking, especially among men. Social stress also resulted in increased drinking, again more often in men than women. Interestingly, the type of stress most commonly reported—health related—had no effect on alcohol use. And stress didn't seem to drive people to drink every day. As Dawson and co concluded:

> Stress does not so much lead individuals to drink more often as to substitute larger quantities of alcohol on the days when they do drink.[10]

NESARC is a high-quality epidemiological study—large scale, well designed, and professionally implemented. And it suggests that part of the reason why men experience more problems with alcohol than women lies in the sexes' differing responses to stress. However, for all its virtues, NESARC is a cross-sectional study. And it relies on participants being able to remember accurately what occurred in their life over the previous year. Would you be confident estimating your alcohol consumption twelve months ago? How clearly can you remember the level of stress you were under back then? Individuals might well have a vague memory, but vague memories aren't great raw material for scientific research. Moreover, a cross-sectional study can only show associations: it isn't well suited to discovering cause and effect. The data may indicate that the frequency of heavy drinking days increases during stressful periods, but it doesn't prove that the former is a result of the latter. Maybe some stressful situations are actually caused by excessive drinking.

This is why research that examines the psychological effects of disasters such as 9/11 is so valuable: rates of alcohol consumption could not have caused these catastrophes. Between 16 October and 15 November 2001, a team led by David Vlahov contacted a random selection of 988 New Yorkers living south of 110th Street in Manhattan. Almost a quarter of these people (24.6 per cent) reported that their drinking had increased in the weeks following the attack on the World Trade Center. (The individuals also smoked more cigarettes and used more marijuana.) This certainly seems to substantiate what Dawson's study suggests: stress leads to higher levels of alcohol consumption. And yet Vlahov and colleagues found no difference between the sexes: men and women were affected to the same degree.

How do we square this finding with the NESARC data? Well, clearly Vlahov's research focuses on a very specific type of stress; as Dawson's analysis demonstrated, whether or not people escalate their drinking depends on the kind of problem they're facing. So the response to disasters such as 9/11 may be atypical; and the stressor itself is atypical because these kinds of events are so rare. We also have to bear in mind that a few weeks' increased drinking does not amount to a clinical problem. Although consumption certainly seems to increase in the immediate aftermath of a catastrophe, it's far from clear that this leads to an upswing in rates of disorder.

What can we deduce from longitudinal studies of alcohol use and stress? Kathleen Rospenda and colleagues from the University of Illinois at Chicago interviewed 1,418 people on two occasions a year apart. For both men and women, stress could lead to higher rates of problem drinking. But there were big differences in the way each sex responded to particular types of stressors. Take sexual harassment, for example: men who were experiencing this problem when first contacted by Rospenda and her team were, a year later, likely to be prone to problem drinking. But not so in the case of women: sexual harassment had no effect on their level of drinking.

And the same was true for workplace harassment, a category which includes a range of unpleasant behaviours such as bullying, ridicule, unjust criticism, humiliation, and malicious gossiping, but excludes sexual harassment. It too seemed to prompt excessive drinking in men only. Rospenda and colleagues speculate that 'when men perceive problems to be non-normative (as they may with sexual harassment), they are less likely to seek help, and thus may be more at risk for problem drinking'.[11] This seems plausible. Sexual harassment, or workplace bullying, is stressful for anyone, of course. But perhaps some men will experience greater feelings of shame and humiliation, fuelled by a sense that 'real' men don't face these kinds of problem.

On the other hand, Rospenda found that a variety of other types of life stress—such as serious illness or injury affecting oneself or a loved one, bereavement, serious relationship problems, and unemployment—were associated with problem drinking in women and not men. Both sexes, then, are liable to respond to stress by drinking more. But stress is a highly varied phenomenon and what drives women to drink is not necessarily the same as what triggers problems in men.

A more sophisticated way to approach the issue is to track alcohol use and stress on a daily basis. Then, with the help of some fairly complex statistical analyses, one can look for patterns of association in the fluctuation of the two variables. This is what's known as a 'daily process design' and it was used in a study by Stephen Armeli and colleagues at the University of Connecticut Health Center. For sixty days, eighty-eight regular drinkers (people who drank four times a week on average, but who had no history of alcohol dependence) kept a diary of life events, how much they drank, and how strongly they wanted a drink. Did stress lead to consumption of greater amounts of alcohol? Not for women, though their desire for a drink did increase. And not for certain men either. Those men who expected alcohol to hamper their ability to get things done actually decreased their drinking on stressful days, presumably because of a worry that alcohol would make it more difficult to handle a tough situation. On the other hand, men with strongly positive beliefs about alcohol—that it aids relaxation, for instance, or helps in a social situation—tended to drink more on stressful days.

The results of Armeli's research were published in 2000. Since then a number of other daily process studies have been carried out, and most of them have found some kind of gender difference in mood-related alcohol use. But the exact nature of that difference varies depending on the demographic profile of the individuals, what's being assessed, and over how long. All of which only adds to the ambiguity surrounding the issue of gender, stress, and alcohol use. Do men drink to cope with difficult situations? Sometimes. Does this help explain the gender difference in rates of alcohol disorder? Perhaps, but the hypothesis is far from nailed down. As we've seen, whether or not men and women reach for the bottle may depend on the kind of stress they're facing. And the problems that trigger the heaviest drinking may well differ for each sex (for some stressors, women probably drink more). Age may be a factor too. And we must keep in mind that increased drinking during or just after a stressful event is different from an alcohol disorder, which is by definition a chronic, persistent problem. Even if we accept that, overall, men are more likely than women to respond to stress by upping their alcohol consumption, we're still left with the crucial question: why? Perhaps, as we'll see in a moment, it's to do with social expectations about how men and women should behave.

One thing is for sure: it's a gross oversimplification to assume that if a couple endures an acrimonious split or faces financial pressures the woman will develop depression and the man turn to drink.

Indeed, anxiety and depression are very highly comorbid with substance disorders—it's not necessarily one or the other but often both together. Many studies have shown that people with substance disorders are very likely also to suffer from depression and/or anxiety. Moreover, emotional disorders can precede—and predict—alcohol problems; and vice versa. One study followed up a nationally representative sample of 34,000 individuals who'd been interviewed three years before as part of the US National Epidemiologic Survey on Alcohol and Related Conditions (NESARC). People who'd been suffering from anxiety and depression at the time of NESARC were more likely to have developed a substance disorder. Those who'd reported a substance problem three years previously were at greater risk of later anxiety disorders, though not depression. A separate prospective study that covered only women came up with a similar finding, with depression predicting later heavy drinking. Almost 1,400 women from Baltimore, who had been assessed as part of the National Institute of Mental Health Epidemiologic Catchment Area project in the mid-1980s, were interviewed a year later. Women who'd been suffering from depression when first surveyed were 2.6 times more likely to have developed a drinking problem than women without depression. When you look at the literature overall, it appears the relationship can work both ways: anxiety and depression can sometimes be a consequence of substance disorders; on other occasions, they can help cause these problems.

Some people may start drinking in order to cope with stressful events and feelings. But it's not a wise strategy, especially over the long term, because alcohol is a depressant. A vicious circle can form in which low mood triggers heavy drinking, which in turn lowers mood even further—and on it goes. Temporary stress can spiral into chronic depression and anxiety. For some people, on the other hand, emotional problems are already deeply entrenched before they start drinking heavily. Again, the alcohol can't help: it merely exacerbates the feelings that lead to drinking in the first place.

All of which means that the picture is complicated. Certainly men are more likely to develop alcohol problems, just as women seem to be more vulnerable to emotional disorders. And in both cases stress may play a big part in triggering those problems. But it's not inevitable that men will respond to that stress by drinking more, nor that women will become depressed or anxious. For a start, the type of stress experienced can make a big difference. We have to bear in mind too that biological factors—and specifically the reactivity of the HPA axis—may help determine whether or not stress leads to psychological problems. As we saw in Chapter 4, how the HPA axis functions may differ in men and women. Moreover, for many people it's not a question of one or the other: emotional problems and alcohol abuse are interlinked.

Social Factors

The ladette culture epitomises everything that is wrong with young British women. Why do women feel it necessary to act like 'one of the boys', are they not satisfied or proud of their own gender? Generally these girls might be good for a 'bit of fun' but they are certainly not relationship material![12]

Sun, 11 December 2008

For a pithy reminder of how social attitudes towards male and female drinking can differ, one need look no further than the above comment featured in a *Sun* story about ladette culture from a few years back. The word 'ladette' first appeared in the 1990s, defined by the *Oxford English Dictionary* as 'a young woman who behaves in a boisterously assertive or crude manner and engages in heavy drinking sessions'. It is not, of course, a compliment. Excessive drinking may not always be applauded in young men, but it is generally regarded as normal. In young women, on the other hand, the same behaviour is deplored by some as yet another symptom of society's inexorable moral decline.

'In many cultures,' write Marja Holmila and Kirsimarja Raitasalo, 'alcohol is one of the more powerful symbols of gender roles and identities.'[13] It's an assertion that certainly seems credible for Western societies, where alcohol and masculinity seem almost inseparably intertwined. Men have licence to drink—regularly and to excess. Indeed, being able to hold your drink is seen as a mark of a 'real' man. Where do men socialize? In the pub. (Even alcoholic drinks themselves are sometimes seen as gendered. Although attitudes and behaviour may be changing, a woman sipping a pint of real ale, or a man ordering a small glass of white wine can still in certain circumstances seem like acts of quiet transgression.)

For women, things are not so clear cut. For centuries, abstinence has been celebrated as an essentially feminine virtue—hence the power and notoriety of Hogarth's *Gin Lane*, at the centre of which is a mother so drunk that she doesn't notice or care that she's dropped her terrified infant. It's not so long ago that pubs, for example, were almost exclusively male preserves. And while attitudes have clearly changed in some respects, concerns about female drinking—and particularly drunkenness—persist: witness, for example, the furore over the antics of 'ladettes', the title itself an indication that these young women are perceived to be behaving in a decidedly unfeminine way.

Given the acres of newsprint dedicated to the admittedly rising rate of female alcohol consumption, it's hard not to conclude that women's drinking touches a cultural raw nerve. (And, as the quotation at the start of this chapter indicates, has done so for many years.) Nothing, it seems, shocks like a drunken woman. How will she take care of her children, her husband, her home? Particular opprobrium is reserved for the woman who drinks while pregnant. Experts do not know how much alcohol it is safe to drink during pregnancy: guidelines vary across the world. But the picture that emerges from newspaper headlines is apocalyptic: 'Glass or two of wine a week "could damage baby"'; 'Drinking alcohol while pregnant weakens mother's bond with child'; 'Moderate drinking while pregnant doubles risk of child becoming depressed'; and perhaps worst of all: 'Mothers who drink while pregnant "can give their children a taste for alcohol"'.[14]

There's certainly evidence that women *believe* that female drunkenness is perceived more negatively than excessive drinking by men. In one study in the United States, for example, the women questioned thought that 50 per cent of other people would strongly disapprove of a woman drinking too much at a party; a drunken man, on the other hand, would offend just 30 per cent. Maybe society's dim view of female drinking partly explains why women tend to reduce their alcohol intake when they become mothers (just the time, you might think, when a couple of glasses of wine at the end of the day are more welcome than ever). Fathers, incidentally, do not alter their drinking habits with the arrival of their offspring. And perhaps it's one of the reasons why women typically reduce their drinking when they start work, while men increase it. Women may be acutely aware that, in society's eyes, alcohol and the role allotted to them—particularly as wives and mothers—do not mix.

Could these cultural attitudes partly explain the difference between male and female rates of alcohol disorder? It's entirely plausible: traditionally, men have been pushed towards alcohol, while women have been pulled away. Drinking and especially drunkenness have been regarded as normal for men and abnormal for women. And there's reasonable evidence to support such a hypothesis, though it's far from proven. We haven't come across any really powerful tests of the theory, possibly because such a test would be so difficult to design. Defining gender roles and measuring social beliefs about them are a tricky business. It's made more complicated by the fact that these beliefs vary so much both within and between countries, meaning that it's difficult to compare like with like. Despite this, several studies seem to bear out the idea that rates of alcohol disorder reflect social views about drink and gender.

The husband-and-wife team of Richard and Sharon Wilsnack have spent decades investigating the interactions between gender, culture, and alcohol use. (Richard Wilsnack is a sociologist; Sharon Wilsnack, a clinical psychologist. Both are based at the University of North Dakota.) One of their early studies, conducted in the 1970s, covered 13,000 girls and 5,000 boys. Those girls who rejected conventional ideas of female behaviour tended to drink more, and were at greater risk of alcohol-related problems. And a number of other cross-sectional studies have shown that, if you take out the effect of gender roles, the gap between male and female alcohol use and abuse narrows. The masculine stereotype normalizes excessive drinking; the feminine stereotype, on the other hand, encourages abstinence or at least moderation. It's no wonder that men are more prone to alcohol disorders.

We can see this effect at work from the other direction as it were. The traditional female role is one of relative powerlessness. Men have a career; a salary; a public role. And the liberty to drink regularly and to excess. Women, conventionally, have none of these things. What happens to the gender difference in alcohol use when these traditional roles are challenged? A team led by Giora Rahav of Tel Aviv University (and including, incidentally, Richard Wilsnack) analysed data from twenty-nine countries across the globe, ranging from the UK and the United States to Costa Rica and Argentina, Japan and India to Nigeria and Uganda. They concluded:

> In all the participating societies men's drinking was more prevalent and heavier than women's drinking.... The most important finding seems to be that the gender ratios between men's and women's rates of drinking and of its consequences are negatively correlated with women's position within society: the higher women's position, the smaller the difference between men['s] and women['s] drinking rates.... [S]ocietal differences between men's and women's drinking are largely a function of the differentiation between men's and women's positions in society. As the roles of men and women are becoming increasingly similar in many social areas, the differences in drinking behaviour tend to diminish.[15]

And it's very clear that, among younger age groups, women are catching up with men in alcohol consumption—presumably as a result of these social changes. In their review of current research on the topic, Columbia University epidemiologist Katherine Keyes and colleagues noted that:

> Younger birth cohorts in North America and Europe are engaging in more episodic and problem drinking. The gender gap in alcohol problems is narrowing in many countries, suggesting shifting social norms surrounding gender and alcohol consumption.[16]

We shall have to wait to see whether the gap will increase again as these cohorts age. But higher rates of alcohol-related problems are a very high price for women to pay in order to enjoy greater social equality.

There's a long way to go before we fully understand why men drink more, and use more drugs, than women. The amount of research on the issue is much less than that on gender differences in depression and anxiety—and, as we've already seen, even the much greater volume of work on emotional disorders hasn't solved that particular conundrum.

And yet we do have some pointers on alcohol problems (and quite probably drug issues too). We know, for instance, that women have a stronger biological reaction. The buzz of alcohol is swiftly replaced by unpleasant physical sensations, meaning that women learn to drink less. Women may also find it easier to control the desire to drink. And they may generally prefer to cope with stress in other ways. Finally, though things are changing, social pressures have strongly discouraged heavy drinking among women.

For men, on the other hand, a greater physiological tolerance of alcohol means that they can enjoy more of the stuff before experiencing the downsides. Drinking, in other words, may simply be more fun for men. And because it makes them feel good, at least in the short term, men may tend to use alcohol to deal with stress. Men also tend to be more impulsive, so they're less able to resist the temptation to have a drink. Lastly, as we've just seen, traditional ideas of masculinity put alcohol in a central position: *men drink*.

But though all these factors might help explain the higher rates of substance abuse among men, the conventional assumption that men respond to distress by drinking and taking drugs while women get depressed and anxious doesn't do the issue justice. As ever with mental health issues, it's far more complicated than that.

6

Less Common Problems
Eating Disorders, Antisocial Personality Disorder, and Autism

In this chapter we look at three problems with large, and contrasting, gender differences. Eating disorders are predominately seen in women, while antisocial personality disorder and autism are much more common among men. All are relatively rare, so they're not going to account for the disparity between the sexes in overall rates of psychological disorders. They're complex problems too, and we don't have the scope here to do more than offer an overview. But the fact that, in each case, the gender difference is so marked may help us get a much clearer insight into the differing factors behind men's and women's mental health problems.

Eating Disorders

Stop the average person in the street and it's doubtful they'd know whether rates of depression are higher among men or women. Perhaps they could make a pretty good guess on substance problems.

But ask someone about eating disorders and we bet they'd tell you straight away, and with total confidence, that anorexia and bulimia are female problems. They'd be correct, too (more or less).

Before we get into the figures, let's first define what we mean by an eating disorder. *Anorexia nervosa* used to be known, dismissively, as the 'slimmer's disease'. Actually it is one of the most dangerous psychological disorders: at its worst, stubbornly resistant to therapy and with potentially catastrophic consequences for the physical—let alone mental—health of affected individuals. The *Diagnostic and Statistical Manual* (DSM) lists four criteria for a diagnosis:

- Refusal to maintain body weight at or above a minimally normal weight for age and height
- Intense fear of gaining weight or becoming fat, even though underweight
- Disturbance in the way one's body weight or shape is experienced, undue influence of body weight or shape on self-evaluation, or denial of the seriousness of the current low body weight
- In postmenarchael females [i.e. those who menstruate] the absence of at least three consecutive menstrual cycles.[1]

The term *bulimia nervosa* was coined in the late 1970s. Doctors had noticed significant numbers of people (almost all of them women) who were prone to regular bouts of frenzied eating. After bingeing, these individuals would attempt to undo the effects on their weight by vomiting, taking laxatives or other medications, dieting, fasting, or exercising. And underlying this behaviour was an intense concern—an obsession, even—with weight and appearance. This is pretty much how the DSM defines bulimia today:

- Recurrent episodes of binge eating... [i.e.]:

  (1) eating, in a discrete period of time... an amount of food that is definitely larger than most people would eat during a similar period of time and under similar circumstances.

  (2) a sense of lack of control over eating during the episode.

- Recurrent inappropriate compensatory behavior in order to prevent weight gain.

- The binge eating and inappropriate compensatory behaviors both occur, on average, at least twice a week for three months.

- Self-evaluation is unduly influenced by body shape and weight.[2]

Anorexia is probably around three to ten times more frequent in women than in men. Reading through the literature, that 'ten times' figure crops up a lot (maybe partly because it sounds so dramatic). But it's difficult to judge exactly how widespread anorexia is among men. This is because very few men with the disorder actually turn up in surveys. Even the upper estimates of lifetime prevalence put the figure at 0.3 per cent—that is, three out of every thousand men may experience the symptoms of anorexia at some stage of their life. It's hardly surprising, then, that epidemiological studies that focus on the current situation (typically the previous twelve months) sometimes don't pick up any men at all. And when a disorder is *that* uncommon, any positive results that do emerge have to be treated with a degree of caution. The statistics on gender difference are very similar for bulimia nervosa. The US National Comorbidity Survey Replication, for example, estimated that 0.5 per cent of women and 0.1 per cent of men had suffered from bulimia during the previous twelve months.

Anorexia and bulimia have much in common. Both, of course, revolve around issues of weight and appearance. Both usually begin during adolescence. And both are partly caused by genetic factors, with heritability thought to be around 50 per cent. Some experts argue that cultural factors—the pressure on women to look thin, for instance, or the availability of sufficient food to enable bingeing—play a bigger role in bulimia than anorexia. But the two disorders clearly overlap, with many people moving from one to the other, or experiencing both simultaneously. Indeed, the classification of eating disorders is a contested topic (actually, classification in general is a red rag to many mental health professionals, with the argument over the latest edition of the DSM—published in May 2013—becoming sufficiently heated to spill over into the mainstream media). The internationally renowned eating disorder researchers Chris Fairburn and Zafra Cooper at Oxford University point out:

> It is not uncommon to encounter individuals who initially met the diagnostic criteria for anorexia nervosa, then those of bulimia nervosa and now have a mixed state. Technically speaking, they have had three distinct psychiatric disorders (anorexia nervosa, then bulimia nervosa and now eating disorder NOS [not otherwise specified]), whereas both common sense and the individual's subjective experience suggest that they have had a single eating disorder that has evolved over time.[3]

As with many other disorders listed in the DSM, the lines of demarcation for eating problems can sometimes seem a little arbitrary. One, however, does seem rather more distinct from the others. Individuals with *binge eating disorder* overeat in much the same way as people with bulimia. Crucially, though, they don't then try to vomit or purge themselves. Age of onset is typically a little later than for the other eating disorders, with most cases developing towards the end of adolescence or during the early twenties. And the gender balance is different too. Women outnumber men, for sure. But the gap is much smaller than for anorexia or bulimia, with binge eating disorder being roughly twice as prevalent in women as in men. For all these reasons, we're not going to dwell on binge eating disorder in this chapter. Instead we'll focus on the eating problems with the largest gender imbalance: anorexia nervosa and bulimia nervosa. Why are these illnesses so much more common in women? Might it, for example, be partly a question of biology?

Biological Factors

At the risk of starting with the punchline, scientists don't appear to have been falling over themselves to investigate possible biological explanations for the gender imbalance in eating disorders.

There are some indications that genes play a bigger part in dissatisfaction with body shape, and in the drive for thinness, in females than they do in males. As we'll see in a moment, environmental factors—such as social pressure to be slim—are likely to be the most important cause for both sexes, but they may be especially potent for men. We know that eating disorders have a genetic component: perhaps this is stronger for women than it is for men.

But most biological research on gender differences in eating disorders has focused on the possible role of female sex hormones, principally oestrogen and progesterone. (As we saw in Chapter 4, some scientists have suggested that these hormones may help increase women's vulnerability to depression and anxiety, though the theory is far from proven.) Could these hormones be responsible, at least in part, for the fact that anorexia and bulimia are so prevalent among women? (Men are also exposed to female sex hormones, but typically in much smaller quantities.) Is this why these problems usually begin during puberty—a time when sex hormones flood in—and tend to disappear once the individual reaches the menopause? And, of course, sex hormones don't simply appear out of the blue during puberty: they play a hugely important role in determining our gender while we're in our mother's womb. Could a vulnerability to eating disorders be created even before birth?

It was this exposure to sex hormones that a team led by Kelly Klump at Michigan State University set out to gauge. But how does one go about measuring prenatal exposure? For all sorts of reasons, taking a reading while a foetus is in the womb is not really an option. Well, you can compare the lengths of an adult's second and fourth (index and ring) fingers. In most men, the ring finger tends to be longer than the index finger; in most women, however, these fingers are roughly equal in length. Why the difference? It's believed to be due to the effect of the male sex hormone testosterone: the more testosterone a foetus is exposed to, the longer their ring finger. (Readers may wish to pause here in order to inspect their own digits.)

Klump and colleagues measured the fingers of 113 female twins aged 18 to 26. They assessed the participants for eating disorders. And they also measured present levels of oestrogen. Women with the least difference between their second and fourth fingers, and the highest amount of current oestrogen, were most likely to display the symptoms of an eating disorder. Perhaps, Klump and co speculated:

> the relatively low level of testosterone before birth in females permits
> their brains to respond to estrogens at puberty, when the hormones
> activate the genes contributing to disordered eating in vulnerable girls.[4]

Klump admits, however: 'This theory remains largely untested.'[5] (For one thing, no one knows which genes contribute to eating disorders, though some candidates have been identified.)

There is, though, a better way of estimating prenatal exposure to sex hormones, and it's a relatively recent innovation. Like the finger ratio test, this new method is what's known as a proxy examination. But this time the proxy for hormone exposure is not the length of one's fingers: it's the sex of one's twin (naturally this test can't be applied to everyone...). The theory is this: if a person's twin is female, that person will have been exposed to greater levels of oestrogen in the womb, thereby elevating their chances of developing an eating disorder.

But the results of research using this test seem to knock that theory firmly on the head, at least for now. In the best, and most up-to-date, analysis of the evidence, a team led by Janet Lydecker at Virginia Commonwealth University assessed data from three studies from the United States, Norway, and Sweden, covering a total of almost 22,000 people. They found that, when it came to eating disorders, the sex of a person's twin was immaterial—which made their conclusion inevitable:

> The prenatal sex hormone hypothesis, which proposes that prenatal hormone exposure is associated with later eating disorder symptomatology, was not supported in these three population-based twin samples.[6]

Whatever biological factors lie behind the gender difference in eating disorders, it seems we may have to wait a while to find out.

Environmental Factors

Lorraine's new bikini body fight! Flat tummy fast! Gabby and Clare on Size Zero...! Stress-free summer diet plan! New body shrink diet! Get a sexy summer body!

These are just some of the headlines, taken from newspapers and magazines, we spotted on a visit to the local newsagent. It was not a research trip that required precise timing: we could have found similar headlines on any other day. What they bear witness to, of course, is society's preoccupation with female weight, size, and body shape. In the eyes of many, it seems, a woman's priority should be to look attractive—for which, read 'slim'. And woe betide those who do not come up to the mark.

Yet of course the odds are stacked against women. For all but a minority, the thin ideal simply isn't realistic. Given the power and reach of today's media, resisting the pressure to measure yourself against this ideal is a challenge for most people. We are, after all, bombarded by images of the young, slim, and beautiful. Perhaps this explains why studies have shown that around half of US girls and young women are unhappy with their bodies. For individuals with eating disorders the compulsion to conform to the ideal is acute. Self-esteem becomes inextricably bound up with looks. The body seems bloated and repulsive. Life revolves around food, weight, shape. An obsession with exercise develops. Strict diets are adopted—so strict in fact that slips are pretty much inevitable. Once the brakes are off, those momentary slips can easily turn into uncontrolled binges, followed by vomiting or purging. (According to one study, the average binge lasts an hour and a quarter, contains 3,415 calories, and most often comprises, in descending order, ice cream, bread, sweets, doughnuts, salads, sandwiches, biscuits, popcorn, cheese, and cereal.) In the aftermath, exercise routines are intensified. And diets grow even more austere.

All the evidence suggests that this preoccupation with appearance, and especially the idea that self-worth derives from the way one looks, is absolutely central to eating disorders. But where do these beliefs come from? Is it right simply to pin them on social pressures? After all, the great majority of women do not develop eating disorders. And, though anorexia and bulimia have become much more prevalent since the 1960s (partly, no doubt, because they are being reported more often), cases of disordered eating have been noted throughout the centuries, long before the rise of modern mass media and the cult of thinness. The term anorexia nervosa was first used in 1874, but medical doctoral theses on the illness were being written in the 17th century. In the Middle Ages, self-starvation was often justified for religious reasons, though this doesn't mean that worries about weight weren't also a factor. Pamela Keel and Kelly Klump have described two such cases:

> St. Catherine of Siena entered a pattern of self-starvation at around 16 years of age that continued until her death in 1380 (at age 32 or 33). Her death was brought on by her refusal to consume food or water.... She portrayed herself as feeling unable to eat and claimed that 'I prayed continually and I pray to God and will pray that he will grace me in this matter of eating so that I may live like other creatures.' ... St. Catherine refused to eat because she viewed herself as afflicted by an inability to eat. St. Veronica (Veronica Giuliani) began a pattern of self-starvation at age 18 that may have represented a relapse from a previous episode at age 15. Fellow nuns reported seeing St. Veronica sneaking into the kitchen and gorging herself on food when she thought no one else was around, and she was placed repeatedly in the infirmary where she was forced to eat and prevented from binge eating. Although St. Veronica wrote several diaries, little information is given concerning the motivation behind her food refusal. The closest revelation on this point is that she felt she was 'in a race against all the other novices to show who loved God the most.'[7]

If we want to gauge the potency of social pressure on women to be slim, perhaps we should start by looking at those jobs for which thinness has been a prerequisite, such as modelling and ballet dancing. Are women in these roles more likely to develop eating disorders? In 2012 Mariafrancesca Garritano was fired from Milan's La Scala after alleging that one in five ballerinas at the company were anorexic. Eating disorders were so widespread, she said, because dancers were expected to conform to impossible ideals of physical perfection:

> When I was training as a teenager, the instructors would call me 'mozzarella' and 'Chinese dumpling' in front of everyone ... I reduced my eating so much that my period stopped for a year and a half when

I was 16 and 17, and I dropped to 43 kilos ... I would get by on an apple and a yoghurt a day, relying on adrenaline to make it through rehearsal ... Some dancers were rushed to hospital to be fed through tubes, others were hit by depression and still need counselling today. I still get serious intestinal pains and frequent bone fractures, which I think are linked to dieting.[8]

La Scala dismissed Garritano for damaging its image. In a statement that was perhaps less reassuring than intended, its spokesman explained: 'Saying that La Scala is similar to what Garritano says she experienced 15 years ago is false. Educational methods used then are not used today and the school now has a course on nutrition.'[9] Garritano, on the other hand, received support from dancers around the world, suggesting that if there was a problem it was not confined to Milan.

Research certainly indicates that models and ballerinas do show higher rates of eating disorder than other women. But it's not clear that the job produces the problem. For instance, young women are presumably more likely to be selected for a modelling career if they are thin. It's possible that some of those young women are thin because of their disordered eating habits. Perhaps women who are already prone to eating disorders—or to associated traits such as perfectionism— are the ones who tend to become successful in these fields.

More convincing evidence of the power of the media to influence attitudes comes from work by Shelly Grabe, L. Monique Ward, and Janet Shibley Hyde at the University of Wisconsin-Madison. They analysed the results of seventy-seven studies that had investigated the links between exposure to mass media and body dissatisfaction, internalization of the thin ideal, and eating habits. Their conclusion was unequivocal:

these findings provide strong support for the notion that exposure to mass media depicting the thin-ideal body is related to women's vulnerability to disturbances related to body image.... Taken

together, the findings from these analyses suggest that media exposure is linked to women's generalized dissatisfaction with their bodies, increased investment in appearance, and increased endorsement
of disordered eating behaviors.[10]

Grabe and colleagues point out that thin people are over-represented
among television characters and that the women in the media today
are slimmer than ever before, thinner than average women, and often
so thin that they meet the criteria for anorexia (less than 85 per cent
of normal body weight for age and height). 'Thus, media aimed at
girls, adolescents, and young women are replete with extremely thin
models that portray an ideal that is unattainable to most.'[11] It's no
surprise, therefore, that the more women are exposed to these
images, the greater their dissatisfaction with their own bodies. Show
a woman a series of adverts featuring thin models (as some researchers have done) and she's more likely to express a negative opinion
about her own size and shape than if the adverts feature models of
average weight or a neutral image (furniture, for example). If just one
short session of ad viewing can influence women's views in this
way, it's easy to imagine the cumulative effect of years of exposure to
media celebrating thinness.

Now just because someone is unhappy with their appearance
doesn't mean that they have an eating disorder (if it did, the statistics
on prevalence would skyrocket). But body dissatisfaction is a core
feature of anorexia and bulimia. Not only that, but people who feel
this way about themselves are at greater risk of developing an eating
problem—it's a vulnerability marker, in other words.

What about the impact of mass media on how men view themselves? There is evidence that men are affected too. Media featuring
the supposedly ideal male body are likely to make men feel worse
about their own physique. But the situation is a little different for
men, for whom being thin is generally deemed less important than

being muscular, with wide shoulders, strong chest and arms, and a relatively small waist—though, as for women, the ideal is never going to be feasible for most individuals. As Timothy Judge and Daniel Cable have noted:

> Like the Barbie doll (which symbolizes an unrealistic female body ideal), today's G. I. Joe figure is just as unattainable, with a bicep almost as big as the waist and bigger than that of the greatest body-builders of all time.[12]

The kind of thinness so prized in women is frequently cultural shorthand for wimpiness in men. So, though men certainly get anxious about their appearance, weight loss may be less of a priority than it is for women. Indeed, they may want to 'bulk up'.

Moreover, the stakes tend to be lower for men. A man is simply less likely than a woman to be judged on his looks, so there's even less reason to worry about that beer belly. In fact, there may even be a financial incentive for men to let things spread a little. A recent study by Timothy Judge and Daniel Cable of employees in Germany and the United States showed that, as thin men get heavier, their earnings increase (though the trend stops if they become obese). Women—and especially thin women—actually earn less when they put on weight. Indeed Judge and Cable calculate that 'a woman who is average weight earns $389,300 less across a 25-year career than a woman who is 25 lbs below average weight'.[13] For men, on the other hand, being very thin is no way to secure that promotion: 'a man who is 25 lbs below average weight is predicted to earn $210,925 less across a 25-year career than a man who is of average weight'.[14] Why is this? Judge and Cable argue that it's to do with gender norms: society values thin women, but isn't terribly concerned about larger men. Fulfil expectations and you'll be able to look forward to a generous pay rise; flout them, on the other hand, and you can count the cost—literally.

Let's summarize where we've got to. What do we know about the possible reasons behind the gender difference in rates of eating disorder? Well, the evidence suggests that social factors play the most significant role. Women are presented with an unattainable physical ideal, of which thinness is a central component. For some women, attempting to live up to these unrealistic expectations causes huge stress, and their eating habits spiral out of control. Perhaps these social pressures combine with a genetic vulnerability, further elevating the risk of women developing a disorder.

But there may also be an overlap between eating disorders and emotional problems. Perhaps the very stark disparity between male and female rates of anorexia and bulimia is an exaggerated version of the difference between male and female rates of depression and anxiety—with many of the same underlying causes. It's not at all unusual for a person with an eating disorder to be also battling depression and/or anxiety. This is no coincidence: certain environmental and genetic factors are involved in both.

Self-esteem, for example, clearly plays a major role in eating disorders. For people with anorexia or bulimia, thinness becomes the ultimate—indeed perhaps the only—criterion of self-worth. As we saw in Chapter 4, low self-esteem is a proven risk factor for depression. And women's self-esteem, on average, tends to be lower than men's. (We also discovered in Chapter 4 that one of the reasons why women's self-esteem can take a hit is worries about appearance: another indication of how eating problems and emotional disorders can often intertwine.) Childhood sexual abuse is another well-established risk factor for eating disorders—just as it is for depression and anxiety. Again, women are more likely to have experienced this kind of trauma than men. There are biological similarities too. Some studies involving people with eating disorders have picked up irregularities in the brain's HPA axis. Again, this is often a feature of depression and anxiety. And it's something that, once more, may be more common in women than men.

Finally, experts now believe that, for some individuals, eating disorders may be a means of coping with unpleasant feelings, by helping them 'blank out' these sensations, or providing a sense of control. We saw in Chapter 4 that men and women differ in the way they respond to negative moods, with women more prone to rumination and pessimism. And women may be more likely to react by adopting unhelpful eating habits too.

Psychological problems, then, are seldom as neatly demarcated as the diagnostic handbooks imply. Instead, they often share symptoms, causes, and remedies. It may be that women experience more eating disorders for at least some of the same reasons that they experience more psychological disorders in general. And among those reasons, environmental factors may be key. But it's too soon to be sure because so few studies have directly investigated the influence of these shared factors on eating disorders.

Antisocial Personality Disorder

> What are little girls made of?
> What are little girls made of?
>   Sugar and spice
>   And everything nice,
>   That's what little girls are made of.
> What are little boys made of?
> What are little boys made of?
>   Slugs and snails
>   And puppy-dogs' tails,
>   That's what little boys are made of.

Malcolm Gladwell calls it the 'law of the few': a relatively small number of people can make a big impact on the world. The 2000 UK survey of Psychiatric Morbidity Among Adults Living in Private Households estimated that 1 per cent of men and 0.2 per cent of women meet the criteria for antisocial personality disorder (ASPD). But that tiny minority may be responsible for up to a quarter of violent incidents causing injury to others. Clearly, ASPD is a force to be reckoned with. And, as the UK survey indicates, it's one that's more often seen in men than women. (Estimates of the prevalence of ASPD vary quite a bit across surveys, partly because it's difficult to diagnose.)

ASPD is part of a nexus of behavioural problems that also includes *conduct disorder* and *oppositional-defiant disorder*, and before we discuss why it may be more common in men it's worth spending a few moments clarifying what these disorders are and how they relate to one another. ASPD, according to the DSM, is characterized by 'a pervasive pattern of disregard for and violation of the rights of others'.[15] The DSM lists seven examples of this behaviour (three are sufficient for a diagnosis):

(1) failure to conform to social norms with respect to lawful behaviors as indicated by repeatedly performing acts that are grounds for arrest

(2) deceitfulness, as indicated by repeated lying, use of aliases, of conning others for personal profit or pleasure

(3) impulsivity or failure to plan ahead

(4) irritability and aggressiveness

(5) reckless disregard for the safety of self or others

(6) consistent irresponsibility, as indicated by repeated failure to sustain consistent work behavior or honor financial obligations

(7) lack of remorse, as indicated by being indifferent to or rational-
     izing having hurt, mistreated, or stolen from another.[16]

It's not much of a character reference. Indeed the five pages that the
DSM devotes to ASPD are filled with a litany of callous, violent, and
downright criminal acts. If you could see this kind of person coming,
you'd get out of the way. Quickly.

ASPD is an adult problem, but it has a childhood counterpart:
conduct disorder. 'The essential feature of Conduct Disorder,' the
DSM states, 'is a repetitive and persistent pattern of behavior in
which the basic rights of others or major age-appropriate societal
norms or rules are violated.'[17] What this means in practice is aggression, vandalism, lying, theft, and serious transgressions such as tru-
ancy or running away from home. A child with conduct disorder has
an above-average chance of being diagnosed later in life with ASPD.
This isn't surprising: one of the DSM's criteria for ASPD is evidence
of conduct disorder before the age of 15. So the two are, by definition,
directly related. And just as with ASPD, conduct disorder is mainly
seen in boys. (Although conduct disorder is generally regarded as a
childhood problem, strictly speaking it isn't. Adults who don't meet
the full criteria for ASPD may sometimes be diagnosed with conduct disorder.)

Conduct disorder is a precursor of ASPD, but scientists have pos-
ited an even earlier link in the psychiatric chain: oppositional-defiant
disorder. ODD usually develops by the age of 8 and, according to the
DSM, is marked by 'a pattern of negativistic, hostile, and defiant
behavior lasting at least 6 months'.[18] Many of the symptoms may be
familiar to parents:

(1) often loses temper

(2) often argues with adults

(3) often actively defies or refuses to comply with adults' requests or rules

(4) often deliberately annoys people

(5) often blames others for his or her mistakes or misbehaviour

(6) is often touchy or easily annoyed by others

(7) is often angry and resentful

(8) is often spiteful or vindictive.[19]

Most children with ODD or conduct disorder outgrow their problems. There's nothing inevitable about a progression to ASPD. And indeed the relationship between these disorders is much debated by specialists. For all the parallels, there are also dissimilarities. The gender difference isn't as stark in ODD, for instance. A strong argument is made by Terrie Moffitt, one of the foremost experts on conduct disorder and antisocial behaviour. Moffitt stresses that we can't take a 'one size fits all' approach to these problems. And she highlights two distinct profiles of people with behavioural issues.

On the one hand there are those whose conduct problems begin—and often end—during adolescence. For these individuals, behaving badly is a highly effective way of signalling a desire for independence from parents and gaining respect from peers, and many of us have tried it at least a little during our teenage years. In most cases these youngsters outgrow their problems with no lasting damage (just like another group of children whose antisocial behaviour is confined to their early years). On the other hand, for a small minority of kids behavioural problems begin early in childhood and get steadily worse. These are the children who grow up into adults with ASPD. (Moffitt calls this the 'childhood-onset life-course persistent type' of disorder.) Unsurprisingly, life is much more difficult for individuals in this second group—for one thing, there's a fair chance they'll end up in prison.

Now the make-up of this second group is overwhelmingly male. Indeed a study by Moffitt and her husband, Avshalom Caspi, suggested that males were ten times more likely than females to develop persistent behavioural problems during childhood. For adolescent onset, the ratio was just 1.5 in favour of boys. In other words, the most serious, deeply engrained, and long-lasting behavioural issues are principally seen in men. (This fits with what we saw in Chapter 3: boys' psychological problems tend to start early in childhood, whereas girls are mainly affected by disorders that begin during adolescence, such as depression, and—as we saw earlier in this chapter—eating disorders.)

Why is this? Fortunately, the best and most extensive research into the causes of conduct problems has focused on children. It is, after all, much easier to help a child to change their behaviour than an adult. Moreover, the wider social costs of antisocial conduct—such as the impact of crime—have made this work a priority. So what does this research have to tell us about gender differences in antisocial behaviour?

We'll start by looking at possible biological explanations, but before we do so a word of caution. Behavioural disorders are pretty diverse; as with most labels, this one can mask some important differences. As we've just seen, for example, in certain individuals problems begin and end during childhood. In others, they start during adolescence but peter out by adulthood. And for still others, difficult behaviour first shows itself during early childhood and then grows increasingly entrenched and damaging. Some individuals' behaviour is very aggressive, while other people with these conditions are not aggressive at all. Scientists are still exploring what these differences mean and why they occur. Their significance for questions of gender has been investigated even less. It's a fair bet, though, that it'll add another layer or two of complexity to the account that follows in the next few pages.

Biological Factors

Are boys genetically vulnerable to behavioural problems? The evidence suggests not: the relative contributions of genes and environment are on the whole very similar for males and females.

That's the broad picture, but within it may lurk some interesting details. For example, as with many other disorders, exactly which of the two factors is more influential in antisocial behaviour can vary according to age: at a particular point in life environment has a more significant effect, while at another genes are more decisive. There's some indication that this age-related pattern may be different in the sexes. It has also been suggested that the genes involved in these disorders may not be the same for men and women. But this is currently little more than a tantalizing hypothesis. Finally, some research has indicated that male antisocial behaviour may be partly influenced by a gene × environment interaction. Specifically: men who possess a variant form of a sex-linked gene (*MAO-A*), and who have been mistreated during childhood, may be more prone to conduct problems than those with either the gene or the maltreatment alone. Whether or not this is a factor in female antisocial behaviour is unclear. And matters are complicated by the fact that in sex-linked genes like *MAO-A* men and women can have differing variant forms, meaning that it's tricky to compare their effect across gender.

The picture is clearer (fortunately) with *temperament*. Psychologists use the term to refer to a child's personality and, as most parents will tell you, it seems to be largely innate. Now there's good evidence to suggest that boys and girls vary in certain aspects of temperament.

In a meta-analysis of 189 studies covering children aged from 3 months to 13 years, Nicole Else-Quest and colleagues at the University of Wisconsin-Madison found that, although overall differences between boys and girls were small, there were some striking exceptions. Boys scored relatively highly for what's known as 'surgency': they were active, impulsive, sociable, and enthusiastic, with a liking for rough-and-tumble play. (We might think of surgency as the 'puppy' ratio.) Girls, on the other hand, proved much better at 'effortful control': they were persistent, adept at concentrating on a given task, and able to resist acting on impulse.

We can't simply equate surgency with antisocial behaviour, of course. But one can imagine how a combination of high energy and relatively low emotional control could help lead to problems. And Else-Quest's findings do chime with evidence that boys are generally more physically aggressive than girls. One can detect the difference in children as young as 1. For example, from about the age of 12 months boys show a willingness to use force against their peers in order to get what they want.

We get a sense of these behavioural differences between boys and girls in an experiment led by Claire Hughes, a professor of developmental psychology at Cambridge University's Centre for Family Research. Hughes and colleagues asked 800 5-year-olds to take part in a game of SNAP!, using cards that depicted farm animals. (Tempting though it is to imagine all these children playing simultaneously—what a game that would be—in fact they did so in same-sex pairs while being supervised by a researcher.) The game was videotaped so that the researchers could study the children's behaviour. And both parents and teachers completed a questionnaire designed to assess whether the child was prone to externalizing problems such as disobedience, aggression, and antisocial behaviour.

As you might guess, this was no ordinary game: the cards were rigged. Each child would experience both a winning and a losing streak. But though every child was confronted with the frustration of seeing their opponent winning card after card, how they reacted depended on their gender. Boys were much more likely than girls to become disruptive, for example by trying to snatch the cards, storming out, or being verbally aggressive. Predictably, the children most given to externalizing problems in general were also the most disruptive during the game—and again these were predominately boys. What Hughes and colleagues found in the SNAP! experiment corroborates the theory that boys are more likely to indulge in externalizing behaviour than girls and, when the red mists descend, are less able to control themselves. It's a combination that makes them especially vulnerable to conduct problems.

Whether these gender differences in temperament are truly innate is debatable. But there are at least a couple of biological factors that merit consideration. First is the male sex hormone, testosterone. In the popular imagination testosterone enjoys a somewhat mixed reputation: it is regarded as both the essence of virile masculinity, and the culprit when men behave badly. There's probably something in this: relatively high levels of prenatal testosterone, for example, have been linked to a later preference for rough-and-tumble play and a propensity for aggression. (This very early wave of sex hormones has a big effect on how the brain is organized and therefore how it functions; in effect, it helps set the brain's hard wiring.)

But, in humans at least, the relationship between testosterone and aggression isn't nearly as straightforward as the media often suggest. For example, once boys and girls reach about 3 to 6 months of age, the level of testosterone in their bodies is quite similar, and it stays that way until puberty when, of course, boys experience a huge surge of the stuff. (Yes, male sex hormones are found in females, just as female hormones are present in males.) So current testosterone levels can't explain why pre-teen boys are typically more aggressive than pre-teen girls. Even in adolescent and adult males, the link between testosterone and aggression is quite modest. Inject young men with testosterone, as some scientists have done, and they don't suddenly metamorphose into Incredible Hulk-type creatures, roaring and brawling and breaking the furniture. Contrary to what we might expect, the extra testosterone doesn't in fact make them any more aggressive.

All of which suggests that simply blaming testosterone for male conduct problems is far too simplistic. Instead, we need to be much more nuanced, recognizing that the hormone seems to produce different effects at different stages of life: prenatal, postnatal, and during adolescence. And remembering too that testosterone probably affects males and females in different ways.

Let's turn now to the second biological factor: the frontal lobes. It's well established that in girls this part of the brain develops faster than in boys (it continues to grow and change right until late adolescence). Why is this significant? Well, the frontal lobes—which lie directly behind the eyes—are responsible for such key tasks as planning, decision-making, and conscious thought. It's our control centre, analysing the stream of information generated by the other parts of the brain and judging how best to respond—and, importantly, how best *not* to respond. Clearly, if your frontal lobes are functioning efficiently you're going to be skilled at effortful control: persistent, focused, and well disciplined. And you'll find it relatively easy to control your emotions. So this may explain, at least in part, why girls are less likely to behave antisocially than boys: their frontal lobes are simply better developed.

And perhaps this female advantage doesn't end in childhood: recent research has indicated that the frontal lobes may also help explain the gender difference in adult conduct problems. A team led by Adrian Raine at the University of Pennsylvania conducted MRI scans of the brains of ninety men and twelve women from Los Angeles. Men with antisocial personality disorder proved to have smaller frontal lobes than men without the disorder. Moreover, the frontal lobes of the women in the study tended to be more developed than those of the men. Raine and colleagues concluded:

> Findings indicate that a significant proportion (77.3%) of the gender difference in antisocial behavior can be accounted for by gender differences in ventral prefrontal gray matter. Strikingly, gender differences were found in frontal sectors that are associated with antisocial behavior, but not in those sectors that were not associated with antisocial behavior.[20]

It's only one study, of course, and the number of women scanned was small. But it certainly looks like there's enough going on here to warrant further research on the role of the frontal lobes in conduct disorders.

A Brief Word on Psychopathy

If we were to tell you that the person sitting opposite you on the bus had just been diagnosed with antisocial personality disorder, you might well feel a little wary. Were we to announce, however, that they had just scored highly on a psychopathy test you might prefer to leave the bus at the very next stop. Or perhaps sooner. But you won't find psychopathy listed as a disorder in the DSM. It's described instead as an aspect of ASPD:

> Individuals with Anti-Social Personality Disorder frequently lack empathy and tend to be callous, cynical, and contemptuous of the feelings, rights, and sufferings of others. They may have an inflated and arrogant self-appraisal (e.g., feel that ordinary work is beneath them or lack a realistic concern about their current problems or their future) and may be excessively opinionated, self-assured, or cocky.

They may display a glib, superficial charm and can be quite voluble and verbally facile (e.g., using technical terms or jargon that might impress someone who is unfamiliar with the topic). Lack of empathy, inflated self-appraisal, and superficial charm are features that have been commonly included in traditional conceptions of psychopathy.[21]

This doesn't mean that everyone with ASPD is psychopathic, but a proportion will be callous, unemotional, highly manipulative, and devoid of guilt: the hallmarks of psychopathy. Although the term may conjure up nightmare visions of remorseless serial killers, like all psychological traits psychopathy exists on a spectrum, running from the relatively mild to the very severe. And you'll find all points on that spectrum among the general population.

Given its intensely negative associations, 'psychopathy' is a hugely emotive and controversial term. Consequently it's seldom used to describe children: 'callous-unemotional traits' is preferred instead. Experts think a subgroup of children with conduct disorder may possess these traits. These youngsters seem to have a markedly different profile from others with conduct disorder: their antisocial behaviour is more extreme; genetic factors may play a bigger role in causing the disorder; they seem less sensitive to punishment or feelings of guilt; and their behaviour is less likely to improve over time. Among children, boys tend to score higher than girls for callous-unemotional traits (just as studies among adults have found more psychopathic tendencies among men). This isn't surprising, of course, given that males are more prone to conduct problems.

Psychopathy is an under-researched area in general. And the work that has been done has generally focused on males, with not a lot of attention being devoted to these characteristics in females. This lack of a comparative analysis means that, although we know these kinds of traits are more common among males, we don't really know why. Nevertheless, two possible factors have been suggested. The first picks up on the fact that those who score highly for psychopathy are typically regarded as cold and heartless, indifferent to the distress they inflict on others. There seems to be a biological basis for this lack of sensitivity. For example, the HPA axis of individuals with psychopathic traits shows a reduced response to stress. Expose them to an unpleasant event—such as a loud noise or an electric shock—and their physiological reactions will be weaker than those of people who don't possess these tendencies. And even when they're not having to respond to these kinds of pressure, their system seems under-aroused: their heart rate is lower, there's less variability in their heart rate, and less cortisol is detectable in their blood. There is some recent evidence that this lack of responsiveness is found only among boys, and not girls. This doesn't seem completely far-fetched: if you remember back to Chapter 4 we saw that HPA reactivity may well vary between men and women. On the other hand, no one has actually proven beyond doubt that boys are less physiologically responsive.

One of the other theories about psychopathy is that it's a disorder marked by an impaired ability to understand the intentions of others (to possess what psychologists call a 'theory of mind'), and particularly to comprehend the feelings of others (a so-called 'affective theory of mind'). It's what the journalist Jon Ronson is describing in this excerpt from his best-selling *The Psychopath Test*:

> In a third office I saw a woman with a *Little Miss Brainy* book on her shelf. She seemed cheerful and breezy and good-looking.
> 'Who's that?' I asked James.
> 'Essi Viding,' he said.
> 'What does she study?' I asked.

'Psychopaths,' said James.

I peered in at Essi. She spotted us, smiled and waved.

'That must be dangerous,' I said.

'I heard a story about her once,' said James. 'She was interviewing a psychopath. She showed him a picture of a frightened face and asked him to identify the emotion. He said he didn't know what the emotion was but it was the face people pulled just before he killed them.'[22]

If you can't read other people's emotions, you're going to find it more or less impossible to empathize with them—and lack of empathy is seen as a hallmark of psychopathy.

It has to be said that the evidence for this theory-of-mind take on psychopathy is patchy. Nonetheless, are there differences between males and females? Well, some studies have suggested that from late childhood and adolescence girls generally perform better on theory-of-mind tests than boys. And from an even earlier age girls are more adept at empathy. Perhaps this is partly why males are more vulnerable to psychopathy (and antisocial behaviour in general): they're less skilled at imagining what it feels like to be on the receiving end of their actions. And maybe this is because their frontal lobes are less well developed. But if these weaknesses are indeed a factor in male psychopathy, they're unlikely to provide a complete explanation. Some experts have pointed out that it's not the absence of theory-of-mind skills that distinguishes people with psychopathy: it's their failure to take the next step into empathy (though again, it's a skill in which women may outperform men). Moreover, psychopathic individuals tend to be extremely good at manipulating and deceiving others. This is the kind of behaviour that requires a pretty sophisticated sense of how people think and feel. Without a theory of mind, other people would seem mystifyingly strange: how then would you persuade them to do what you'd like? Again, it seems that individuals with psychopathy have no trouble judging what another person is feeling: they simply don't care.

Environmental Factors

As we've seen, antisocial personality disorder doesn't suddenly appear out of the blue in adults. It's the culmination of behavioural problems often stemming back to early childhood. And generally kids with this profile are from troubled backgrounds. Maltreatment, poverty, parental conflict, parental alcoholism—all are clearly linked to conduct disorder in children (which doesn't mean that these problems *cause* the conduct issues, merely that the two usually go hand in hand). Style of parenting—either overly strict or, to a lesser extent, excessively laissez-faire—seems to be associated too. Yet although childhood adversity and unsatisfactory parenting are well-established predictors of conduct disorder, there's no difference in their effect on girls and boys. Expose a child of either sex to these influences and the end result is likely to be the same.

However, are boys and girls equally likely to encounter such experiences? Studies show, for example, that parents are much more likely to use excessive physical force to discipline boys. Perhaps this is because it's less socially acceptable to hit girls, or because of a belief that boys need to be 'toughened up'. Whatever the reason, the disparity is thought to account for at least some of the difference—estimates vary from 4 per cent to 38 per cent—between male and female rates of conduct disorder. But let's imagine that boys were disciplined in the same way as girls. Would this really reduce their aggressive, antisocial behaviour by up to a third? Alas, it's probably more complicated than that. Parenting isn't a one-way process. Parent and child influence each other's behaviour. And at least some of this behaviour—especially on the part of the child—may be deeply rooted in genetics. There's a good deal of evidence, for instance, that genetically influenced aggression by children can actually cause negative parenting (presumably because exhausted parents don't know what else to try or simply lash out in frustration). Unfortunately, this negative parenting tends to elicit more antisocial behaviour in the child and the miserable cycle goes on. Parents and child alike can become trapped in, to use the jargon, an 'evocative gene–environment correlation', with genetic factors causing a situation that only intensifies the effect of those same genetic factors.

Just to add to the complexity, it's possible that this works in a different way depending on whether the parenting is being done by the child's mother or father—though it has to be said that very little work has been done on the issue. An exception is a recent study that looked at the links between behavioural problems in Swedish adolescents and parental criticism (assessed by a questionnaire including items like 'I find fault with him/her'; 'He/she makes me irritated'; 'I have to ask him/her to behave differently'; 'I try to influence his/her behavior'[23]). Mothers' criticism seemed to be largely a response to the child's behaviour: there was, in other words, an evocative gene–environment correlation. Paternal criticism, on the other hand, emerged less as a reaction to a child's genetically influenced disruptiveness. Instead, this disruptiveness was triggered, in a much more direct way, by dads criticizing their offspring.

There's some evidence too that boys and girls may respond a little differently to environmental factors, though there's so little research that it's impossible to make any definitive statement. But one US study followed 500 children from pre-kindergarten to third grade—roughly ages 5 to 9. Mothers who showed a lack of affection, or who typically reacted negatively to their child's misbehaviour (for example, by criticizing and scolding, yelling, threatening, and warning, physically restraining, or smacking), tended to trigger aggression in sons and daughters alike. But whereas the boys became increasingly aggressive over time, the girls' aggression steadily waned.

Of course, as we've just seen, conceptualizing children's bad behaviour as a straightforward response to parental input is generally too simplistic. The relationship is far more dynamic and reciprocal than that, with parent and child continually influencing each other. So some researchers have highlighted a failure of what they call 'mutual emotion regulation'—for example, little Tom's refusal to eat his supper produces an enraged response from his parent, which only makes Tom even more determined not to consume a mouthful of the delights upon his plate. At least one study has suggested that when it comes to anger, this process may work rather differently between mothers and daughters than between mothers and sons. (The children in the sample were, on average, 5 years old; the response of fathers wasn't measured.) If mothers were annoyed by the antics of their angry daughter, they tended to make it plain. But for boys, the response was rather different:

> The findings suggest that, when faced with a son's angry distress, mothers may not convey their actual feelings or may communicate anger that is not really felt. . . . Parents often expressed disapproval of a son's poorly regulated anger but confusion about how to handle it because they did not want to 'turn him into a wimp'.[24]

As we saw in Chapter 4, social expectations about the kind of emotions it is permissible for boys and girls to display often vary. Showing anxiety, for instance, may be less acceptable in boys than girls. With anger, on the other hand, it's the other way around: giving full rein to one's annoyance may be seen as normal masculine behaviour. In the US study, this kind of attitude seems to have been a factor in mothers' ambivalent response to their sons' anger. Unfortunately, reacting in this way may do little to stop the bad behaviour.

Indulging boys' temper tantrums; encouraging girls to be pretty and thin like the women on TV—both are examples of the way in which gender norms shape our behaviour. And perhaps they also help trigger 'gender-appropriate' mental health problems: that is, eating disorders for women and behavioural disorders for men.

Yet when you read the scientific literature, a different emphasis seems to emerge. For women, social pressures do indeed take centre stage. Anorexia and bulimia are largely seen as a response to the stress of attempting to live up to an impossible feminine ideal. For men, however, persistent conduct problems are typically portrayed as rooted in biology. Men, the argument runs, are naturally aggressive; when they can't control these drives, anti-social behaviour results. Given that conduct problems often show themselves very early in life, while eating disorders don't usually develop until much later, it's easy to see how such an approach has come about: the younger a person is, it's assumed, the more likely it is that their behaviour is innate rather than culturally determined. Beyond the first few months of life, however, this is often a pretty dubious assumption. And at times the literature can give the impression of excusing men's anti-social behaviour (*they can't help it, poor things: it's all that testosterone coursing through their veins*), while women are implicitly criticized for being too easily pressured by silly media kerfuffle about female body shape (*so you don't look like Keira Knightley: what's the big deal?*).

Our coverage in this chapter reflects the overall balance of research: male conduct disorders are principally seen as biologically driven; female eating problems have their roots in social pressures. But of course there isn't actually a great deal of work on gender difference in either type of disorder, and the choice of what does take place may be skewed by this conventional view. As a corrective, it would be fascinating to see a concerted effort to investigate both cultural influences on antisocial behaviour and biological factors in eating disorders. Were such work to take place, maybe we would witness a repeat of the scenario we have observed with depression and substance problems, in which potential biological vulnerabilities in each sex seem to be exacerbated by environmental factors.

Autism

Our final port of call in this survey of gender difference is a very different type of disorder. But just like the other conditions we've discussed in Part 2—depression, anxiety, substance disorders, eating problems, and conduct disorders—there is a marked disparity between male and female rates of autism. And this, as we'll see in a moment, has made it the battleground for an intensely heated debate about sex differences in the brain.

Autism has experienced a heightened public profile in recent years. This has come about partly through its representation in high-profile movies like *Rain Man* and best-selling fiction such as Mark Haddon's *The Curious Incident of the Dog in the Night-Time*; partly because of the publicity surrounding its alleged link to the MMR vaccine; and also partly because research into autism has told us a lot about certain absolutely central psychological processes: namely, how we understand other people. But though almost everyone will now have heard of the condition, we may have a rather sketchy knowledge of the details. Autism is defined by three major forms of impairment: in a person's ability to interact socially, to communicate, and to sustain a broad range of interests. Often there are more general learning disabilities too. An individual with autism may struggle to form friendships, or to master the gamut of non-verbal techniques used to relate to other people, such as meeting the eye or adopting an appropriate facial expression. They may struggle with spoken language. And they may become obsessed with one or two very narrow subjects (dates, for example, or phone numbers), and insist on very clearly delineated and unchanging routines.

The dominant view of autism—the view you'll find in the psychiatric manuals—is that it exists on a spectrum, encompassing a range of conditions from low to high function (Asperger's syndrome, for instance). Approximately 1.8 per cent of men in England fall somewhere on this autism spectrum; for women the figure is just 0.2 per cent. Yet experts are beginning to question the coherence of autism as a concept. Research by London psychologists Francesca Happé, Angelica Ronald, and Robert Plomin suggests that the triad of impairments that defines autism—relating to social interaction, communication, and range of interests—is 'fractionable'. Each impairment has different genetic, neurological, and cognitive causes. And they don't always appear together: indeed, there is only a modest association between the three in the general population. As a result:

> The question arises whether one should conceptualize autism and related disorders as lying on one spectrum, or whether each individual should be mapped in a three dimensional space along three, perhaps orthogonal, dimensions: social interaction, communication, and RRBIs [restricted and repetitive behaviours and interests].[25]

Autism, then, may have its weaknesses as a concept. Even so, there's no getting away from the fact that it's an overwhelmingly male condition. Why is this? Well, autism is unlike any of the other disorders we've so far covered in this book. This is because it's so unequivocally rooted in biology, showing up very early in a child's life (by definition, before the age of 3) and having nothing whatsoever to do with upbringing. As Carolyn Zahn-Waxler and colleagues have written: 'disorders such as autism result primarily from genetic, neurological, hormonal, constitutional, and other biological abnormalities'.[26] Clearly, the same can't be said for depression or substance disorders, for example. Biological factors are certainly emphasized in research on conduct problems, though even there debate about the effects of social factors continues. In the case of autism, things are relatively clear-cut. Heritability is very high, at around 80 per cent, indicating how influential genes are in determining who does or does not develop the disorder.

But hang on, you might object: what about the other 20 per cent? Doesn't this figure suggest that environmental factors are involved after all? In fact, even the non-genetic causes are probably physical in nature: maternal infection during pregnancy, for example, or complications during birth. All of which means that if we want to understand why autism is so much more common in males than females we'd best focus on possible biological explanations. Attributing the disparity to differences in the way boys and girls are raised, and specifically the gender roles they are taught, would be what Simon Baron-Cohen has called a 'ludicrous position'.[27] And, as far as we're aware, no one in the scientific community now does so.

One theory is that boys are more vulnerable for genetic reasons. But Baron-Cohen—director of Cambridge University's Autism Research Centre—suggests that sex-related brain differences lie at the heart of the matter. There's ample evidence, some of it arising from Baron-Cohen's own pioneering work, that autism involves a basic cognitive problem. Individuals with the condition struggle to develop a theory of mind (which as we saw earlier in this chapter may play a part in certain types of antisocial behaviour). This results in a kind of 'mindblindness': an inability to understand that other people have thoughts and feelings. And it explains why children with autism find it hard, for example, to build social relationships or to communicate with others, and why they don't typically engage in imaginative play.

That people with autism have major problems with theory of mind is pretty universally accepted. What's proved controversial is Baron-Cohen's development of the idea of mindblindness. We're seeing in autism, he argues, an 'extreme form of the male brain'.[28] Here's how it works. There are two key types of cognitive processing, or ways of thinking. One is 'systemizing', which Baron-Cohen describes as:

> the drive to analyse the variables in a system, to derive the underlying rules that govern the behaviour of a system. Systemising also refers to the drive to construct systems. Systemising allows you to predict the behaviour of a *system*, and to control it.[29]

The other is 'empathizing', or:

> the drive to identify another person's emotions and thoughts, and to respond to these with an appropriate emotion. Empathising allows you to predict a person's behaviour, and to care about how others feel.[30]

At a crude level, systemizing is essentially about dealing with *things* while empathizing focuses on building relationships with *people*. In Baron-Cohen's view, men and women differ in their aptitude for systemizing and empathizing. On the whole, men are better at the first and women more skilled at the second. (Baron-Cohen has tested these theories by asking people to fill in questionnaires that assess their competence at systemizing and empathizing. A couple of example questions: 'I can easily tell if someone else wants to join in a conversation'; 'I am fascinated by how machines work'.[31]) Indeed, as we saw in Chapter 4, there is evidence that girls are more accomplished at empathy than boys. And at age 3, argues Baron-Cohen, girls display more ability at theory-of-mind tasks. Boys, on the other hand, seem to prefer mechanical toys. Moreover, men are more proficient at imagining how an object will look when it's rotated (an essential skill, obviously) and at spatial navigation.

Nowhere is the contrast between these two differing cognitive abilities more starkly displayed, Baron-Cohen states, than in autism. Individuals with the condition are poor at empathizing, which is unsurprising given their underdeveloped theory of mind. On the other hand, they can be very strong at systemizing. (Baron-Cohen notes, for example, that people with autism 'are strongly drawn to structured, factual and rule-based information'[32] and show an extreme attention to detail.) In other words, people with autism possess strongly 'male' brains—which explains why they happen to be predominately male themselves.

But why is the male brain so strong at systemizing? In Baron-Cohen's view, a major contributor is prenatal testosterone: the more testosterone in a foetus's system, the more skewed their brains will be towards systemizing (Baron-Cohen notes 'a wealth of data relating prenatal hormones to masculinisation of the mind and the brain'[33]). After just a few weeks of life, the human foetus experiences a surge of sex hormones. Testosterone doesn't just occur in male foetuses, as we know. But boys are generally exposed to a lot more of it. The likelihood of experiencing the kind of hefty dose that could perhaps lead to autism is therefore greater for boys: hence the gender difference in rates of the condition.

Is there such a thing as an extreme female brain? Can empathy ever become so excessive that it qualifies as a psychological disorder? Perhaps there are people whose ability to sense and share other people's distress, caused by abnormally large amounts of prenatal female sex hormones, is so acute that it makes them unwell, or prevents them from living a normal life. Maybe this helps explain why women are more vulnerable to depression and anxiety, for example. To date, however, there's no evidence that this is the case.

Reaction to Baron-Cohen's theory has been mixed. In the view of the psychologist Cordelia Fine:

higher foetal testosterone in nonclinical populations has not been convincingly linked with better mental rotation ability, systemising ability, mathematical ability, scientific ability or worse mind reading.[34] ... [T]here are question marks over whether he [Baron-Cohen] is measuring fetal testosterone, whether he is measuring 'empathising' and 'systemising', and whether males and females even differ in these skills.[35]

Other experts have questioned the focus on autism. After all, autism isn't the only neuro-developmental disorder to begin early in life and to predominately affect males: dyslexia and attention deficit hyperactivity disorder (ADHD), for example, do the same. So the question becomes not why are males more vulnerable to autism, but why are they susceptible to this particular set of disorders? Moreover, a recent study in Sweden found that, though women with autism spectrum disorders showed elevated levels of male sex hormones and less feminine facial features, men with the disorder actually looked less masculine and had higher voices than a control group of men without the disorder. Clearly, this isn't what one would expect if the men had been exposed to abnormally large quantities of prenatal testosterone. (Because it was a cross-sectional study with adults, the researchers had no way of knowing what the prenatal levels of testosterone had been; current levels for the men with autism were no higher than those of the control group.)

Perhaps as a result of such criticism, Baron-Cohen has taken pains to point out recently that his theory hasn't been 'fully confirmed or refuted'[36] (though he also asserts that the weight of evidence is increasing). Baron-Cohen's research on autism has been groundbreaking. Time will tell whether extending that work into a theory of essential sex differences has been a step too far.

7

Conclusion
Putting the Pieces Together

You can look at a piece of a puzzle for three whole days, you can
believe that you know all there is to know about its colouring and
shape, and be no further on than when you started. The only thing
that counts is the ability to link this piece to other pieces. The pieces
are readable, take on a sense, only when assembled; in isolation, a
puzzle piece means nothing—just an impossible question, an opaque
challenge.

Georges Perec, *Life: A User's Manual*[1]

Having looked at the pieces of this particular puzzle for rather longer
than three days, and having attempted to fit them together in a meaningful fashion, what do we see?

Our initial hunch, formed during research for our A to Z guide to
common emotional and psychological problems, seems to have
been right. We analysed the best evidence currently available (a big
caveat): twelve large-scale, national epidemiological surveys. And a
remarkably consistent picture emerged: in any given year, women
appear to experience higher overall rates of psychological disorder
than men. The most comprehensive of these surveys—the Mental
Health Supplement of the German National Health Interview and
Examination Survey—found that 25 per cent of men had experienced
a psychological disorder in the previous twelve months; the figure

for women was 37 per cent. Remember the statement from the World Health Organization we quoted in Chapter 1: 'Overall rates of psychiatric disorder are almost identical for men and women'[2]? That just doesn't square with the evidence. Instead, the figures bear out the contention of many feminist writers that women outnumber men for mental illness.

But let's be clear. The data does *not* show that women outnumber men for all types of disorder. As we've seen, several are more common among men, and even those that are more common in women also afflict very significant numbers of men (depression being just one example). Categorizing mental health troubles as essentially a female problem would be wildly inaccurate. According to a 2012 report by the UK Centre for Economic Performance, 'at least one third of all families (including parents and their children) include someone who is currently mentally ill'.[3] Indeed, psychological problems account for almost half of all ill health among the under-65s. Overall, approximately ten million adults in the UK may be suffering from a disorder. And millions of those individuals are male.

Nevertheless, though men tend to be prone to so-called externalizing disorders such as substance problems and antisocial personality disorder, while women are more susceptible to emotional problems like depression and anxiety, the figures aren't equal. If the epidemiological data is reliable, women outnumber men for psychological disorders as a whole. Indeed, according to the best of the national surveys (the German study), rates are almost 50 per cent higher in women than in men. And the problems that really tip the balance—that is, depression and anxiety—are those for which environmental factors are most influential.

But we need more evidence. To really be sure of what's going on, a large-scale, comprehensive epidemiological survey is required, assessing recent—rather than lifetime—prevalence and including the full range of disorders. As you might remember from Part 1, even the best of the currently available studies leave out important—and common—conditions, such as sleep and sexual disorders. (In both these instances, the data we do have suggests they're more often seen in women than in men.) Problems must be measured dimensionally too. That way we include people who may not meet the DSM criteria for a diagnosis, but who nonetheless may be struggling with very real problems.

This kind of survey is the only way to discover whether women really do have greater rates of disorder than men. And the stakes are high. If the findings of the current studies hold up, we're witnessing a major public health issue. Let's imagine that the statistics we highlighted in Chapter 2 turn out to be reasonably accurate. At a conservative estimate, that means the odds on women experiencing a psychological disorder are approximately 1.2 times those for men. At first glance, this might not seem like a very significant difference. And indeed if mental illness were very rare, the extra number of women affected would be pretty small. But of course these are problems that affect vast numbers of people. (The World Health Organization estimates that 121 million people worldwide suffer from depression alone.) As a result, that relatively modest odds ratio translates into a huge numerical imbalance. On a global scale, that means millions more women than men are experiencing psychological disorders.

If these statistics prove to be anywhere near correct, we have a problem that demands urgent action. Most immediately, we can provide the kind of treatment that has been proven to work. But we'll be better placed to reduce the likelihood of problems developing in the first place if we take the next step, and discover *why* men and women differ in their vulnerability to psychological problems. What does the evidence suggest right now?

What's striking straight away is how under-researched an issue this is. In the case of certain disorders—depression, most notably—some useful work has been done on gender. For most conditions, however, we have little evidence for why men and women are affected differently. (Even in the case of depression, we lack an established, integrated theory of gender difference.) There has been a degree of theoretical speculation, for sure. But no one, as far as we've been able to discover, has successfully used empirical tests—that is, drawing on real-world experiences—to explain why the burden of distress is not shared equally between men and women (or, more precisely, why women's greater rates of internalizing disorders aren't balanced by men's greater rates of externalizing problems).

This may be partly because understanding the causes of mental illness is such a complex and challenging task, even before you start factoring in variables like gender. Determining what proportion of the population is suffering from a particular condition is no small undertaking. It's the metaphorical equivalent, let's say, of construct-ing a rocket. But working out *why* these people have developed the disorder is like getting that rocket to the moon—and back. It can be done, but not quickly, and not without huge amounts of concerted, coordinated effort and plentiful resources.

This is because mental illness is seldom the result of just one factor. Instead, its causes are usually what are known as 'inus conditions': that is—take a deep breath—'an insufficient but non-redundant part of an unnecessary but sufficient condition'.[4] The theory of inus conditions was developed by the Australian philosopher John Mackie—a man reputedly so courteous and pleasant that it was easy to assume he warmly supported one's point of view when in fact he utterly disagreed. Mackie argued that most events—and psychological disorders are surely a prime example—are the result of an interaction between mul-tiple causes. Moreover, the same outcome can follow from varying combinations of causes. So a single factor is rarely enough: all it does is increase the chances of something occurring. Imagine, for instance, a lighted match. You can certainly use it to start a fire in your office (you may have your reasons). But in fact it's merely an inus condition. The lighted match is insufficient because other factors are needed too (oxygen, for example, and materials to burn). It's non-redundant because these other factors aren't enough on their own. Even if you have all these elements in place—the lighted match, the oxygen, and the flammable material—they are unnecessary in the sense that you could start a fire by another means (leaving your electric heater on, for instance). Yet they are nevertheless sufficient: it's not the only way to get the job done, but it'll work.

This is the level of complexity we often face when trying to explain mental illness. When we add gender into the mix, things can appear even more opaque. On a bad day, it can seem like a quicksand of ifs, ands, buts, and maybes. Yet patterns do emerge. In general, the research highlights the stress caused by life events and social roles: remember, for example, the link between childhood sexual abuse and depression, or the psychological impact of cultural attitudes to weight or alcohol. Indeed, the importance of environmental factors is indicated by the fact that the conditions to which women seem especially vulnerable are the least heritable: that is, those for which genetic factors are much less significant than environmental influences. Conditions with relatively high heritability—such as schizophrenia and bipolar disorder—tend to occur equally in men and women. So if we were to highlight one principal explanation for the gender difference in overall rates of disorder, it would be the environment.

It's certainly plausible that women experience higher levels of stress because of the demands of their social role. Increasingly, women are expected to function as carer, homemaker, and breadwinner—all while being perfectly shaped and impeccably dressed: 'superwoman' indeed. Given that domestic work is undervalued, and considering that women tend to be paid less, find it harder to advance in a career, have to juggle multiple roles, and are bombarded with images of apparent female 'perfection', it would be surprising if there weren't some emotional cost. (There's actually quite a bit of evidence that people in vulnerable social situations are prone to mental health problems, though this work has tended to focus on socio-economic status and ethnic identity rather than gender.) Indeed, when Katarina Boye analysed data on 13,000 people from twenty-five countries, she discovered that 'European women have higher well-being the longer their paid working hours and the shorter their housework hours are'.[5] Unfortunately, Boye also found that the women in her study performed three times as much housework as men, while men did twice as much paid work. Hence her conclusion that: 'differences between women's and men's paid working hours and housework hours are one reason why European women have lower well-being than European men have'.[6] (In Boye's study men's well-being was unaffected by hours spent doing paid and unpaid work.) Women are also, of course, much more likely to have experienced childhood sexual abuse, a trauma that all too often results in lasting damage.

How do these environmental factors affect the individual? At a psychological level, the evidence suggests that they can undermine women's self-concept—that is, the way a person thinks about themselves. These are the kind of pressures that can leave women feeling as if they've somehow failed; as if they don't have what it takes to be successful; as if they've been left behind. Body image worries may be especially damaging. And then there's the fact that women are taught to place such importance on social relationships. Such relationships can be a fantastic source of strength, of course. But to some extent we're relying on other people for our happiness: a risky business. If things don't work out, our self-concept can take a knock.

Negative self-concept—and the cognitive biases that go with it, such as pessimism—have been established as key vulnerability factors for many psychological problems. It won't necessarily cause a problem on its own, but in certain circumstances it can make it more likely to develop. There's good evidence that women's self-esteem tends to be lower than that of men (self-esteem is closely related to self-concept). So it's likely that one of the key psychological processes underpinning gender differences in psychological disorders is how individuals see themselves, and how they think they measure up to the people around them. Thanks to the unique combination of pressures faced by women in contemporary society, they may be particularly vulnerable to negative self-concept and thus to psychological disorders.

As this point our argument becomes more speculative. Maybe the disparity between male and female rates of disorder isn't only the result of environmental stresses affecting individuals' psychology. When we look at the literature as a whole, it seems that there may be—perhaps—a toxic synergy between negative events, cultural values, and psychological and biological vulnerabilities. And that toxic synergy may occur more frequently for women than for men.

The old idea that stress causes women to worry and men to drink is simplistic. But it does contain a kernel of truth. Certainly, the evidence suggests that the kind of stress that produces psychological problems is often different for men and women—and for plausible sociocultural reasons. Losing one's job often has more of an impact on men, for example, since what a man does for a living is conventionally seen as central to his identity. That a child is experiencing significant problems at school, on the other hand, may be especially distressing for women: mothers still tend to do most of the childcare, after all, and thus will often be the parent most involved in dealing with the issue. It's also true that drink and emotional problems often go together. Nevertheless, men's and women's response to stress does vary somewhat. Men truly are more likely to drink excessively, and women to develop anxiety and depression. (We should remember, however, that millions of men suffer from emotional problems, just as large—and arguably increasing—numbers of women struggle with alcohol abuse.)

Now there are good social reasons for this divergence. In the West, drinking is regarded as a mark of masculinity; women, on the other hand, are expected to be in touch with their feelings. Yet there may also be differing biological vulnerabilities. Men, for example, may be more impulsive; women may be more susceptible to certain types of stress because of the way the HPA axis functions. If we think of stress as a chisel striking a rock, the blows women receive from the environment may sometimes be stronger (think childhood sexual abuse), more persistent (think social role burden), and differently angled (think relationships). This might explain why women experience more psychological problems than men. But where exactly the rock splits—that is, the specific disorder that develops—may depend on psychological and biological fault lines. And perhaps these fault lines differ by gender. (Bear in mind, though, that these factors are often interlinked. Biological vulnerabilities can emerge from environmental pressures: childhood sexual abuse, for instance, can affect the reactivity of the HPA axis. So the chisel doesn't merely exploit existing weaknesses in the rock: it can help cause those weaknesses.)

But we're hypothesizing. It's impossible to be more conclusive, because the research has done little more than scratch the surface. How do we obtain a clearer sense of what's going on? The best answers will come from longitudinal studies: following representative cohorts over a number of years from childhood into adulthood, and carefully measuring the interaction between biological factors, life events, and mental illness. (These are the kind of studies that researchers dream about, but they're very expensive and thus rarely undertaken.) It's crucial that such projects start when the participants are babies or children. Not only do many disorders first show themselves during childhood or adolescence, but what happens early in life can have a significant effect on adult mental health.

These surveys must be designed with gender in mind, recognizing its potential importance and assessing a range of social factors, such as parenting, media consumption, and relationships, and covering experience both at school and at home. Moreover, let's not confine ourselves to flagging up the disparities between the sexes. Research that doesn't find differences can be seen as some sort of failure: it's certainly less newsworthy. It may also struggle to find an academic journal that will publish its results. Yet the similarities between men and women can tell us as much about the nature of mental illness as the differences.

But we're not kidding ourselves: clearly this is a controversial area. As a recent headline in *The Psychologist* put it: 'Studying sex differences is not for the faint-hearted'.[7] Some readers may question our approach. The research we've highlighted focuses on individuals, analysing how genetic, biological, social, and psychological factors can help produce mental health problems. This can be a very powerful way to apply scientific principles to the study of individual distress. But it's not without its pitfalls, certainly when dealing with neurological factors. As Cordelia Fine has noted:

> The sheer complexity of the brain, together with our assumptions about gender, lend themselves beautifully to over-interpretation and precipitous conclusions.[8]

This is true—which is why it's so important to proceed with caution, repeatedly testing hypotheses until the evidence is clear-cut.

Others may argue that the answers are best sought in broad social structures. From such a perspective, perhaps, women's psychological problems result from the inequalities of a patriarchal society. We believe social factors may play a significant part in many disorders. But, in our view, they don't provide a total explanation. For that, we need to link these social influences to an individual's life history, genetic make-up, biology, and psychological processes. After all, people exposed to the same social pressures respond in different ways; the goal is to figure out why, to understand how environmental factors play out on an individual level. Mental health is too tangled a web for anything less.

There may be those who feel that mental health problems are too elusively personal to be studied scientifically. Or who take issue with the range of conditions we cover. You won't be surprised to learn that we are quite sure these disorders can be analysed scientifically: which clinical academic researcher would argue otherwise? And not only is it possible; this kind of research represents our best hope of understanding and treating these problems. As to the selection of disorders, we follow the established psychiatric handbooks. They're far from perfect, and arguments about categorization are a dime a dozen. But for all the debate, the DSM and ICD are the definitive reference works, used—albeit sometimes grudgingly—by mental health professionals worldwide. And though the diagnostic details may sometimes be questionable, with literally hundreds of separate conditions now listed, the actual experiences these handbooks highlight describe a very wide range of mental health problems.

One fairly common view of the gender difference in rates of disorder is that they are simply a consequence of under-reporting by men. There's doubtless some truth in this. We know that men are less likely to visit a doctor for a physical ailment, and psychological problems don't fit well with conventional masculinity. But hardly any research has been done on the issue. (Not that it's an easy phenomenon to study: how do you measure what people are not telling you—or indeed, in some cases, not admitting even to themselves?) In the absence of any proper data, it's just not possible to know how big a factor male under-reporting is. Given the possible contribution of the other social and biological factors we've discussed in Part 2, we think it's likely that under-reporting explains only a small proportion of the difference between men and women in the overall rate of psychological problems. Time will tell.

Finally, it may be that we will be accused of labelling women as somehow innately 'mad' or 'crazy'. This kind of language isn't helpful. Indeed it's based on a fundamental misunderstanding of mental illness. And it stigmatizes everyday problems experienced by millions of people, male and female alike. These are problems that are usually neither innate nor inevitable, difficulties that wouldn't occur if it weren't for the contribution of social pressures. Whether or not women truly are more susceptible to psychological disorders in the current environment—and we certainly need more sophisticated epidemiological surveys to be sure—we gain nothing by simply assuming there's no case to answer. Difference need not be a pejorative concept.

People certainly seem used to the idea that gender plays a role in many physical ailments. And indeed the book-buying population seems to possess a healthy appetite for books on gender difference: think *Men Are From Mars…*, *The Female Brain*, *The Essential Difference*, *Delusions of Gender*, and so on. And on. But when it comes to mental health issues, a curious silence has prevailed. (We looked eagerly, for example, at a new textbook on gender to see whether it mentioned the issue. It didn't.) Mental health professionals, psychiatrists, and psychologists don't tend to discuss gender differences, and our guess is that they aren't talked about by the general public either.

As we saw in Chapter 1, there may be good historical reasons for this reticence. Perhaps the topic has become taboo. Yet by ignoring the influence of gender, we deprive ourselves of the opportunity to change the situation for the better—and for both sexes.

If, for example, cultural ideas about masculinity are pushing men into alcohol abuse, we can seek to modify those ideas. If women are indeed subject to additional stress because of lower social status, there's even more reason to address these inequalities. And we don't have to look far to see what can be achieved when a mental health issue is tackled head on. Having acknowledged how widespread psychological disorders are, and accepted the efficacy of cognitive behavioural therapy, in 2007 the UK government launched the Improving Access to Psychological Therapies (IAPT) scheme. Since then, 3,600 new therapists have been trained in evidence-based treatments and many thousands of people helped to overcome their problems. In financial terms, if nothing else, IAPT is surely money well spent. According to the UK Health and Safety Executive, almost eleven million working days are lost each year to stress, depression, or anxiety. (Presumably many more are lost to other disorders.) The overall costs to the economy have been estimated at £77 billion for England alone.

Given the extent of the burden on society and individuals alike, understanding what causes mental illness, and thus being better placed to prevent and treat it, should need no justification. But our ability to do that is going to be hampered if we assume that gender is, at most, merely a marginal issue. In fact, it may often be a crucial element of the puzzle. Without gender, perhaps, the pieces simply won't link up.

NOTES

CHAPTER 1

1. McManus, S., Meltzer, H., Brugha, T., Bebbington, P., and Jenkins, R. (2009). *Adult Psychiatric Morbidity in England, 2007: Results of a Household Survey* (National Centre for Social Research), p. 12.
2. American Psychiatric Association (2000). *Diagnostic and Statistical Manual of Mental Disorders*. Fourth Edition. Text Revision (Arlington: APA), p. 372.
3. Williams, M. et al. (2007). *The Mindful Way Through Depression* (New York: Guilford Press), p. 16.
4. Ohayon, M. (2002). Epidemiology of insomnia. *Sleep Medicine Review*, 6, p. 97.
5. <http://www.who.int/mental_health/prevention/genderwomen/en/>, accessed 4 September 2012.
6. <http://www.mentalhealth.org.uk/help-information/mental-health-a-z/W/women/>, accessed 4 September 2012.
7. <http://www.priorygroup.com/Conditions/Mental-Health-and-Addictions-Conditions/Womens-mental-health-issues.aspx>, accessed 4 September 2012.
8. Centre for Economic Performance's Mental Health Policy Group (2012). *How Mental Illness Loses Out in the NHS* (London: LSE), p. 1.
9. Gove, W. and Tudor, J. (1977). Sex differences in mental illness: A comment on Dohrenwend and Dohrenwend. *American Journal of Sociology*, 82, p. 1327.
10. American Psychiatric Association (2000). *Diagnostic and Statistical Manual of Mental Disorders*. Fourth Edition. Text Revision (Arlington: APA), p. 686.
11. Gove and Tudor, p. 1329.
12. Showalter, E. (1995). *The Female Malady* (London: Virago), pp. 3–4.

13. Showalter, p. 8.
14. Showalter, p. 17.
15. Showalter, p. 51.
16. Showalter, p. 19.
17. Ussher, J. (2011). *The Madness of Women* (Hove: Routledge), p. 1.
18. Ussher, pp. 1–2.
19. Kaplan, M. (1983). A woman's view of DSM-III. *American Psychologist*, 38, p. 786.
20. Williams, J. and Spitzer, R. (1983). The issue of sex bias in DSM-III. *American Psychologist*, 38, p. 797.
21. Widiger, T. and First, M. (2007). Gender and diagnostic criteria. In *Age and Gender Considerations in Psychiatric Diagnosis* (Arlington: APA), p. 135.
22. Widiger and First, p. 129.
23. Ussher, pp. 4–5.
24. Ussher, p. 88.
25. Rutter, M. et al. (2003). Using sex differences in psychopathology to study causal mechanisms. *Journal of Child Psychology and Psychiatry*, 44, pp. 1092–3.

CHAPTER 2

1. Barlow, D. H. and Durand, V. M. (2005). *Abnormal Psychology: An Integrative Approach*. (Belmont, CA: Thomas Wadsworth), p. 89.
2. American Psychiatric Association (2000). *Diagnostic and Statistical Manual of Mental Disorders*. Fourth Edition. Text Revision (Arlington: APA), p. 356.
3. DSM, p. 663.
4. DSM, p. 686.
5. McManus, S., Meltzer, H., Brugha, T., Bebbington, P., and Jenkins, R. (2009). *Adult Psychiatric Morbidity in England, 2007: Results of a Household Survey* (National Centre for Social Research), p. 18.
6. <http://www.who.int/mental_health/prevention/genderwomen/en/>, accessed 4 September 2012.

7. Field, A. (2005). *Discovering Statistics Using SPSS*. Second Edition (London: Sage), p. 739.

8. Field, p. 739.

9. Kessler, R. et al. (2005). Prevalence, severity, and comorbidity of 12-month DSM-IV disorders in the National Comorbidity Survey Replication. *Archives of General Psychiatry*, 62, p. 625.

10. <http://www.hcp.med.harvard.edu/wmh/>, accessed 4 September 2012.

11. Kessler, R. et al. (2005). Lifetime prevalence and age-of-onset distributions of DSM-IV disorders in the National Comorbidity Survey Replication. *Archives of General Psychiatry*, 62, p. 594.

CHAPTER 3

1. <http://www.dsm5.org/Pages/Default.aspx>, accessed 4 September 2012.

2. Narrow et al. (eds) (2007). *Age and Gender Considerations in Psychiatric Diagnosis* (Arlington: APA), p. 16.

3. Narrow et al., p. 135.

4. Narrow et al., p. 135.

5. Narrow et al., p. 135.

6. Andrews et al. (2009). Exploring the feasibility of a meta-structure for DSM-V and ICD-11. *Psychological Medicine*, 39, pp. 1993–4.

7. Kendell, R. and Jablensky, A. (2003). Distinguishing between the validity and utility of psychiatric diagnoses. *American Journal of Psychiatry*, 10, p. 4.

8. Plomin, R. et al. (2009). Common disorders are quantitative traits. *Nature Reviews Genetics*, 10, p. 873.

9. Goldberg, D. (2000). Plato versus Aristotle: Categorical and dimensional models for common mental disorders. *Comprehensive Psychiatry*, 41 (s1), p. 8.

10. Goldberg (2000), p. 9.

11. Hu, Y. et al. (2007). Can the 12-item General Health Questionnaire be used to measure positive mental health? *Psychological Medicine*, 37, p. 1009.

12. Hu, p. 1009.

13. Simpson, B. and Wolfers, J. (2009). The paradox of declining female happiness. *American Economic Journal*, 2, pp. 190–1.

14. 'The Pink Floyd Story: Which One's Pink?', documentary broadcast on BBC4, 16 September 2011.

15. Pierce, K. and Kirkpatrick, D. (1992). Do men lie on fear surveys? *Behaviour Research and Therapy*, 30, p. 415.

16. Seedat, S. et al. (2009). Cross-national associations between gender and mental disorders in the World Health Organization World Mental Health Surveys. *Archives of General Psychiatry*, 66, p. 793.

17. Rutter, M. et al. (2003). Using sex differences in psychopathology to study causal mechanisms. *Journal of Child Psychology and Psychiatry*, 44, p. 1093.

18. Crick, N. and Zahn-Waxler, C. (2003). The development of psychopathology in females and males. *Development and Psychopathology*, 15, pp. 720–1.

19. Crick and Zahn-Waxler, p. 732.

20. Crick and Zahn-Waxler, p. 724.

21. Rose, A. J. (2002). Co-rumination in the friendships of boys and girls. *Child Development*, 73, p. 1830.

22. Merikangas, K. et al. (2010). Lifetime prevalence of mental disorders in U.S. adolescents. *Journal of the American Academy of Child and Adolescent Psychiatry*, 49, p. 980.

CHAPTER 4

1. Hume, D. (1748). *An Enquiry Concerning Human Understanding and Other Writings* (Cambridge: Cambridge University Press), p. 70.

2. <http://grants.nih.gov/grants/guide/pa-files/pa-09-108.html>, accessed 4 September 2012.

3. Wizemann, T. M. and Pardue, M.-L. (eds.) (2001) *Exploring the Biological Contributions to Human Health: Does Sex Matter?* (Washington, DC: National Academy Press), p. x.

4. Wizemann and Pardue., p. x.

5. Blehar, M. (2006). Women's mental health research. *Annual Review of Clinical Psychology*, 2, p. 135.

6. Quoted in Fine, C. (2010). *Delusions of Gender* (London: Icon Books), p. xxiv.

7. Cahill, L. (2006). Why sex matters for neuroscience. *Nature Reviews Neuroscience*, 7, p. 477.

8. Cosgrove, K. et al. (2007). Evolving knowledge of sex differences in brain structure, function and chemistry. *Biological Psychiatry*, 62, p. 847.

9. Davies, W. and Wilkinson, L. (2006). It is not all hormones: Alternative explanations for sexual differentiation of the brain. *Brain Research*, 1126, p. 37.

10. Cahill, p. 483.

11. Hyde, J. et al. (2008). The ABCs of depression: Integrating affective, biological, and cognitive models to explain the emergence of the gender difference in depression. *Journal of Abnormal Psychology*, 115, p. 295.

12. Kendler, K. et al. (2006). A Swedish national twin study of lifetime major depression. *American Journal of Psychiatry*, 163, p. 112.

13. Roca, C. A. et al. (2005). Sex-related differences in stimulated hypothalamic-pituitary-adrenal axis during induced gonadal suppression, *Journal of Clinical Endocrinology and Metabolism*, 90, p. 4228.

14. Taylor, S. (2006). Tend and befriend. *Current Directions in Psychological Science*, 15, p. 273.

15. Taylor, p. 274.

16. McGuffin, P. et al. (2011). The truth about genetic variation in the serotonin gene and response to stress and medication. *British Journal of Psychiatry*, 198, p. 426.

17. Nolen-Hoeksema, S. et al. (1999). Explaining the gender difference in depressive symptoms. *Journal of Personality and Social Psychology*, 77, pp. 1062 and 1069.

18. Nolen-Hoeksema, S. and Morrow, J. (1991). A prospective study of depression and distress following a natural disaster. *Journal of Personality and Social Psychology*, 61, p. 115.

19. Nolen-Hoeksema (1999), p. 1071.

20. Brown, G. et al. (1995). Loss, humiliation and entrapment among women developing depression. *Psychological Medicine*, 25, p. 11.

21. Sanathara, V. et al. (2003). Interpersonal dependence and major depression. *Psychological Medicine*, 33, p. 927.

22. Kendler, K. et al. (1999). Causal relationships between stressful life events and the onset of major depression. *American Journal of Psychiatry*, 156, p. 838.

23. Hankin, B. et al. (2007). Sex differences in adolescent depression. *Child Development*, 78, p. 283.

24. Bebbington, P. et al. (2009). Suicide attempts, gender, and sexual abuse. *American Journal of Psychiatry*, 166, p. 1138.

25. Chaplin, T. et al. (2005). Parental socialization of emotion expression. *Emotion*, 5, pp. 81 and 85.

26. Wichstrøm, L. (1999). The emergence of gender difference in depressed mood during adolescence. *Developmental Psychology*, 35, p. 232.

27. American Psychiatric Association (2000). *Diagnostic and Statistical Manual of Mental Disorders*. Fourth Edition. Text Revision (Arlington: APA), p. 449.

28. Gerull, F. and Rapee, R. (2002). Mother knows best: Effects of maternal modelling on the acquisition of fear and avoidance behaviour in toddlers. *Behaviour Research and Therapy*, 40, p. 285.

29. Chen, Y.-Y. et al. (2005). Can social factors explain sex differences in insomnia? Findings from a National Survey in Taiwan. *Journal of Epidemiology and Community Health*, 59, p. 492.

30. Klose, M. and Jacobi, F. (2004). Can gender differences in the prevalence of mental disorders be explained by sociodemographic factors? *Archives of Women's Mental Health*, 7, p. 133.

CHAPTER 5

1. Lifestyle of the Modern Girl Condemned, *Manchester Guardian*, 18 February 1926; <http://www.guardian.co.uk/theguardian/2012/feb/18/archive-1926-modern-girls-lifestyle-condemned>, accessed 4 September 2012.

2. Caspi, A. and Moffitt, T. E. (2006). Gene-Environment Interactions in Psychiatry: Joining Forces with Neuroscience. *Nature Reviews Neuroscience*, 7, p. 583.

3. Nolen-Hoeksema, S. and Hilt, L. (2006). Possible contributors to the gender differences in alcohol use and problems. *Journal of General Psychology*, 133, p. 359.

4. Castelnuovo, A. et al. (2006). Alcohol dosing and total mortality in men and women. *Archives of Internal Medicine*, 166, p. 2442.

5. Dick, D. et al. (2010). Understanding the construct of impulsivity and its relationship to alcohol use disorders. *Addiction Biology*, 15, p. 220.

6. Cross, C. et al. (2011). Sex differences in impulsivity: a meta-analysis. *Psychological Bulletin*, 137, p. 102.

7. Cross et al., p. 121.

8. Keyes, K. et al. (2011). Stressful life experiences, alcohol consumption, and alcohol use disorders. *Psychopharmacology*, 218, p. 8.

9. Dawson, D. et al. (2005). The association between stress and drinking: Modifying effects of gender and vulnerability. *Alcohol and Alcoholism*, 40, p. 454.

10. Dawson et al., p. 453.

11. Rospenda, K. et al. (2008). Workplace harassment, stress, and drinking behaviour over time. *Addictive Behaviors*, 33, p. 966.

12. *The Sun*, 11 December 2008.

13. Holmila, M. and Raitasalo, K. (2005). Gender differences in drinking. *Addiction*, 100, p. 1767.

14. Glass or two of wine a week 'could damage baby'. *The Telegraph*, 11 April 2011; <http://www.telegraph.co.uk/health/healthnews/8441176/Glass-or-two-of-wine-a-week-could-damage-baby.html>, accessed 4 September 2012. Drinking alcohol while pregnant weakens mothers bond with child. *The Telegraph*, 22 April 2009; <http://www.telegraph.co.uk/health/healthnews/5197463/Drinking-alcohol-while-pregnant-weakens-mothers-bond-with-child.html, accessed 4 September 2012. Moderate drinking while pregnant doubles risk of child becoming depressed. *The Telegraph*, 23 November 2009; <http://www.telegraph.co.uk/health/healthnews/6630115/Moderate-drinking-while-pregnant-doubles-risk-

of-child-becoming-depressed.html>, accessed 4 September 2012. Mothers who drink while pregnant 'can give their children a taste for alcohol'. *The Telegraph*, 9 March 2009; <http://www.telegraph.co.uk/health/women_shealth/4962536/Mothers-who-drink-while-pregnant-can-give-their-children-a-taste-for-alcohol.html>, accessed 4 September 2012.

15. Rahav, G. et al. (2006). The influence of societal level factors on men's and women's alcohol consumption and alcohol problems. *Alcohol and Alcoholism*, 41 (S1), pp. i47 and i54.

16. Keyes, K. et al. (2011). Birth cohort effects and gender differences in alcohol epidemiology. *Alcoholism: Clinical and Experimental Research*,35, p. 1.

CHAPTER 6

1. American Psychiatric Association (2000). *Diagnostic and Statistical Manual of Mental Disorders*. Fourth Edition. Text Revision. (Arlington, VA: American Psychiatric Association), p. 589.

2. DSM, p. 594.

3. Fairburn, C. and Cooper, Z. (2011). Eating disorders, DSM-5 and clinical reality. *British Journal of Psychiatry*, 198, p. 9.

4. Klump, K. et al. (2006). Preliminary evidence that gonadal hormones organise and activate disordered eating. *Psychological Medicine*, 36, p. 539.

5. Klump et al., p. 545.

6. Lydecker, J. et al. (2012). Association between co-twin sex and eating disorders in opposite sex twin pairs. *Journal of Psychosomatic Research*, 72, p. 73.

7. Keel, P. and Klump, K. (2003). Are eating disorders culture-bound syndromes? Implications for conceptualizing their etiology. *Psychological Bulletin*, 129, pp. 752–3.

8. One in five ballerinas at La Scala is anorexic, leading dancer claims. *The Observer*, 4 December 2011; <http://www.guardian.co.uk/world/2011/dec/04/ballerinas-la-scala-anorexic-claim>, accessed 4 September 2012.

9. Italian ballerina sacked in anorexia row. *The Guardian*, 4 February 2012; <http://www.guardian.co.uk/stage/2012/feb/05/italian-ballerina-sacked-anorexia-row>, accessed 4 September 2012.

10. Grabe, S. et al. (2008). The role of the media in body image concerns among women. *Psychological Bulletin*, 134, pp. 470–1.

11. Grabe et al. p. 460.

12. Judge, T. and Cable, D. (2011). When it comes to pay, do the thin win? The effect of weight on pay for men and women. *Journal of Applied Psychology*, 96, p. 97.

13. Judge and Cable, p. 109.

14. Judge and Cable, p. 109.

15. American Psychiatric Association (2000). *Diagnostic and Statistical Manual of Mental Disorders*, p. 701.

16. DSM, p. 706.

17. DSM, p. 93.

18. DSM, p. 102.

19. DSM, p. 102.

20. Raine, A. et al. (2011). Sex differences in orbitofrontal gray as a partial explanation for sex differences in antisocial personality. *Molecular Psychiatry*, 16, p. 234.

21. American Psychiatric Association (2000). *Diagnostic and Statistical Manual of Mental Disorders*, p. 703.

22. Ronson, J. (2011). *The Psychopath Test* (London: Picador), p. 10.

23. Narusyte, J. et al. (2011). Parental criticism and externalising behaviour problems in adolescents. *Journal of Abnormal Psychology*, 120, pp. 367–8.

24. Cole, P. et al. (2003). Mutual emotion regulation and the stability of conduct problems between preschool and early school age. *Development and Psychopathology*, 15, p. 16.

25. Happé, F. and Ronald, A. (2008). The 'fractionable autism triad'. *Neuropsychological Review*, 18, p. 299.

26. Zahn-Waxler, C. et al. (2008). Disorders of childhood and adolescence: Gender and psychopathology. *Annual Review of Clinical Psychology*, 4, p. 277.

27. Baron-Cohen, S. (2010). Book review: Delusions of gender—'neurosexism', biology and politics. *The Psychologist*, 23, p. 904.

28. Baron-Cohen, S. (2002). The extreme male brain theory of autism. *Trends in Cognitive Sciences*, 6, p. 251.

29. Baron-Cohen (2002), p. 248.

30. Baron-Cohen (2002), p. 248.

31. Baron-Cohen, S. (2003). *The Essential Difference* (London: Penguin), pp. 200 and 207.

32. Baron-Cohen, S. (2002), p. 252.

33. Baron-Cohen, S. et al. (2011). Why are autism spectrum conditions more prevalent in males? *PLoS Biology*, 9, e1001081, p. 7.

34. Fine, C. (2010). *Delusions of Gender* (London: Icon Books), p. 130.

35. Sutton, J. (2010). The battle of the sex differences. Jon Sutton interviews Cordelia Fine about neurosexism and more. *The Psychologist*, 23, p. 901.

36. Baron-Cohen, S. et al. (2011), p. 1.

CHAPTER 7

1. Perec, G. (1988). *Life: A User's Manual* (London: Collins Harvill), p. xv.

2. <http://www.who.int/mental_health/prevention/genderwomen/en/>, accessed 4 September 2012.

3. Centre for Economic Performance's Mental Health Policy Group (2012). *How Mental Illness Loses Out in the NHS* (London: LSE), p. 6.

4. Shadish, W. et al. (2002). *Experimental and Quasi-Experimental Designs for Generalised Causal Inference* (Boston, MA: Houghton Mifflin), p. 4.

5. Boye, K. (2009). Relatively different? How do gender differences in well-being depend on paid and unpaid work in Europe? *Social Indicators Research*, 93, p. 522.

6. Boye, p. 522.

7. British Psychological Society (2010). The battle of the sex differences. *The Psychologist* (November), 23, pp. 900–03.

8. Fine, C. (2010). *Delusions of Gender* (London: Icon Books), p. xxviii.

SOURCES

CHAPTER 1

American Psychiatric Association (2000). *Diagnostic and Statistical Manual of Mental Disorders.* Fourth Edition. Text Revision. Arlington: APA.

Appignanesi, L. (2008). *Mad, Bad and Sad: A History of Women and the Mind Doctors from 1800.* London: Virago.

Busfield, J. (1996). *Men, Women and Madness.* Hampshire: Palgrave Macmillan.

Centre for Economic Performance's Mental Health Policy Group (2012). *How Mental Illness Loses Out in the NHS.* London: LSE.

Dohrenwend, B. and Dohrenwend, B. (1976). Sex differences and psychiatric disorders. *American Journal of Sociology,* 81, 1447–54.

Freeman, D. and Freeman, J. (2009). *Know Your Mind: Everyday Emotional and Psychological Problems and How to Overcome Them.* London: Pan Macmillan.

Gomberg, E. and Franks, V. (eds) (1979). *Gender and Disordered Behavior.* New York: Brunner/Mazel.

Gove, W. and Tudor, J. (1973). Adult sex roles and mental illness. *American Journal of Sociology,* 78, 812–35.

—— (1977). Sex Differences in Mental Illness: A Comment on Dohrenwend and Dohrenwend. *American Journal of Sociology,* 82, 1327–36.

Guttentag, M. et al. (eds) (1980). *The Mental Health of Women.* New York: Academic Press.

Kaplan, M. (1983). A woman's view of DSM-III. *American Psychologist,* 38, 786–92.

Kessler, E. et al. (2005). Prevalence, severity, and comorbidity of 12-month DSM-IV disorders in the National Comorbidity Survey Replication. *Archives of General Psychiatry,* 62, 617–27.

Kohen, D. (ed.) (2000). *Women and Mental Health.* London: Routledge.

Laumann, E. O. et al. (1999). Sexual dysfunction in the United States. *Journal of the American Medical Association*, 281, 537–44.

McManus, S., Meltzer, H., Brugha, T., Bebbington, P., and Jenkins, R. (2009). *Adult Psychiatric Morbidity in England, 2007: Results of a Household Survey*. National Centre for Social Research.

Ohayon, M. (2002). Epidemiology of insomnia. *Sleep Medicine Review*, 6, 97–111.

Rutter, M. et al. (2003). Using sex differences in psychopathology to study causal mechanisms. *Journal of Child Psychology and Psychiatry*, 44, 1092–115.

Showalter, E. (1995). *The Female Malady*. London: Virago.

Ussher, J. (2011). *The Madness of Women*. Hove: Routledge.

üstün, T. and Kessler, R. (2002). Global burden of depressive disorders. *British Journal of Psychiatry*, 181, 181–3.

Wang, P. et al. (2005). Twelve-month use of mental health services in the United States. *Archives of General Psychiatry*, 62, 629–40.

Widiger, T. and First, M. (2007). Gender and Diagnostic Criteria. In *Age and Gender Considerations in Psychiatric Diagnosis: A Research Agenda for DSM-V.* (eds W. Narrow, M. First, P. Sirovatka, D. Regier). Arlington: APA.

Williams, J. and Spitzer, R. (1983). The issue of sex bias in DSM-III. *American Psychologist*, 38, 793–8.

Williams, M. et al. (2007). *The Mindful Way Through Depression*. New York: Guilford Press.

<http://www.who.int/mental_health/prevention/genderwomen/en/>, accessed 4 September 2012.

<http://www.mentalhealth.org.uk/help-information/mental-health-a-z/W/women/>, accessed 4 September 2012.

<http://www.priorygroup.com/Conditions/Mental-Health-and-Addictions-Conditions/Womens-mental-health-issues.aspx>, accessed 4 September 2012.

CHAPTER 2

American Psychiatric Association (2000). *Diagnostic and Statistical Manual of Mental Disorders*. Fourth Edition. Text Revision. Arlington: APA.

Andrews, G. et al. (2001). Prevalence, comorbidity, disability and service utilisation. *British Journal of Psychiatry*, 178, 145–53.

Barlow, D. H. and Durand, V. M. (2005). *Abnormal Psychology: An Integrative Approach*. Belmont, CA: Thomas Wadsworth.

Bijl, R. et al. (1998). Prevalence of psychiatric disorder in the general population. *Social Psychiatry and Psychiatric Epidemiology*, 33, 587–95.

Bourdon, K. et al. (1992). Estimating the prevalence of mental disorders in U.S. adults from the Epidemiologic Catchment Area Survey. *Public Health Report*, 107, 663–8.

ESEMeD/MHEDEA 2000 Investigators (2004). Prevalence of mental disorders in Europe. *Acta Psychiatrica Scandinavica*, 109, 21–7.

Field, A. (2005). *Discovering Statistics Using SPSS*. Second Edition. London: Sage.

Freeman, D., Brugha, T., Meltzer, H., Jenkins, R., Stahl, D., and Bebbington, P. (2010). Persecutory ideation and insomnia: Findings from the second British National Survey of Psychiatric Morbidity. *Journal of Psychiatric Research*, 44, 1021–6.

de Graaf, R. et al. (2002). Predictors of first incidence of DSM-III-R psychiatric disorders in the general population. *Acta Psychiatrica Scandinavica*, 106, 303–13.

Grant, B. et al. (2009). Sociodemographic and psychopathologic predictors of first incidence of DSM-IV substance use, mood and anxiety disorders. *Molecular Psychiatry*, 14, 1051–66.

Haro, J. M. et al. (2006). Concordance of the Composite International Diagnostic Interview Version 3.0 (CIDI 3.0) with standardised clinical assessments in the WHO Mental Health Surveys. *International Journal of Methods in Psychiatric Research*, 15, 167–80.

Jacobi, F. et al. (2004). Prevalence, co-morbidity and correlates of mental disorders in the general population. *Psychological Medicine*, 34, 597–611.

Jenkins, R., Meltzer, H., Bebbington, P., Brugha, T., Farrell, M., McManus, S., and Singleton, N. (2009). The British Mental Health Survey Programme: achievements and latest findings. *Social Psychiatry and Psychiatric Epidemiology*, 44, 899–904.

Kessler, R. et al. (1994). Lifetime and 12-month prevalence of DSM-III-R psychiatric disorders in the United States. *Archives of General Psychiatry*, 51, 8–19.

—— (1998). Methodological studies of the Composite International Diagnostic Interview (CIDI) in the US National Comorbidity Survey. *International Journal of Methods in Psychiatric Research*, 7, 33–55.

—— (2005). Lifetime prevalence and age-of-onset distributions of DSM-IV disorders in the National Comorbidity Survey Replication. *Archives of General Psychiatry*, 62, 593–602.

—— (2005). Prevalence, severity, and comorbidity of 12-month DSM-IV disorders in the National Comorbidity Survey Replication. *Archives of General Psychiatry*, 62, 617–27.

Kessler, R. and ŭstŭn, T. (2008). *The WHO World Mental Health Surveys*. New York: Cambridge University Press.

Martini, J. et al. (2009). New women-specific diagnostic modules. *Archives of Women's Mental Health*, 12, 281–9.

McManus, S., Meltzer, H., Brugha, T., Bebbington, P., and Jenkins, R. (2009). *Adult Psychiatric Morbidity in England, 2007: Results of a Household Survey*. National Centre for Social Research.

Meltzer, H. et al. (1995). *The Prevalence of Psychiatric Morbidity among Adults Living in Private Households. Report 1. OPCS Surveys of Psychiatric Morbidity in Great Britain*. London: HMSO.

National Centre for Social Research and University of Leicester (2011). *Adult Psychiatric Morbidity Survey, 2007* [computer file]. Third Edition. Colchester, Essex: UK Data Archive [distributor] SN: 6379, <http://dx.doi.org/10.5255/UKDA-SN-6379-1>, accessed 11 October 2012.

Oakley Browne, M.A. et al. (2006). Lifetime prevalence and projected lifetime risk of DSM-IV disorders in Te Rau Hinengaro. *Australian and New Zealand Journal of Psychiatry*, 40, 865–74.

Office for National Statistics (2003). *Psychiatric Morbidity among Adults Living in Private Households, 2000* [computer file]. Colchester, Essex: UK

Data Archive [distributor] SN: 4653, <http://dx.doi.org/10.5255/UKDA-SN-4653-1>, accessed 22 October 2012.

Office of Population Censuses and Surveys. Social Survey Division (1996). *OPCS Surveys of Psychiatric Morbidity: Private Household Survey*, 1993 [computer file]. Colchester, Essex: UK Data Archive [distributor] SN: 3560, <http://dx.doi.org/10.5255/UKDA-SN-3560-1>, accessed 11 October 2012.

Reed, V. et al. (1998). To what degree does the Composite International Diagnostic Interview (CIDI) correctly identify DSM-IV disorders? Testing validity in a clinical sample. *International Journal of Methods in Psychiatric Research*, 7, 142–55.

Regier, D. A. et al. (1988). One-month prevalence of mental disorders in the United States. *Archives of General Psychiatry*, 45, 977–86.

Robins, L. and Regier, D. (eds) (1991). *Psychiatric Disorders in America*. New York: Free Press.

Seedat, S. et al. (2009). Cross-national associations between gender and mental disorders in the World Health Organization World Mental Health Surveys. *Archives of General Psychiatry*, 66, 785–95.

Singleton, N., Bumpstead, R., O'Brien, M., Lee, A. and Meltzer, H. (2001). *Psychiatric Morbidity among Adults Living in Private Households*. TSO London.

Slade, T. et al. (2009). 2007 National Survey of Mental Health and Wellbeing. *Australian and New Zealand Journal of Psychiatry*, 43, 594–605.

Tsuang, M.T. and Tohen, M. (eds) (2002). *Textbook in Psychiatric Epidemiology*. Second Edition. New York: Wiley.

Vicente, B. et al. (2006). Lifetime and 12-month prevalence of DSM-III-R disorders in the Chile Psychiatric Prevalence Study. *American Journal of Psychiatry*, 163, 1362–70.

Wells, J.E. et al. (2006). Te Rau Hinengaro: The New Zealand Mental Health Survey. *Australian and New Zealand Journal of Psychiatry*, 40, 835–44.

<http://www.who.int/mental_health/prevention/genderwomen/en/>, accessed 4 September 2012.

<http://www.hcp.med.harvard.edu/wmh/>, accessed 4 September 2012.

CHAPTER 3

Andrews, G. et al. (2009). Exploring the feasibility of a meta-structure for DSM-V and ICD-11. *Psychological Medicine*, 39, 1993–2000.

Bolton, D. (2009). What is mental disorder? *Psychiatry*, 8, 468–70.

Crick, N. and Zahn-Waxler, C. (2003). The development of psychopathology in females and males. *Development and Psychopathology*, 15, 719–42.

Ekman, P. (1992). An argument for basic emotions. *Cognition and Emotion*, 6, 169–200.

Fine, C. (2010). *Delusions of Gender*. London: Icon Books.

Goldberg, D. (2000). Plato versus Aristotle: Categorical and dimensional models for common mental disorders. *Comprehensive Psychiatry*, 41 (s1), 8–13.

—— (2010). Should our major classifications of mental disorders be revised? *British Journal of Psychiatry*, 196, 255–6.

Hu, Y. et al. (2007). Can the 12-item General Health Questionnaire be used to measure positive mental health? *Psychological Medicine*, 37, 1005–13.

Kendler, R. et al. (2001). Are there sex differences in the reliability of a lifetime history of major depression and its predictors? *Psychological Medicine*, 31, 617–25.

Kendell, R. and Jablensky, A. (2003). Distinguishing between the validity and utility of psychiatric diagnoses. *American Journal of Psychiatry*, 10, 4–12.

Korten, A. and Henderson, S. (2000). The Australian National Survey of Mental Health and Well-Being. *British Journal of Psychiatry*, 177, 325–30.

Leach, L. et al. (2008). Gender differences in the endorsement of symptoms for depression and anxiety: Are gender-biased items responsible? *Journal of Nervous and Mental Disease*, 196, 128–35.

McManus, S., Meltzer, H., Brugha, T., Bebbington, P., and Jenkins, R. (2009). *Adult Psychiatric Morbidity in England, 2007: Results of a Household Survey*. National Centre for Social Research.

Meltzer, H. et al. (2000). *The Mental Health of Children and Adolescents in Great Britain*. London: National Statistics Office.

Merikangas, K. et al. (2010). Lifetime prevalence of mental disorders in U.S. adolescents. *Journal of the American Academy of Child and Adolescent Psychiatry*, 49, 980–9.

Narrow, W. E. et al. (eds) (2007). *Age and Gender Considerations in Psychiatric Diagnosis*. Arlington: APA.

Oakley Browne, M. et al. (2010). The Kessler Psychological Distress Scale in Te Rau Hinengaro. *Australian and New Zealand Journal of Psychiatry*, 44, 314–22.

Ostrov, J.M., Crick, N., and Keating, C. (2005). Gender-biased perceptions of preschoolers' behavior. *Sex Roles*, 52, 393–8.

Pierce, K. and Kirkpatrick, D. (1992). Do men lie on fear surveys? *Behaviour Research and Therapy*, 30, 415–18.

Plomin, R. et al. (2009). Common disorders are quantitative traits. *Nature Reviews Genetics*, 10, 872–8.

Rose, A. J. (2002). Co-rumination in the friendships of boys and girls. *Child Development*, 73, 1830–43.

Rutter, M. et al. (2003). Using sex differences in psychopathology to study causal mechanisms. *Journal of Child Psychology and Psychiatry*, 44, 1092–115.

Seedat, S. et al. (2009). Cross-national associations between gender and mental disorders in the World Health Organization World Mental Health Surveys. *Archives of General Psychiatry*, 66, 785–95.

Simpson, B. and Wolfers, J. (2009). The paradox of declining female happiness. *American Economic Journal*, 2, 190–225.

'The Pink Floyd Story: Which One's Pink?' Documentary broadcast on BBC4, 16 September 2011.

The politics of mental health. *The Guardian*, 29 July 2012; <http://www.guardian.co.uk/society/2012/jul/29/politics-mental-health>, accessed 11 September 2012.

Weich, S. et al. (2011). Mental well-being and mental illness. *British Journal of Psychiatry*, 199, 23–8.

Wells, J. and Horwood, L. (2004). How accurate is recall of key symptoms of depression? A comparison of recall and longitudinal reports. *Psychological Medicine*, 34, 1001–11.

<http://www.dsm5.org/Pages/Default.aspx>, accessed 4 September 2012.

CHAPTER 4

American Psychiatric Association (2000). *Diagnostic and Statistical Manual of Mental Disorders*. Fourth Edition. Text Revision. Arlington: APA.

Antony, M. and Stein, M. (eds) (2009). *Oxford Handbook of Anxiety and Related Disorders*. New York: Oxford University Press.

Balbo, M. et al. (2010). Impact of sleep and its disturbances on hypothalamo-pituitary-adrenal axis activity. *International Journal of Endocrinology*. Doi: 10.1155/2010/759234.

Bao, A. M. et al. (2008). The stress system in depression and neurodegeneration. *Brain Research Reviews*, 57, 531–53.

Bebbington, P. (1996). The origins of sex differences in depressive disorder. *International Review of Psychiatry*, 8, 295–332.

—— et al. (2009). Suicide attempts, gender, and sexual abuse. *American Journal of Psychiatry*, 166, 1135–40.

Benas, J. S. et al. (2010). Body dissatisfaction and weight-related teasing. *Journal of Behavior Therapy and Experimental Psychiatry*, 41, 352–6.

Blehar, M. (2006). Women's mental health research. *Annual Review of Clinical Psychology*, 2, 135–60.

Brown, G. et al. (1986). Social support, self-esteem and depression. *Psychological Medicine*, 16, 813–31.

—— (1995). Loss, humiliation and entrapment among women developing depression. *Psychological Medicine*, 25, 7–21.

Burke, H. et al. (2005). Depression and cortisol responses to psychological stress. *Psychoneuroendocrinology*, 30, 846–56.

Cahill, L. (2006). Why sex matters for neuroscience. *Nature Reviews Neuroscience*, 7, 477–84.

Caspi, A. et al. (2010). Genetic sensitivity to the environment: The case of the serotonin transporter gene and its implications for studying complex diseases and traits. *American Journal of Psychiatry*, 167, 509–27.

Castle, D. et al. (eds) (2006). *Mood and Anxiety Disorders in Women*. Cambridge: Cambridge University Press.

Chaplin, T. et al. (2005). Parental socialization of emotion expression. *Emotion*, 5, 80–8.

Chen, Y.-Y. et al. (2005). Can social factors explain sex differences in insomnia? Findings from a National Survey in Taiwan. *Journal of Epidemiology and Community Health*, 59, 488–94.

Connolly, K. et al. (2008). Evidence for disgust sensitivity mediating the sex differences found in blood-injection-injury phobia and spider phobia. *Personality and Individual Differences*, 44, 898–908.

Corra, M. et al. (2009). Trends in marital happiness by gender and race, 1973 to 2006. *Journal of Family Issues*, 20, 1379–404.

Cosgrove, K. et al. (2007). Evolving knowledge of sex differences in brain structure, function and chemistry. *Biological Psychiatry*, 62, 847–55.

Cowen, P. (2010). Not fade away: The HPA axis and depression. *Psychological Medicine*, 40, 1–4.

Cyranowski, J. et al. (2000). Adolescent onset of the gender difference in lifetime rates of major depression. *Archives of General Psychiatry*, 57, 21–7.

Dalgard, O. et al. (2006). Negative life events, social support and gender difference in depression. *Social Psychiatry and Psychiatric Epidemiology*, 41, 444–51.

Das-Munshi, J. et al. (2008). Public health significance of mixed anxiety and depression. *British Journal of Psychiatry*, 192, 171–7.

Davies, W. and Wilkinson, L. (2006). It is not all hormones: Alternative explanations for sexual differentiation of the brain. *Brain Research*, 1126, 36–45.

Davis, M. et al. (1999). Is life more difficult on Mars or Venus? A meta-analytic review of sex differences in major and minor life events. *Annals of Behavioral Medicine*, 21, 83–97.

Eisenberg, N. et al. (1998). Parental socialization of emotion. *Psychological Inquiry*, 9, 241–73.

Eley, T. et al. (2004). Gene-environment interaction analysis of serotonin system markers with adolescent depression. *Molecular Psychiatry*, 9, 908–15.

Eley, T. and Stevenson, J. (1999). Exploring the covariation between anxiety and depression symptoms. *Journal of Child Psychology and Psychiatry*, 40, 1273–82.

Escribá-Agűir, V. & Artazcoz, L. (2011). Gender differences in postpartum depression: A longitudinal cohort study. *Journal of Epidemiological and Community Health*, 65, 320–6.

Fanous, A. et al. (2002). Neuroticism, major depression and gender. *Psychological Medicine*, 32, 719–28.

Fine, C. (2010). *Delusions of Gender*. London: Icon Books.

Fivush, R. et al. (2000). Gender differences in parent-child emotion narratives. *Sex Roles*, 41, 233–53.

Gerull, F. and Rapee, R. (2002). Mother knows best: Effects of maternal modelling on the acquisition of fear and avoidance behaviour in toddlers. *Behaviour Research and Therapy*, 40, 279–87.

Goodwin, R. and Gotlib, I. (2004). Gender differences in depression: The role of personality factors. *Psychiatry Research*, 126, 135–42.

Goodyer, I. et al. (2009). Serotonin transporter genotype, morning cortisol and subsequent depression in adolescents. *British Journal of Psychiatry*, 95, 39–45.

Gotlib, I. et al. (2008). HPA axis reactivity: a mechanism underlying the associations among 5-HTTLPR, stress, and depression. *Biological Psychiatry*, 63, 847–51.

Hammen, C. et al. (2010). Chronic and acute stress, gender, and serotonin transporter gene-environment interactions predicting depression symptoms in youth. *Journal of Child Psychology and Psychiatry*, 51, 180–7.

Hankin, B. et al. (2007). Sex differences in adolescent depression. *Child Development*, 78, 279–95.

—— (2009). Developmental origins of cognitive vulnerabilities to depression. *Journal of Clinical Psychology*, 65, 1327–38.

—— (2010). Hypothalamic-pituitary-adrenal axis dysregulation in dysphoric children and adolescents. *Biological Psychiatry*, 68, 484–90.

Hankin, B. and Abramson, L. (2001). Development of gender differences in depression. *Psychological Bulletin*, 127, 773–96.

Harris, T. (2001). Recent developments in understanding the psychosocial aspects of depression. *British Medical Bulletin*, 57, 17–32.

Heim, C. et al. (2008). The link between childhood trauma and depression. *Psychoneuroendocrinology*, 33, 693–710.

Hettema, J. (2008). What is the genetic relationship between anxiety and depression? *American Journal of Medical Genetics Part C*, 148C, 140–6.

—— et al. (2005). The structure of genetic and environmental risk factors for anxiety disorders in men and women. *Archives of General Psychiatry*, 62, 182–9.

Hines, M. (2011). Gender development and the human brain. *Annual Review of Neuroscience*, 34, 69–88.

Hume, D. (1748). *An Enquiry Concerning Human Understanding and Other Writings*. Cambridge: Cambridge University Press.

Hyde, J. et al. (2008). The ABCs of depression: Integrating affective, biological, and cognitive models to explain the emergence of the gender difference in depression. *Journal of Abnormal Psychology*, 115, 291–313.

Johnson, E. et al. (2006). Epidemiology of DSM-IV insomnia in adolescence. *Pediatrics*, 117, e247–56.

Kajantie, E. and Phillips, S. (2006). The effects of sex and hormonal status on the physiological response to acute psychosocial stress. *Psychoneuroendocrinology*, 31, 151–78.

Karg, K. et al. (2011). The serotonin transporter promoter variant (5-HTTLPR), stress, and depression meta-analysis revisited. *Archives of General Psychiatry*, 68, 444–54.

Keenan, K. and Shaw, D. (1997). Developmental and social influences on young girls' early problem behaviour. *Psychological Bulletin*, 121, 95–113.

Kendler, K. et al. (1999). Causal relationships between stressful life events and the onset of major depression. *American Journal of Psychiatry*, 156, 837–41.

—— (2000). Stressful life events and previous episodes in the etiology of major depression in women. *American Journal of Psychiatry*, 157, 1243–51.

—— (2001). Gender differences in the rates of exposure to stressful life events and sensitivity to their depressogenic effects. *American Journal of Psychiatry*, 158, 587–93.

Kendler, K. et al. (2003). Life event dimensions of loss, humiliation, entrapment, and danger in the prediction of onset of major depression and generalised anxiety. *Archives of General Psychiatry*, 60, 789–96.

—— (2004). Childhood sexual abuse, stressful life events and risk for major depression in women. *Psychological Medicine*, 34, 1475–82.

—— (2006). A Swedish national twin study of lifetime major depression. *American Journal of Psychiatry*, 163, 109–14.

Keyes, C. and Goodman, S. (eds) (2006). *Women and Depression*. New York: Cambridge University Press.

Kirschbaum, C., Pirke, K-M., and Hellhammer, D. H. (1993). The 'Trier' Social Stress Test: A tool for investigating psychobiological stress responses in a laboratory setting. *Neuropsychobiology*, 28, 76–81.

Kling, K. C. et al. (1999). Gender differences in self-esteem. *Psychological Bulletin*, 125, 470–500.

Klose, M. and Jacobi, F. (2004). Can gender differences in the prevalence of mental disorders be explained by sociodemographic factors? *Archives of Women's Mental Health*, 7, 133–48.

Kudielka, B. and Kirschbaum, C. (2005). Sex differences in HPA axis responses to stress. *Biological Psychology*, 69, 113–32.

Kuehner, C. (2003). Gender differences in unipolar depression. *Acta Psychiatrica Scandinavica*, 108, 163–74.

Lake, R. I. et al. (2000). Further evidence against the environmental transmission of individual differences in neuroticism from a collaborative study of 45,850 twins and relatives on two continents. *Behavior Genetics*, 30, 223–33.

Lenroot, R. and Giedd, J. (2010). Sex differences in the adolescent brain. *Brain and Cognition*, 72, 46–55.

Linton, S. (2004). Does work stress predict insomnia? A prospective study. *British Journal of Health Psychology*, 9, 127–36.

McGuffin, P. et al. (2011). The truth about genetic variation in the serotonin gene and response to stress and medication. *British Journal of Psychiatry*, 198, 424–7.

McLaughlin, K. A. et al. (2010). Childhood adversity, adult stressful events, and risk of past-year psychiatric disorder. *Psychological Medicine*, 40, 1647–58.

McLean, C. and Anderson, E. (2009). Brave men and timid women? A review of the gender differences in fear and anxiety. *Clinical Psychology Review*, 29, 496–505.

McLeod, B. et al. (2007). Examining the association between parenting and childhood anxiety: a meta-analysis. *Clinical Psychology Review*, 27, 155–72.

Middeldorp, C. et al. (2005). The co-morbidity of anxiety and depression in the perspective of genetic epidemiology. *Psychological Medicine*, 35, 611–24.

Morin, C. et al. (2003). Role of stress, arousal, and coping skills in primary insomnia. *Psychosomatic Medicine*, 65, 259–67.

Mosing, M. et al. (2009). Genetic and environmental influences on the co-morbidity between depression, panic disorder, agoraphobia, and social phobia. *Depression and Anxiety*, 11, 1004–11.

Munafò, M. R. et al. (2004). Are there sex differences in the association between the 5HTT gene and neuroticism? A meta-analysis. *Personality and Individual Differences*, 37, 621–6.

Muris, P. et al. (2005). The relation between gender role orientation and fear and anxiety in nonclinic-referred children. *Journal of Clinical Child and Adolescent Psychology*, 34, 326–32.

Naragon-Gainey, K. (2010). Meta-analysis of the relations of anxiety sensitivity to the depressive and anxiety disorders. *Psychological Bulletin*, 136, 128–50.

National Centre for Social Research and University of Leicester (2011). *Adult Psychiatric Morbidity Survey, 2007* [computer file]. Third Edition. Colchester, Essex: UK Data Archive [distributor] SN: 6379, <http://dx.doi.org/10.5255/UKDA-SN-6379-1>, accessed 11 October 2012.

Nazroo, J. et al. (1997). Gender differences in the onset of depression following a shared life event. *Psychological Medicine*, 27, 9–19.

Nolen-Hoeksema, S. (2001). Gender differences in depression. *Current Directions in Psychological Science*, 10, 173–6.

—— et al. (1999). Explaining the gender difference in depressive symptoms. *Journal of Personality and Social Psychology*, 77, 1061–72.

Nolen-Hoeksema, S. and Morrow, J. (1991). A prospective study of depression and distress following a natural disaster. *Journal of Personality and Social Psychology*, 61, 115–21.

Ohayon, M. et al. (1998). Comorbidity of mental and insomnia disorders in the general population. *Comprehensive Psychiatry*, 39, 185–97.

Oldehinkel, A. and Bouma, E. (2011). Sensitivity to the depressogenic effect of stress and HPA-axis reactivity in adolescence. *Neuroscience and Biobehavioral Reviews*, 35, 1757–70.

Olff, M. et al. (2007). Gender differences in posttraumatic stress disorder. *Psychological Bulletin*, 133, 183–204.

Orith, U. et al. (2008). Low self-esteem prospectively predicts depression in adolescence and young adulthood. *Journal of Personality and Social Psychology*, 95, 695–708.

Pariante, C. and Lightman, S. (2008). The HPA axis in major depression. *Trends in Neurosciences*, 31, 464–8.

Parker, G. and Brotchie, H. (2010). Gender differences in depression. *International Review of Psychiatry*, 22, 29–436.

Paul, K. et al. (2008). Influence of sex on sleep regulatory mechanisms. *Journal of Women's Health*, 17, 1201–8.

Piccinelli, M. and Wilkinson, G. (2000). Gender differences in depression. *British Journal of Psychiatry*, 177, 486–92.

Plomin, R. et al. (eds). (2008). *Behavioral Genetics*. Fifth Edition. New York: Worth Publishers.

Portella, M. et al. (2005). Enhanced early morning salivary cortisol in neuroticism. *American Journal of Psychiatry*, 162, 807–9.

Rao, U. et al. (2008). Effects of early and recent adverse experiences on adrenal response to psychosocial stress in depressed adolescents. *Biological Psychiatry*, 64, 521–6.

Riemann, D. et al. (2010). The hyperarousal model of insomnia. *Sleep Medicine Reviews*, 14, 19–31.

Risch, N. et al. (2011). Interaction between the serotonin transporter gene (5-HTTLPR), stressful life events, and risk of depression. *JAMA*, 306, 679–781.

Roca, C. A. et al. (2005). Sex-related differences in stimulated hypothalamic-pituitary-adrenal axis during induced gonadal suppression. *Journal of Clinical Endocrinology and Metabolism*, 90, 4224–31.

Sanathara, V. et al. (2003). Interpersonal dependence and major depression. *Psychological Medicine*, 33, 927–31.

Schumm, W. et al. (1998). Gender and marital satisfaction. *Psychological Reports*, 83, 319–27.

Scott, K. et al. (2010). Gender and the relationship between marital status and first onset of mood, anxiety and substance use disorders. *Psychological Medicine*, 40, 1495–505.

Seedat, S. et al. (2009). Cross-national associations between gender and mental disorders in the World Health Organization World Mental Health Surveys. *Archives of General Psychiatry*, 66, 785–95.

Sivertsen, B. et al. (2009). The epidemiology of insomnia. *Journal of Psychosomatic Research*, 67, 109–16.

Slavich, G. et al. (2010). Gender differences in life events prior to onset of major depressive disorder. *Journal of Abnormal Psychology*, 119, 791–803.

Stein, M. et al. (1996). Childhood physical and sexual abuse in patients with anxiety disorders and in a community sample. *American Journal of Psychiatry*, 153, 275–7.

—— (2008). Gene-by-environment (serotonin transporter and childhood maltreatment) interaction for anxiety sensitivity, an intermediate phenotype for anxiety disorders. *Neuropsychopharmacology*, 33, 312–19.

Stroud, L. et al. (2002). Sex differences in stress responses. *Biological Psychiatry*, 52, 318–27.

Taylor, S. (2006). Tend and befriend. *Current Directions in Psychological Science*, 15, 273–7.

Twenge, J. et al. (2003). Parenthood and marital satisfaction: A meta-analytic review. *Journal of Marriage and Family*, 65, 574–83.

Wang, J. et al. (2007). Gender difference in neural response to psychological stress. *Social Cognitive and Affective Neuroscience*, 2, 227–39.

Weiss, E. et al. (1999). Childhood sexual abuse as a risk factor for depression in women. *American Journal of Psychiatry*, 156, 816–28.

Wichstrøm, L. (1999). The emergence of gender difference in depressed mood during adolescence. *Developmental Psychology*, 35, 232–45.

Wizemann, T. M. and Pardue, M.-L. (eds) (2001) *Exploring the Biological Contributions to Human Health: Does Sex Matter?* Washington, DC: National Academy Press.

Zahn-Waxler, C. (2010). Socialization of emotion: Who influences whom and how? In *The Role of Gender in the Socialization of Emotion* (eds A. Kennedy Root and S. Denham). San Francisco: Jossey-Bass.

—— et al. (2008). Disorders of childhood and adolescence. *Annual Review of Clinical Psychology*, 4, 275–303.

Zhang, B. and Wing, Y. (2006). Sex differences in insomnia: a meta-analysis. *Sleep*, 29, 85–93.

<http://grants.nih.gov/grants/guide/pa-files/pa-09-108.html>, accessed 4 September 2012.

CHAPTER 5

Agrawal, A. and Lynskey, M. (2008). Are there genetic influences on addiction: Evidence from family, adoption and twin studies. *Addiction*, 103, 1069–81.

American Psychiatric Association (2000). *Diagnostic and Statistical Manual of Mental Disorders*. Fourth Edition. Text Revision. Arlington, VA: American Psychiatric Association.

Armeli, S. et al. (2000). Stress and alcohol use. *Journal of Personality and Social Psychology*, 78, 979–94.

Bezdjian, S. et al. (2011). Genetic and environmental influences on impulsivity. *Clinical Psychology Review*, 31, 1209–23.

Carney, M. et al. (2000). Positive and negative daily events, perceived stress, and alcohol use. *Journal of Consulting and Clinical Psychology*, 68, 788–98.

Caspi, A. and Moffitt, T.E. (2006). Gene-environment interactions in psychiatry: Joining forces with neuroscience. *Nature Reviews Neuroscience*, 7, 583–90.

Castelnuovo, A. et al. (2006). Alcohol dosing and total mortality in men and women. *Archives of Internal Medicine*, 166, 2437–45.

Cerdá, M. et al. (2008) Comorbid forms of psychopathology. *Epidemiologic Reviews*, 30, 155–77.

Christie-Mizell, C. and Peralta, R. (2009). The gender gap in alcohol consumption during late adolescence and young childhood. *Journal of Health and Social Behavior*, 50, 410–26.

Compton, W. et al. (2007). Prevalence, correlates, disability, and comorbidity of DSM-IV drug abuse and dependence in the United States. *Archives of General Psychiatry*, 64, 566–76.

Cross, C. et al. (2011). Sex differences in impulsivity: A meta-analysis. *Psychological Bulletin*, 137, 97–130.

Dawson, D. et al. (2005). The association between stress and drinking: Modifying effects of gender and vulnerability. *Alcohol and Alcoholism*, 40, 453–60.

Degenhardt, L. et al. (2008). Toward a global view of alcohol, tobacco, cannabis and cocaine use. *PLoS Medicine*, 5(7): e141. doi:10.1371/journal.pmed.0050141.

Dick, D. (2011). Developmental changes in genetic influences on alcohol use and dependence. *Child Development Perspectives*, 5, 223–30.

—— and Bierut, L. (2006). The genetics of alcohol dependence. *Current Psychiatry Reports*, 8, 151–7.

—— et al. (2010). Understanding the construct of impulsivity and its relationship to alcohol use disorders. *Addiction Biology*, 15, 217–26.

Dixit, A. and Crum, R. (2000). Prospective study of depression and the risk of heavy alcohol use in women. *American Journal of Psychiatry*, 157, 751–8.

Do ladettes make you mad? *Sun*, 11 December 2008.

Drinking alcohol while pregnant weakens mothers bond with child. *The Telegraph*, 22 April 2009; <http://www.telegraph.co.uk/health/healthnews/5197463/Drinking-alcohol-while-pregnant-weakens-mothers-bond-with-child.html>, accessed 4 September 2012.

Glass or two of wine a week 'could damage baby'. *The Telegraph*, 11 April 2011; <http://www.telegraph.co.uk/health/healthnews/8441176/Glass-or-two-of-wine-a-week-could-damage-baby.html>, accessed 11 October 2012.

Grant, B. et al. (2009). Sociodemographic and psychopathologic predictors of first incidence of DSM-IV substance use, mood and anxiety disorders. *Molecular Psychiatry*, 14, 1051–66.

Hall, W. et al. (2009). Understanding comorbidity between substance use, anxiety and affective disorders. *Addictive Behaviors*, 34, 526–30.

Hanna, E. et al. (1997). The relationship between drinking and heart disease morbidity in the United States. *Alcoholism*, 21, 111–18.

Hensing, G. and Spak, F. (2009). Introduction: Gendering socio cultural alcohol and drug research. *Alcohol and Alcoholism*, 44, 602–6.

Holmila, M. and Raitasalo, K. (2005). Gender differences in drinking. *Addiction*, 100, 1763–9.

Huselid, R. and Cooper, L. (1992). Gender roles as mediators of sex differences in adolescent alcohol use and abuse. *Journal of Health and Social Behavior*, 33, 348–62.

Hussong, A. (2007). Predictors of drinking immediacy following daily sadness. *Addictive Behaviors*, 32, 1054–65.

—— et al. (2001). Specifying the relations between affect and heavy alcohol use among young adults. *Journal of Abnormal Psychology*, 110, 449–61.

Kendler, K. et al. (2006). Illicit psychoactive substance use, abuse and dependence in a population-based sample of Norwegian twins. *Psychological Medicine*, 36, 955–62.

—— (2007). Specificity of genetic and environmental risk factors for symptoms of cannabis, cocaine, alcohol, caffeine, and nicotine dependence. *Archives of General Psychiatry*, 64, 1313–20.

—— (2008). Genetic and environmental influences on alcohol, caffeine, and nicotine use from early adolescence to middle adulthood. *Archives of General Psychiatry*, 65, 674–82.

—— (2011). Predicting alcohol consumption in adolescence from alcohol-specific and general externalising genetic risk factors, key environmental exposures and their interaction. *Psychological Medicine*, 41, 1507–16.

Kessler, R. et al. (1997). Lifetime co-occurrence of DSM-III-R alcohol abuse and dependence with other psychiatric disorders in the National Comorbidity Survey. *Archives of General Psychiatry*, 54, 313–21.

Kessler, R. et al. (2005). Prevalence, severity and comorbidity of 12-month DSM-IV disorders in the National Comorbidity Survey Replication. *Archives of General Psychiatry*, 62, 617–27.

—— (2007). Lifetime prevalence and age-of-onset distributions of mental disorders in the World Health Organization's World Mental Health Survey Initiative. *World Psychiatry*, 6, 168–76.

Kessler, R. & Üstün, T. (2008). *The WHO World Mental Health Surveys*. New York: Cambridge University Press.

Keyes, K. et al. (2010). Telescoping and gender differences in alcohol dependence. *American Journal of Psychiatry*, 167, 969–76.

—— (2011). Birth cohort effects and gender differences in alcohol epidemiology. *Alcoholism: Clinical and Experimental Research*, 35, 1–12.

—— (2011). Stressful life experiences, alcohol consumption, and alcohol use disorders. *Psychopharmacology*, 218, 1–17.

Liang, W. and Chikritzhs, T. (2011). Affective disorders, anxiety disorders and the risk of alcohol dependence and misuse. *British Journal of Psychiatry*, 119, 219–24. Doi: 10.1192/bjp.bp.110.086116.

Lifestyle of the Modern Girl Condemned, *Manchester Guardian*, 18 February 1926; <http://www.guardian.co.uk/theguardian/2012/feb/18/archive-1926-modern-girls-lifestyle-condemned>, accessed 11 October 2012.

Lynskey, M. et al. (2002). Genetic and environmental contributions to cannabis dependence in a national young adult twin study. *Psychological Medicine*, 32, 195–207.

Merikangas, K. R. et al. (1998). Comorbidity of substance use disorders with mood and anxiety disorders. *Addictive Behaviors*, 23, 893–907.

Magid, V. et al. (2007). Differentiating between sensation seeking and impulsivity through their mediated relations with alcohol use and problems. *Addictive Behaviors*, 32, 2046–61.

Miller, M. et al. (2009). Gender differences in alcohol impairment of simulated driving performance and driving-related skills. *Alcohol and Alcoholism*, 44, 586–93.

Moderate drinking while pregnant doubles risk of child becoming depressed. *The Telegraph*, 23 November 2009: <http://www.telegraph.co.uk/health/

healthnews/6630115/Moderate-drinking-while-pregnant-doubles-risk-of-child-becoming-depressed.html>, accessed 11 October 2012.

Morean, M. and Corbin, W. (2010). Subjective response to alcohol. *Alcoholism: Clinical and Experimental Research*, 34, 385–95.

Mothers who drink while pregnant 'can give their children a taste for alcohol'. *The Telegraph*, 9 March 2009; <http://www.telegraph.co.uk/health/women_shealth/4962536/Mothers-who-drink-while-pregnant-can-give-their-children-a-taste-for-alcohol.html>, accessed 11 October 2012.

Mumenthaler, M. et al. (1999). Gender differences in moderate drinking effects. *Alcohol Research & Health*, 23, 55–64.

Nolen-Hoeksema, S. (2004). Gender differences in risk factors and consequences for alcohol use and problems. *Clinical Psychology Review*, 24, 981–1010.

—— and Hilt, L. (2006). Possible contributors to the gender differences in alcohol use and problems. *Journal of General Psychology*, 133, 357–74.

Plant, M. (2008). The role of alcohol in women's lives. *Journal of Substance Abuse*, 13, 155–91.

Plomin, R. et al. (eds). (2008). *Behavioral Genetics*. Fifth Edition. New York: Worth Publishers.

Quinn, P. and Fromme, K. (2011). Subjective response to alcohol challenge. *Alcoholism*, 35, 1759–70.

Rahav, G. et al. (2006). The influence of societal level factors on men's and women's alcohol consumption and alcohol problems. *Alcohol and Alcoholism*, 41 (S1), i47–i55.

Rospenda, K. et al. (2008). Workplace harassment, stress, and drinking behaviour over time. *Addictive Behaviors*, 33, 964–7.

Saunders, B. et al. (2008). Impulsive errors on a Go-NoGo reaction time task. *Alcoholism*, 32, 888–94.

Schroder, K. and Perrine, M. (2007). Covariations of emotional states and alcohol consumption. *Social Science and Medicine*, 65, 2588–602.

Schulte, M. et al. (2009). Gender differences in factors influencing alcohol use and drinking progression among adolescents. *Clinical Psychology Review*, 29, 535–47.

Seedat, S. et al. (2009). Cross-national associations between gender and mental disorders in the World Health Organization World Mental Health Surveys. *Archives of General Psychiatry*, 66, 785–95.

Shivendra, S. et al. (2008). Emerging role of epigenetics in the actions of alcohol. *Alcoholism*, 32, 1525–34.

Slutske, W. et al. (2002). Personality and the genetic risk for alcohol dependence. *Journal of Abnormal Psychology*, 111, 124–33.

Stinson, F. et al. (2005). Comorbidity between DSM-IV alcohol and specific drug use disorders in the United States. *Drug and Alcohol Dependence*, 80, 105–16.

Stoltenberg, S. et al. (2008). Does gender moderate associations among impulsivity and health-risk behaviours? *Addictive Behaviors*, 33, 252–65.

Sugarman, D. et al. (2009). Are women at greater risk? An examination of alcohol-related consequences and gender. *American Journal on Addictions*, 18, 194–7.

Swendsen, J. and Merikangas, K. (2000). The comorbidity of depression and substance use disorders. *Clinical Psychology Review*, 20, 173–89.

Swendsen, J. et al. (2000). Mood and alcohol consumption. *Journal of Abnormal Psychology*, 109, 198–204.

Veenstra, M. et al. (2006). A literature overview of the relationship between life-events and alcohol use in the general population. *Alcohol and Alcoholism*, 41, 455–63.

Verdejo-Garcia, A. et al. (2008). Impulsivity as a vulnerability marker for substance-use disorders. *Neuroscience and Biobehavioral Reviews*, 32, 777–810.

Verweij, K. et al. (2010). Genetic and environmental influences on cannabis use initiation and problematic use. *Addiction*, 105, 417–30.

Vlahov, D. et al. (2002). Increased use of cigarettes, alcohol, and marijuana among Manhattan, New York, residents after the September 11th terrorist attacks. *American Journal of Epidemiology*, 165, 988–96.

Vlahov, D. et al. (2004). Sustained increased consumption of cigarettes, alcohol, and marijuana among Manhattan residents after September 11, 2001. *American Journal of Public Health*, 94, 253–4.

Wang, G.-J. et al. (2003). Alcohol intoxication induces greater reductions in brain metabolism in male than in female subjects. *Alcoholism*, 27, 909–17.

Wilsnack, R. and Wilsnack, S. (1978). Sex roles and drinking among adolescent girls. *Journal of Studies on Alcohol*, 39, 1855–74.

Wilsnack, R. et al. (2000). Gender differences in alcohol consumption and adverse drinking consequences. *Addiction*, 95, 251–65.

Wong, C. et al. (2011). Drugs and addiction: An introduction to epigenetics. *Addiction*, 106, 480–9.

CHAPTER 6

Alexander, G. and Saenz, J. (2011). Postnatal testosterone levels and temperament in early infancy. *Archives of Sexual Behavior*, 40, 1287–92.

American Psychiatric Association (2000). *Diagnostic and Statistical Manual of Mental Disorders*. Fourth Edition. Text Revision. Arlington, VA: American Psychiatric Association.

Archer, J. (2006). Testosterone and human aggression. *Neuroscience and Biobehavioral Reviews*, 30, 319–45.

Baillargeon, R. et al. (2007). Gender differences in physical aggression. *Developmental Psychology*, 43, 13–26.

Baker, J. et al. (2009). Genetic risk factors for disordered eating in adolescent males and females. *Journal of Abnormal Psychology*, 118, 576–86.

Barlett, C. et al. (2008). Meta-analyses of the effects of media images on men's body-image concerns. *Journal of Social and Clinical Psychology*, 27, 279–310.

Baron-Cohen, S. (2002). The extreme male brain theory of autism. *Trends in Cognitive Sciences*, 6, 248–54.

—— (2010). Book review: Delusions of gender—'neurosexism', biology and politics. *The Psychologist*, 23, pp. 904–5.

—— et al. (1999). Recognition of faux pas by normally developing children and children with Asperger syndrome or high-functioning Autism. *Journal of Autism and Developmental Disorders*, 29, 407–18.

Baron-Cohen, S. et al. (2005). Sex differences in the brain: Implications for explaining autism. *Science*, 310, 819–23.

—— (2011). Why are autism spectrum conditions more prevalent in males? *PLoS Biology*, 9, e1001081.

Berkout, O. et al. (2011). Mean girls and bad boys: Recent research on gender differences in conduct disorder. *Aggression and Violent Behavior*, 16, 503–11.

British Psychological Society (2010). The battle of the sex differences. *The Psychologist* (November), 23, 900–3.

Brockmeyer, T. et al. (2011). Starvation and emotion regulation in anorexia nervosa. *Comprehensive Psychiatry*, doi:10.1016/j.comppsych.2011.09.003.

Brugha, T. et al. (2011). Epidemiology of autism spectrum disorders in adults in the community in England. *Archives of General Psychiatry*, 68, 459–66.

Cale, E. and Lilienfeld, S. (2002). Sex differences in psychopathy and antisocial personality disorder. *Clinical Psychology Review*, 22, 1179–207.

Coid, J. et al. (2006). Prevalence and correlates of personality disorder in Great Britain. *British Journal of Psychiatry*, 188, 423–31.

—— (2006). Violence and psychiatric morbidity in the national household population of Britain. *British Journal of Psychiatry*, 189, 12–19.

Cole, P. et al. (2003). Mutual emotion regulation and the stability of conduct problems between preschool and early school age. *Development and Psychopathology*, 15, 1–18.

Crick, N. et al. (2006). A longitudinal study of relational aggression, physical aggression, and children's social-psychological adjustment. *Journal of Abnormal Child Psychology*, 34, 131–42.

Dadds, M. et al. (2005). Disentangling the underlying dimensions of psychopathy and conduct problems in childhood. *Journal of Consulting and Clinical Psychology*, 73, 400–10.

Davey, G. (2008). *Psychopathology*. Chichester: Wiley.

Dellava, J. et al. (2011). Generalised anxiety disorder and anorexia nervosa. *Depression and Anxiety*, 28, 728–33.

Diamantopoulou, S. et al. (2010). Testing developmental pathways to antisocial personality problems. *Journal of Abnormal Child Psychology*, 38, 91–103.

Dolan, M. and Fullam, R. (2004). Theory of mind and mentalizing ability in antisocial personality disorders with and without psychopathology. *Psychological Medicine*, 34, 1093–102.

Else-Quest, N. et al. (2006). Gender differences in temperament: A meta-analysis. *Psychological Bulletin*, 132, 33–72.

Esme, R. (2007). Sex differences in child-onset, life-course-persistent conduct disorder. *Clinical Psychology Review*, 27, 607–27.

Fairburn, C. and Cooper, Z. (2011). Eating disorders, DSM-5 and clinical reality. *British Journal of Psychiatry*, 198, 8–10.

Fairburn, C. and Harrison P. (2003). Eating disorders. *Lancet*, 361, 407–16.

Fairburn, C. et al. (2003). Cognitive behaviour therapy for eating disorders. *Behaviour Research and Therapy*, 41, 509–28.

Farah, A. and Chamorro-Premuzic, T. (2010). Investigating theory of mind in nonclinical psychopathy and Machiavellianism. *Personality and Individual Differences*, 49, 169–74.

Fine, C. (2010). *Delusions of Gender*. London: Icon Books.

Giedd, J. et al. (1999). Brian development during childhood and adolescence: A longitudinal MRI study. *Nature Neuroscience*, 2, 861–3.

Gladwell, M. (2000). *The Tipping Point*. Boston: Little, Brown.

Grabe, S. et al. (2008). The role of the media in body image concerns among women. *Psychological Bulletin*, 134, 460–76.

Happé, F. and Ronald, A. (2008). The 'fractionable autism triad'. *Neuropsychological Review*, 18, 287–304.

Harrison, A. et al. (2010). Emotional functioning in eating disorders. *Psychological Medicine*, 40, 1887–97.

Hines, M. (2011). Gender development and the human brain. *Annual Review of Neuroscience*, 34, 69–88.

Hoek, H. and van Hoeken, D. (2003). Review of the prevalence and incidence of eating disorders. *International Journal of Eating Disorders*, 34, 383–96.

Hudson, J. et al. (2007). The prevalence and correlates of eating disorders in the National Comorbidity Survey Replication. *Biological Psychiatry*, 61, 348–58.

Hughes, C. (2011). *Social Understanding and Social Lives*. Hove: Psychology Press.

—— et al. (2002). 'I'm gonna beat you!' SNAP! An observational paradigm for assessing young children's disruptive behaviour in competitive play. *Journal of Child Psychology and Psychiatry*, 43, 507–16.

—— et al. (2011). Individual differences in false belief understanding are stable from 3 to 6 years and predict children's mental state talk with school friends. *Journal of Experimental Child Psychology*, 108, 96–112.

Isen, J. et al. (2010). Sex-specific association between psychopathic traits and electrodermal reactivity in children. *Journal of Abnormal Psychology*, 119, 216–25.

Italian ballerina sacked in anorexia row. *The Guardian*, 4 February 2012; <http://www.guardian.co.uk/stage/2012/feb/05/italian-ballerina-sacked-anorexia-row>, accessed 11 October 2012.

Jacobi, C. et al. (2004). Coming to terms with risk factors for eating disorders. *Psychological Bulletin*, 130, 19–65.

Javdani, S. et al. (2011). Expanding our lens: Female pathways to antisocial behaviour in adolescence. *Clinical Psychology Review*, 31, 1324–48.

Judge, T. and Cable, D. (2011). When it comes to pay, do the thin win? The effect of weight on pay for men and women. *Journal of Applied Psychology*, 96, 95–112.

Kaye, W. et al. (2009). New insights into symptoms and neurocircuit function of anorexia nervosa. *Nature Reviews Neuroscience*, 10, 573–84.

Keel, P. and Klump, K. (2003). Are eating disorders culture-bound syndromes? Implications for conceptualizing their etiology. *Psychological Bulletin*, 129, 747–69.

Kendler, K. et al. (1995). The structure of the genetic and environmental risk factors for six major psychiatric disorders in women. *Archives of General Psychiatry*, 52, 374–83.

Kerr, M. and Schneider, B. (2008). Anger expression in children and adolescents. *Clinical Psychology Review*, 28, 559–77.

Klump, K. et al. (2006). Preliminary evidence that gonadal hormones organise and activate disordered eating. *Psychological Medicine*, 36, 539–46.

Lydecker, J. et al. (2012). Association between co-twin sex and eating disorders in opposite sex twin pairs. *Journal of Psychosomatic Research*, 72, 73–7.

McFadyen-Ketchum, S. A. et al. (1996). Patterns of change in early childhood aggressive-disruptive behaviour. *Child Development*, 67, 2417–33.

Meier, M. et al. (2009). The role of harsh discipline in explaining sex differences in conduct disorder. *Journal of Abnormal Child Psychology*, 37, 653–64.

—— (2011). Sex differences in the genetic and environmental influences on childhood conduct disorder and adult antisocial behavior. *Journal of Abnormal Psychology*, 120, 377–88.

Merikangas, K. et al. (2009). Lifetime prevalence of mental disorders in U.S. adolescents. *Journal of the American Academy of Child and Adolescent Psychiatry*, 49, 980–9.

Mitchell, J. E. et al. (1981). Frequency and duration of binge-eating episodes in patients with bulimia. *American Journal of Psychiatry*, 138, 835–6.

Moffitt, T. and Caspi, A. (2001). Childhood predictors differentiate life-course persistent and adolescence-limited antisocial pathways among males and females. *Development and Psychopathology*, 13, 355–75.

Moffitt, T. et al. (2008). Research review: DSM-V conduct disorder. *Journal of Child Psychology and Psychiatry*, 49, 3–33.

Narusyte, J. et al. (2007). Aggression as a mediator of genetic contributions to the association between negative parent-child relationships and adolescent antisocial behaviour. *European Child & Adolescent Psychiatry*, 16, 128–37.

—— (2011). Parental criticism and externalising behaviour problems in adolescents. *Journal of Abnormal Psychology*, 120, 365–76.

O'Connor, D. et al. (2004). Effects of testosterone on mood, aggression, and sexual behavior in young men. *Journal of Clinical Endocrinology and Metabolism*, 89, 2837–45.

Odgers, C. et al. (2008). Female and male antisocial trajectories. *Development and Psychopathology*, 20, 673–716.

O'Leary, M. et al. (2007). Gender differences in the association between psychopathic personality traits and cortisol response to induced stress. *Psychoneuroendocrinology*, 32, 183–91.

Olino, T. (2010). Conduct disorder and psychosocial outcomes at age 30. *Journal of Abnormal Child Psychology*, 38, 1139–49.

One in five ballerinas at La Scala is anorexic, leading dancer claims. *The Observer*, 4 December 2011: <http://www.guardian.co.uk/world/2011/dec/04/ballerinas-la-scala-anorexic-claim>, accessed 11 October 2012.

Polivy, J. and Herman, P. (2002). Causes of eating disorders. *Annual Review of Psychology*, 53, 187–213.

Preti, A. et al. (2008). Eating disorders among professional fashion models. *Psychiatry Research*, 159, 86–94.

—— (2009). The epidemiology of eating disorders in six European countries. *Journal of Psychiatric Research*, 43, 1125–32.

Raine, A. et al. (2011). Sex differences in orbitofrontal gray as a partial explanation for sex differences in antisocial personality. *Molecular Psychiatry*, 16, 227–36.

Rogstad, J. and Rogers, R. (2008). Gender differences in contributions of emotion to psychopathy and antisocial personality disorder. *Clinical Psychology Review*, 28, 1472–84.

Ronald, A. et al. (2006). Phenotypic and genetic overlap between autistic traits at the extremes of the general population. *Journal of the American Academy of Child and Adolescent Psychiatry*, 45, 691–9.

Ronson, J. (2011). *The Psychopath Test*. London: Picador.

Rowe, R. et al. (2010). Developmental pathways in Oppositional Defiant Disorder and Conduct Disorder. *Journal of Abnormal Psychology*, 119, 726–38.

Sauro, C. et al. (2008). Stress, hypothalamic-pituitary-adrenal axis and eating disorders. *Neuropsychobiology*, 57, 95–115.

Shamsay-Tsoory, S. et al. (2010). The role of the orbitofrontal cortex in affective theory of mind deficits in criminal offenders with psychopathic tendencies. *Cortex*, 46, 68–677.

Silberg, J. and Bulik, C. (2005). The developmental association between eating disorders symptoms and symptoms of depression and anxiety in juvenile girls. *Journal of Child Psychology and Psychiatry*, 46, 1317–26.

Striegel-Moore, R. and Bulik, C. (2007). Risk factors for eating disorders. *American Psychologist*, 62, 181–98.

Sutton, J. (2010). The battle of the sex differences. *The Psychologist*, 23, 901–3.

Ringham, R. et al. (2006) Eating disorder symptomatology among ballet dancers. *International Journal of Eating Disorders*, 39, 503–8.

Rowe, R. et al. (2004). Testosterone, antisocial behaviour, and social dominance in boys. *Biological Psychiatry*, 55, 546–52.

—— (2010). Developmental pathways in oppositional defiant disorder and conduct disorder. *Journal of Abnormal Psychology*, 119, 726–38.

Treasure, J. et al. (2008). Models as a high-risk group. *British Journal of Psychiatry*, 192, 243–4.

Van Engeland, H. and Buitelar, J. (2008). Autism spectrum disorders. In *Rutter's Child and Adolescent Psychiatry* (eds M. Rutter et al.). Oxford: Blackwell.

van Goozen, S. et al. (2007). The evidence for a neurobiological model of childhood antisocial behavior. *Psychological Bulletin*, 133, 149–82.

Wade, T. et al. (2000). Anorexia nervosa and major depression. *American Journal of Psychiatry*, 157, 469–71.

Wiebe, S. et al. (2008). Using confirmatory factor analysis to understand executive control in preschool children. *Developmental Psychology*, 44, 575–87.

Zahn-Waxler, C. et al. (2008). Disorders of childhood and adolescence: Gender and psychopathology. *Annual Review of Clinical Psychology*, 4, 275–303.

CHAPTER 7

Boye, K. (2009). Relatively different? How do gender differences in well-being depend on paid and unpaid work in Europe? *Social Indicators Research*, 93, pp. 509–25.

British Psychological Society (2010). The battle of the sex differences. *The Psychologist* (November), 23, 900–3.

Centre for Economic Performance's Mental Health Policy Group (2012). *How Mental Illness Loses Out in the NHS*. London: LSE.

Clark, D. (2011). Implementing NICE guidelines for the psychological treatment of depression and anxiety: The IAPT experience. *International Review of Psychiatry*, 23, 318–27.

Fine, C. (2010). *Delusions of Gender*. London: Icon Books.

Health and Safety Executive. Working days lost: <http://www.hse.gov.uk/statistics/dayslost.htm>, accessed 11 October 2012.

Perec, G. (1988). *Life: A User's Manual*. London: Collins Harvill.

Sainsbury Centre for Mental Health (2003). *Economic and Social Costs of Mental Illness in England*. London: SCMH.

Shadish, W. et al. (2002). *Experimental and Quasi-Experimental Designs for Generalised Causal Inference*. Boston, MA: Houghton Mifflin.

World Health Organization. Mental disorders: <http://www.who.int/whr/2001/media_centre/en/whr01_fact_sheet1_en.pdf>, accessed 22 October 2012.

World Health Organization. Gender and women's mental health: <http://www.who.int/mental_health/prevention/genderwomen/en/>, accessed 4 September 2012.

INDEX